Return to the Motherland

My Journey to Find the Truth

(Memoir)

Ken Kookjoo Choi

ISBN 978-0-578-48376-4

EdgeWise Publishing
P.O. Box 1092
Bellingham, WA 98227

Editor: Kendra Langeteig, PhD
Book design and typesetting: Kathleen Weisel
Cover design: May May Gong

To my parents,
Choi Hyungwoo (Il-chon) and Yoo Taejung,
I bow down

Dong-A Ilbo street fundraising campaign for flood victims of three southern provinces of South Korea. Choi Hyungwoo, author's father (left), wearing a straw hat. Shin Gyeong (Hsinking), China, circa 1934.

Contents

Preface

Do you want to learn what is life?
Listen to your seniors who lived their lives fully and meaningfully.
—Yoo Taejung, "Transformation" (1985)

When I sat down to write my life story, at the encouragement of my family and friends, I didn't know where to begin. It was a daunting prospect, to say the least. I had never written a book. Except for writing business plans and keeping a journal, I had no previous experience as a writer. I had been a businessman my entire life. Besides, I didn't consider myself exceptional or extraordinary in any way, even though people said my story was worth telling. I was regarded as a success by those in my Korean community in Portland, Oregon, someone who had realized the American dream. To succeed in business and give my family a good life in this country was not easy by any means. But my challenges paled by comparison with the sacrifices my parents made for the cause of Korea's independence and freedom while raising me and my siblings. I knew that my memoir could only begin by telling the story of my parents and the years growing up in Seoul before I emigrated to the United States.

By good fortune, my mother Yoo Taejung wrote a memoir in her later years, which amounted to a folder of handwritten pages and loose notes. She also had published a few articles in newspapers. My mother was a gifted writer and storyteller. As children, my sisters and I loved to listen to her stories about growing up as a girl and meeting and marrying our father. She was always reluctant at first to share her trials and tribulations. "There is no sense dwelling in the past," she would say. "Besides, my past is filled with sad stories and I don't care to revisit it." But once she began telling her stories, we were often entertained for hours. These stories left an indelible impression on our young minds and hearts. My parents' married life lasted only ten years, four years in China and six years in Korea, until the terrifying day in 1950 when my father was captured by the soldiers of the People's Army of North Korea, never to be seen again by my family.

Writing my memoir stirred up many poignant memories of growing up in war-torn Korea. It also raised questions about my father that had haunted me since the day he disappeared from our lives. Had I not started writing my memoir, which prompted me to investigate the circumstances of my father's death, the truth that I share in this book would never have been brought to light.

My parents suffered many hardships in their married life during the ruthless Japanese occupation. My father Choi Hyungwoo (Il-chon) was an independence movement activist and journalist. He wrote an important book about the movement before I was old enough to read. After my father's arrest, my mother struggled to raise me and my two sisters, as we moved from place to place in the war-torn country. I have done my best to recreate the scenes from my childhood as told through my mother's eyes and from my own recollections. Through my mother's tireless efforts to support our family, and despite serious health challenges for both of us, I graduated from Korea University with a degree in Political Science and Diplomacy. I was soon hired to work for an international trading company in Seoul. This job opened the door to my career and enabled me to start a new life in America.

When I emigrated from Seoul, Korea, to Portland, Oregon, in 1969, I was a penniless young man of twenty-seven with a three-month visa and poor English. But my heart was set on becoming a successful businessman in America and a naturalized citizen. Soon after arriving, I met my wife and soulmate, Myungki, who was a graduate student in music education at Portland State University. We soon married, and God blessed us with three beautiful daughters. Thanks to their supermom, our daughters thrived in school and pursued their musical talents. I founded K-C International Ltd., in 1976, an import/export company specializing in exporting recycled paper products to more than a dozen countries in Asia, India, and South America. Thanks to my hard-working partners and employees, our company grew quickly and soon we became one of the major exporters in North America.

With my support, my mother and other family members emigrated to Portland. They, too, would find success in America. The lives of our family have been truly blessed, though not without challenges. We were fortunate to have a close network of family and friends in the Portland community. Both Myungki and I volunteered our service to help support new Korean immigrants through the Korean churches and the Korean Society of Oregon. To perform volunteer work in the midst of our busy lives was overwhelming at times, but well worth it.

Forty-three years after my father and half-brothers disappeared, my mother received a letter from her stepsons. We learned that my brothers were still alive and living in North Korea. Soon after, my mother received an invitation from a government official to visit Pyongyang. At her request, I accompanied her on this trip. Little did we know, when we landed in Pyongyang to reunite with my brothers, that we would be treated like VIPs and meet the great leader Kim Il Sung. He had been a friend and comrade of my father during the days of the independence movement.

My father was honored as a patriot at a special luncheon with Kim Il Sung, where my family was presented with an excerpt from my father's book. There was also a memorial service and a medal was awarded on behalf of my father. While my mother and I received wonderful hospitality, and our hosts did everything possible to make our stay comfortable, their well-orchestrated itinerary could not prevent us from observing the miserable life of my brothers and my North Korean compatriots. The degree of surveillance was suffocating, and it saddened my mother and me for the entire duration of our stay.

One year after the trip to Pyongyang, the life of my family was turned completely upside down when my wife Myungki was the victim of a terrible car accident and sustained a traumatic brain injury that put her in coma. My daughters and I spent agonizing months waiting in suspense. By the grace of God, I got my wife back, though her journey to recovery would be long and arduous. To take care of my wife, I sold my business in 1997 and turned my full attention to her recovery. Against the prognosis of the specialists, Myungki surprised everyone, though she would never fully regain her cognitive abilities. Myungki also survived third-stage breast cancer and I had my own journey with cancer. Despite these setbacks, we went on to enjoy our life together as true companions. We had the pleasure of seeing our three daughters graduate from prestigious colleges, marry happily, and achieve brilliant success in their careers. My wife Myungki and I beat the odds and made it all the way to our golden years.

To write the final chapter of my memoir, I returned to South Korea in 2018 to search the libraries for a copy of my father's two-volume book, *A Short History of the Overseas Korean Revolutionary Movement*, in the hope of solving the mysteries surrounding my father's relationship with Kim Il Sung. And at long last, I found the clues that would enable me to pay proper tribute to my father and mother.

The search for the truth about my father turned out to be as much a journey to find the truth about who I am. To tell this story, I shared my personal struggles concerning my faith in God and my issues with the monotheistic religions of the world, including the beliefs of my Korean Presbyterian church. On the day my wife opened her eyes from the coma, I was blessed with a moment of self-realization. I dare profess that in that moment, I learned who God is and who I am. The way I served others in my life was forever changed from that day forward.

It is my parents who are the stars of my story. They showed me through their example to live my life unselfishly and return everything to God before I go. It is my wish for my daughters and our future generations of Korean Americans to understand and honor this important legacy. We must never forget those who came before us. They made it possible for us to have the freedoms we enjoy and the opportunity to pursue our dreams as citizens of a democracy, unlike our relatives in North Korea who still suffer under the yoke of communism. But beyond any national borders, the truth is that all of us are united as one human family.

There are many important things in life. Family, love, hope, faith, money, honor, the list goes on. For me, what is most important is a humble attitude and fully realizing that the spirit of God resides in each of us. I hope those who read this story will be inspired by it and take comfort in knowing there are others who have lived through difficult times and found happiness.

↞ Acknowledgements ↠

Without the prayers, love, and support of my family, I could never have overcome the many trials and challenges or achieved success in my life.

I give my utmost thanks to my late mother, Yoo Taejung, who brought me into this world. Without her unconditional love and sacrifices, I would not be the person I am today, nor would I have been able to endure the terrible ordeal of my wife's tragic accident.

I also must acknowledge my three wonderful daughters, Jennifer, Christine, and DeAnna, who stood by their super mother and me throughout the difficult years and gave their love and always raised our spirits.

I am deeply grateful to my dear wife Myungki, who has been by my side these fifty years. Without her loving presence, my life would have been miserable, and our daughters and I would not have realized our dreams.

Special thanks to my very dear sisters Myungjoo and Hyunjoo. Hyunjoo willingly gave up her own successful business for a year to be Myungki's full-time care giver. She rescued me from depression so I could focus on my business and take care of the needs of my family. Thanks go to my brother-in-law Mike Caravatta, who read initial drafts of my memoir and encouraged me to keep writing. Also, my deepest appreciation goes to all of my family and friends in Portland, Oregon and San Jose, California who did not spare their love and support.

My utmost thanks go to Pat and Jo Connolly of Portland, Oregon. Pat took a chance and hired a FOB (fresh off the boat) like me to work for his company, found an attorney to help me get my green card, and trained me to become a legitimate American salesman.

There were many people who freely gave me their support and encouragement when I was going through the most difficult period of my life. I give thanks to my business associates Frank Crowley, Phil Epstein, Bill Brooks, and Sue Litton, my long time CFO and sister-in-law, who passed away in 2016. Many thanks to all my wonderful employees at K-C International Inc.

Special thanks to Dr. Danielle Erb, of the Legacy Brain Rehabilitation Institute of Oregon, and Meg Munger, the social worker at Kaiser Permanente, who helped me and my family to push Myungki to recover during the most critical period of her rehabilitation. Without the expert treatment at the emergency unit of the Emmanuel Hospital and the wonderful medical system of Kaiser Permanente and their doctors and nurses, Myungki's life could not have been saved and extended this far.

Special thanks to my dear friend and mentor Park Youngju, Chairman of the Eagon Industrial Co., in South Korea, and his beautiful wife Inja. He helped me to get my first decent job with an American importer in 1971, which paved the way to start my own successful business career.

Without the help of my guardian angel, Col. Fred Ruth, retired Commander of U.S. Southern Territory of the Salvation Army, I would never have finished my college education in Korea, which enabled me to become who I am today.

I would like to give my very special thanks to Dr. Kendra Langeteig of EdgeWise Publishing in Bellingham, Washington. Finding her online was a small miracle in itself. She helped guide me through the arduous process of editing, and like a magician, she turned my crude working draft into a beautiful book. Most important, she encouraged me to see that my memoir had stories and messages worthy of publishing. My thanks also go to Kathleen Weisel for the book design and typesetting, and to May May Gong for the cover design and proofreading.

There were many angels in my life. I hope it's not too late for me to become one.

Ken Kookjoo Choi
San Jose, California

Timeline of Modern Korean History

1905:   The Korea-Japan Treaty. Korea became a protectorate of imperial Japan.

1910:   The Korea-Japan Annexation Treaty.

1919:   March 1st Movement. Declaration of Korean Independence. Nationwide peaceful demonstration crushed by Japanese military and police force.

1938:   Japanese Governor General of Korea begins the Japanese name-change policy.

1945:   Surrender of the Japanese Empire to the U.S. and Allies.

1945:   The Korean peninsula is divided between Soviet Union and American occupation forces at the 38th parallel.

1948:   Establishment of the Republic of Korea with Syngman Rhee as president. August 15.

1948:   Establishment of the Democratic People's Republic of Korea (DPRK) with Kim Il Sung as premier. September 9.

1950:   The Korean War begins.

1953:   Korean War Armistice Agreement signed.

1960:   April Revolution of Republic of Korea. Syngman Rhee resigns.

1961:   May 16th Military coup d'état by General Park Chung-hee.

1965: Normalization of Korea-Japan relations.

1972: The first Red Cross talks between South and North Korea.

1978: South Korea achieved $1,117 GNP per capita.

1979: President Park Chung-hee assassinated.

1980: May 18th Gwangju Uprising.

1988: 25th Summer Olympic Games held in Seoul, Korea.

1991: South and North Korea join the United Nations.

1994: Death of Kim Il Sung. Kim Jong Il takes control of North Korea.

2002: FIFA World Cup jointly held by Korea and Japan.

2011: Kim Jong Il dies, Kim Jong Un takes over as the supreme leader of North Korea.

2016: President Park Geun-hye impeached.

2017: Moon Jae-in sworn in as President of South Korea.

2018: South Korea achieved $32,000 GNP per capita.

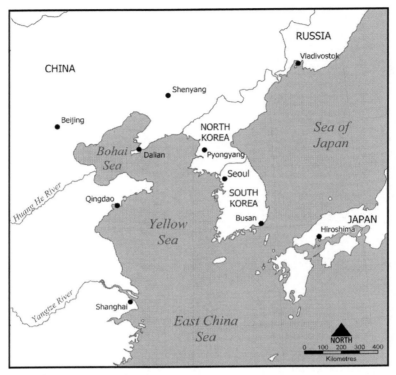

Map of Korean Peninsula, 2005.

PART ONE

UNDIVIDED HEART

Wedding photo of Choi Hyungwoo and Yoo Taejung, Beijing, China, 1940.

CHAPTER 1

BEIJING, OH BEIJING

My father, Choi Hyungwoo (Il-chon), and my mother, Yoo Taejung, met in Beijing, China, in 1940. He was thirty-five and she, twenty-two years old. Both my parents were born in Korea. My father was born in Jeongju, Pyonganbuk-do, North Korea, and my mother in Seoul, South Korea. The Korean peninsula was under the ruthless occupation of imperial Japan. After a brief courtship, my parents married and started life together in Beijing. It was my father's third marriage and the second for my mother.

When my parents married, my father had four children living with him from his two previous marriages. He had two sons, Seokjoo and Chuljoo, and one daughter, Youngjoo, from his first wife (her surname was Byun). She had died at a young age due to complications from a pregnancy. His son Dongjoo was from his second wife, Seung So-ok, who was a fervent member of the independence movement during the Japanese occupation of Korea. It was Seung So-ok's second marriage, too. Her previous husband was the nationally known revolutionary poet, politician, and independence movement activist, Kim Hyuk.

My father was best friends with both Kim Hyuk and Seung So-ok, as he was active in the independence movement as a journalist. Unfortunately, Kim Hyuk's life ended abruptly. He was captured by the Japanese police, brutally tortured, and murdered. Subsequently, his wife Seung So-ok tried to commit suicide by throwing herself into the E-Tong river in Manchuria, but her friends miraculously rescued her in time. She gradually recovered from this ordeal, and would later marry her husband's best friend, my father. Sadly, Seung So-ok never fully recovered from her old wounds and sickness. She passed away at a young age, leaving my father to care for his four children alone. It is difficult to imagine how my father managed to raise his children while working as a journalist and independence movement activist during the harsh Japanese occupation period in Manchuria and China.

My mother's first marriage was not happy, and it ended in divorce. Her husband Hong Soonyoung came from a wealthy family whose relatives were related to Queen Shin Jung, mother of King Heon Jong, the 24th king of the Lee Dynasty. He was from the so-called Yang Ban (noble) class. My mother Yoo Taejung's parents, although not as wealthy, were also from the Yang Ban class. Hong Soonyoung had graduated from Meiji University in Tokyo, Japan. Returning home triumphant, he was highly sought after by many willing bride candidates of the Yang Ban class in Seoul, Korea. The handsome young man was introduced to my mother at the arrangement of both families, and he did not wait long to ask for my mother's hand in marriage.

My mother Yoo Taejung and Hong Soonyoung had two children from this marriage; a son, Sonsik, and a daughter named Woonsik. Unfortunately, not only was this man handsome, but he was a philanderer, too. Against my mother's wishes, three years after they were married, her husband ran off to Beijing, China, with a new young girlfriend, stealthily taking three-year-old Sonsik and six-month-old Woonsik with them.

Bewildered and heart broken, my mother searched for their whereabouts for many months. Eventually, she learned where they were residing in Beijing, and she decided to go after them. After many days of traveling from Seoul to Beijing, by train, jinrikisha, and on foot, she reached the house where her husband lived with her two babies and his new girlfriend.

Exhausted and emotionally drained, she stood outside the door of their house. She hesitated for a moment to regain her composure, then knocked on the door, ready to confront them face-to-face. While standing there, she heard a voice coming from inside of the house. A young woman in modern-style dress with two toddlers appeared from behind the door. Her husband Hong Soonyoung was not with them. The woman was pretty, but she was wearing rather excessive makeup and looked vain and shallow to my mother.

Instantly, my mother recognized her two babies. Startled, the young woman looked at my mother and made a slight motion, as if she wanted to go back inside the house. She was visibly shaken to see the children's real mother standing in front of her. She didn't bother to ask who my mother was, even though they had never met before. Instinctively the young woman knew it was my mother. There was a guilty expression on her face. She murmured a few words in Korean, but my mother could not hear her. Tears started rolling down my mother's cheeks, and she kneeled down to embrace her daughter Woonsik, now one-and-a-half years old.

Woonsik did not recognize her own mother. She was startled and began to cry.

"Woonsik, I am your mommy, what's wrong, baby? Oh baby, I am so sorry I couldn't come sooner. Don't worry, baby, I am here now!"

My mother held her child tightly to her bosom. Woonsik kept crying and wiggled to get out of her mother's arms, calling her father's girlfriend "Mommy" instead. Confused and alarmed, my mother then turned to her four-year-old son, Sonsik, who was hiding behind the young surrogate mother. He, too, looked puzzled and seemed to have forgotten who my mother was. When she reached out her arms to him, he turned away from her and ran inside the house.

My poor mother was totally confused and devastated. She had never imagined that anything like this could happen. How could her children have forgotten who she was in only a year's time? Was it possible?

She could understand Woonsik's innocent reaction, because she was still breastfeeding her baby daughter when they stole her away. But Sonsik was three years old at the time. Perhaps he vaguely remembered who she was but did not know how to react. Perhaps he liked this young mother better than his real mother, who looked tired and grief stricken, and was dressed in baggy clothes.

My mother was utterly speechless. She was unable to think straight. She felt as if her energy was being sucked out of her whole body. The sky appeared to be falling on her head, and she crumbled down onto the ground, feeling she had lost all purpose in life. She wanted to die right there on the spot. How could barely a year of separation make such a difference that her children would forget their own true mother? Utterly bewildered by the situation, she didn't know what to do next. The excruciatingly painful experience of having her babies stolen from her was one thing. But for a mother not to be recognized by her own children was doubly harrowing and it tore her heart into a thousand pieces.

Recognizing the seriousness of the unimaginable situation unfolding before her eyes, the young woman awkwardly approached my mother and tried to say something in Korean to comfort her. She couldn't find the proper words. She knelt down in front of my mother and apologized for what had happened. After a long pause, the girlfriend shamelessly suggested that my mother stay in Beijing and live with her and the babies and Hong Soonyoung. My mother couldn't believe what she had just heard.

Although overwhelmed with anger, my mother did not want to lose her composure. As a woman, she felt sorry for this young woman. My mother knew how easily she herself had fallen prey to her husband's facade. She felt thankful that his girlfriend had been taking good care of her two young babies. Woonsik was clinging to her "stepmother," and stared at her own mother as if she were a stranger. My mother called to her son many times, but Sonsik refused to come out of the house. Swallowing her pride and wiping away her tears, she decided that maybe this young woman could make a better mother than herself.

Quietly, my mother stood up and embraced the young woman. "You will take good care of my babies, won't you? Please, please, promise me," my mother entreated her.

Without speaking, the young woman nodded her head. My mother felt so weak, she was unable to move. Even her tears had frozen. Finally, she found the strength to turn away from the woman and the child in her arms, her own Woonsik, and walked away. She stepped into a dark narrow alley, restraining the urge to look back, and ventured into the windy city. Out of nowhere, tears of grief swelled up again and blurred her vision. There were only a few people passing by on the street. She let the tears flow freely. She didn't care anymore. She kept on walking as the sun set behind her and the streets grew dark. Years later, she would remember how strange it felt to follow the long, sad, soulless shadow that stretched in front of her.

Her incredibly arduous, heart-wrenching journey from Seoul to Beijing had turned out to be a total failure. Without her babies, she no longer saw any reason to live. Even so, she knew it would have been impossible to put up with Hong Soonyoung and live under the same roof with him and his new "bride." She had been abused and manipulated by this cruel, arrogant man for far too long. Nor did she want to stay in Beijing, a desolate city with no heart and no soul. She was devastated. God had forsaken her, she was sure of it.

My sister Hyunjoo later told me that our mother had tried to commit suicide; but alas, she offered my sister no further details. That would have to remain one of the missing pages in the story of our mother's life.

Wedding of Choi Youngjoo (author's eldest half-sister) and husband.
The honorable Mr. Sin Ik-Hui, speaker of the National Assembly of South Korea, officiated the wedding. Seoul, Korea, 1948.
Back row: Mr. Sin (fifth from left), standing next to Choi Hyungwoo (author's father);
standing beside him is Choi Seungjo (father's friend who escaped Namsan execution site in 1950). Front row, second from left: Seokjoo (eldest half-brother), and
Yoo Taewook (author's uncle). Second row, fourth from right: Yoo Taejung (author's
mother) in black skirt. Front row: The small boy at right is author Kookjoo beside
half-brother Dongjoo.

CHAPTER 2

LAWS OF KARMA

In the backwards, feudalistic society of Korea in the 1940s, it was unthinkable and considered taboo for a woman to divorce her spouse. She either remained single and legally bound by marriage, or in a situation like my mother's, she would allow her husband to bring the second wife into the home and raise the children together. My mother Yoo Taejung wanted none of this, and she resolved to get a divorce from Hong Soonyoung. Legally, the custody of the children was automatically given to the husband, regardless of his character or social position. Women had absolutely no rights whatsoever. And yet, at the young age of twenty-one, she adamantly demanded a legal divorce, knowing the social stigma it put on her would be painful to bear.

With the help of her brother Taewook, who was residing in Beijing to participate in the independence movement, she soon managed to get the divorce. My uncle sympathized with my mother's plight and invited her to stay with him temporarily in Beijing rather than return to their parents' house in Seoul. Taewook helped my mother to secure the divorce from her husband by handling all the legal paperwork. The divorce was quickly granted due to the modernized Japanese legal system implemented in Korea.

One sunny day, a few months after her divorce, Taewook, who was two years younger than my mother, called and invited her to lunch at a humble Chinese restaurant in downtown Beijing. He had an outgoing personality and was a progressive thinker like my mother. They shared similar ideology, and both of them hated the oppressive Japanese occupation of Korea. They got along really well together and looked out for each other whenever disputes arose amongst their five siblings.

Taewook was acquainted with my father Hyungwoo, as he was a well-known and respected journalist who wrote for the Korean newspaper *Dong-A Ilbo* in Beijing, whose motto was, "For the people, democracy, and culture." They had met a few times at secret political meetings. He admired my father's articles and his extensive knowledge of Asian history and the new reform movements. Above all, he respected and admired my father for his kind personality and his compassion for the Korean people.

Despite the considerable age difference between my father and my mother, among other shortcomings, Taewook saw the strong integrity and intelligence they had in common and he thought they would make a good match. He had envisioned this lunch with my mother as a perfect opportunity to broach the idea to my mother.

After sharing a nice lunch, with a pot of hot oolong tea, my uncle proposed the idea of introducing my mother to "a nice gentleman." Very cautiously, he explained my father's background, highlighting his important work in the resistance movement, and went on to explain that he was a twice-married man who had lost both his wives at a young age. Last, Taewook mentioned the four children that Hyungwoo was now raising by himself.

My mother almost jumped out of her chair. "Are you out of your mind?" she exclaimed. "Not even one year has passed since my divorce, and yet you expect me to get married again? To someone who is thirteen years older and has four kids? What kind of brother are you? He is almost old enough to be my father. You want your sister to become a slave for the five of them? You must be crazy!"

She was furious and couldn't believe that her dear brother would dare consider such a terrible match for her. She had not even thought of remarrying. But Taewook's idea seems to have grown on my mother, because she grew curious about meeting this important man about whom her brother had spoken so highly.

One day, not long after this conversation, my father invited my mother to his house, located on the outskirts of Beijing. My father Hyungwoo greeted my mother at the door. He was wearing a pair of round black-framed glasses. His dark eyes looked kind but serious. She noticed his high forehead and early signs of receding hair. The two-story home was spacious, though disorderly. Hyungwoo's four teenage children were wearing worn-out clothes and appeared to be suffering from malnutrition. She thought briefly about how hard it must have been for my father to raise these children singlehandedly while also performing the duties of a journalist and independence movement activist.

The furniture and other contents of the house were sparse. The only thing that impressed my mother was the enormous collection of books displayed on the shelves of his study. He apologized for his humble living conditions. It was painfully obvious to my mother that he was trying his best not to disappoint her. In fact, he did not waste any time, but proposed the idea of marriage that very day. He tried to convince her that they could work together to make a comfortable life for the family, albeit it was not going to be easy—that is, if she would accept his proposal.

My father's gentle way of talking to my mother and his cautious, respectful approach toward her was drastically different from the condescending treatment of her ex-husband, who was verbally abusive and frequently beat her. My father impressed my mother as a warm, kind, honest, and highly intelligent man. He was also a fervent patriot who deeply cared about Korea and its people. Without a passion for freedom and strong willpower, it would have been impossible for anyone to pursue higher education and work as a full-time journalist and activist under the

Japanese occupation in China—while also raising four children. Not only had my father completed correspondence courses at the University of Manchuria, he was taking a Western history course at Waseda University in Japan. The second industrial revolution was advancing at a rapid pace in the Western hemisphere, and Japan had become one of the most advanced countries in the world. He was concerned that Korea was lagging behind.

My father did not try to hide anything from my mother. He admitted that there were many uncertainties looming ahead for him and his would-be future wife. During their courtship he pondered the fairness of his decision to marry her and hesitated before officially proposing. Finally, he gathered his courage and made a formal proposal to my mother with a sincere apology for his circumstances. He knew it was unfair of him to bring in such a young wife and expect her to take care of his four teenage children. It would require a herculean effort for her to serve as a housewife and assume duties such as cooking and laundry, while also helping the children with school and coping with the many challenges of living in a foreign land.

Instead of committing herself to a new marriage under these undesirable circumstances, my mother could have chosen an easier path and pursued her dream to attain a higher education and become a writer herself. God was not kind to her. He did not let her choose the easier path. My mother later confessed to me that she had succumbed and accepted my father's proposal out of sympathy for him and his four children, not because of her love for him. Although she would grow to love him deeply, she was more concerned about the wellbeing of his four young children and was willing to sacrifice her freedom to help them. She also had a secret prayer in her heart: if she took good care of these children, perhaps the stepmother of her own two children would love and take care of them as well.

She also told us that she was moved by his passion to fight for Korea's independence from Japan. The story of my father's life, an activist who had survived the tragic death of his wives and was raising four children alone, must have seemed overwhelming to my mother at a still tender age. And yet she felt deep sympathy for him. I must help, she thought. Like my father, she felt a desperate yearning for Korea's independence. She wanted to play a role in the movement by helping this man to raise his children. Swept up in the moment, she forgot about her own dreams and aspirations and naively said yes.

Although I could not say for sure, I believe the character and integrity my father demonstrated during their courtship must have painted a good impression on her heart. For it outweighed her reservations about the challenges ahead that she knew would become routine in their married life.

I witnessed my mother's love. True love can endure and overcome anything and everything. Especially when that love is based on mutual respect, deep empathy, and humility. She committed herself to her God-given destiny and never wavered while performing the duty of a wife and the mother of eventually seven children, after my two sisters and I were born.

Over the years, I never heard any complaints from my mother about her decision to marry my father, even though ten years after they married, she would be forced to raise his children without him. Instead, she often said that she would have been willing to marry again if she could ever find a man with characteristics like my father. Such a man never came into her life.

Choi Hyungwoo (second from left) with fellow journalists in front of the Dong-A Ilbo, Shin Gyeong Bureau building, Hsinking, China, circa 1935.

—ᴡᴡ—

CHAPTER 3

THE PATRIOT'S CALL

My father Choi Hyungwoo was born in Jeongju, Pyonganbuk-do, North Korea in 1905. It was the year Japan crushed Russia's mighty Second Pacific Squadron, formerly called "The Baltic Fleet," in the Battle of Tsushima. The war eventually ended that year with the peace Treaty of Portsmouth negotiated between Russia and Japan, and mediated by Theodore Roosevelt, then President of the United States. It was shocking news to the Western world that a small country like Japan had defeated the giant Russian bear. Up until the treaty, Russia had commanded control of the northern half of Korea above the 39th parallel. Japan wanted to avoid a confrontation with Russia, fearing the provocation of the powerful alliance between Russia, France, and Germany would be too much to handle. However, by now, Japan had become the de facto owner of the Korean peninsula. Subsequently, Japan formally annexed Korea in 1910, without any resistance from the Western powers, including the United States.

My mother vaguely recalled my father telling her that to avoid the Japanese occupation, his family had moved to Manchuria around 1913 when he was eight years old. He had an older brother and sister. His parents could not stand the ruthless and oppressive Japanese colonial rule. Like many poor farmers and fellow compatriots who hated Japan, they decided to relocate to a remote area where they could have their own farmland and build enough strength to fight for the independence of their Korean homeland.

They first settled in the Bong Chon (*Fengtian* in Chinese) prefecture of Manchuria, where my father finished his elementary education. Then he enlisted as a soldier and became a secretary for General Oh Dong Jin, who was commissioned by Jung Eui Bu, a Korean military organization of the Anti-Japanese Resistance Movement established in Manchuria 1924.

To their chagrin, Japan would conquer Manchuria in 1932 and China would cease resistance against the Japanese. The Jung Eui Bu was also disintegrated prior to the Japanese occupation. My father remained in Ogaja, Gilim prefecture, and became a teacher at the Samsung School. He also served as the editor of the revolutionary monthly magazine *Nong Woo* (Farmer's Friend), covering news on the independence movement fighters' success and the progress of the Second World War. He contributed many enlightening articles for the undereducated farmers and compatriots.

In 1926, my father met a brilliant youth leader in the independence movement against the Japanese, who would become known as Kim Il Sung, the future leader of North Korea. My father, seven years older than Kim, liked him and saw a bright future for him. It was my father and his father-in-law, Byon Daewoo, who suggested that he change his name from Kim Song Ju to Kim "Il Sung," which means *like the sun* of a nation. Kim Il Sung later personally acknowledged this name change in his memoir, *With the Century.*

My father and Kim Il Sung had served under Lee Jongnak, who founded a revolutionary organization in Manchuria for overthrowing imperialism, called The Gilheuk Farmers Alliance. According to my mother's recollection, my father said he had high hopes and wishes for Kim Il Sung while he was involved with him in the independence movement. However, my father did not wish to be associated with communism, and there was a parting of the ways between them.

The increasing shift toward communism among the resistance fighters in Beijing was the reason my father moved our family from Beijing to Seoul in 1944, one year prior to the Korean Independence from Japan. Furious guerrilla warfare continued between the followers of the socialistic communism and the parties backed by Syngman Rhee and the United States. The country was divided into two factions: the Labour Party, led by Kim Il Sung, and the Freedom Party, led by Syngman Rhee.

South Korea, which was backed by the United States, was in turmoil, not knowing which direction the country should follow. Syngman Rhee eventually prevailed and set up the Republic of Korea on August 15, 1948.

With the support of both China and Russia, Kim Il Sung quickly seized on the momentum and organized the northern half of the country using the strategy of the big brother government, the same tactics used by Stalin. They formally declared the establishment of the Democratic People's Republic of Korea on September 9, 1948, appointing Kim Il Sung as Chancellor.

Despite the fact that my father did not agree with Kim Il Sung's communist ideology, he was impressed by how fast Kim Il Sung was able to pull the entire northern half of Korea into order. My father, Choi Hyungwoo, along with other great patriots, such as Kim Gu, Kim Kyu-sik, Lyuh Woon-hyung, and Cho Bong-am, strived to create one united nation. He could not bear the idea of his beloved country being split up again, so soon after obtaining independence from Japan. He even volunteered to serve in the "Welcoming Committee for Kim Il Sung" when they announced a meeting between Kim Il Sung and Syngman Rhee in Seoul South Korea. The meeting never materialized.

I have few memories of my father during those years. There was little time for my father to spend with his children, as he was preparing to run for a seat on the National Assembly. I remember that our house was always crowded with people coming and going. My mother was busy tending the family and feeding the visitors. It was like a zoo.

My father ran in the National Assembly race for the second

National election held on May 30, 1950. They were to elect 210 representatives. A total 2,209 candidates vied for the available seats. The results of the election revealed that no majority political party emerged; 60% of the elected representatives were from Independent parties. My father ran as a member of the Federation Korean National Independence Party. The party head was Dr. Kim Kyu-sik, whose party platform advocated a middle of the road policy. They supported neither the proletarian socialists nor capitalistic government. They had proposed immediate meetings between the representatives of the North and South to find ways for a compromise, vowing never to allow the country to be divided. Alas! They failed in their efforts toward reconciliation.

My mother said that in the beginning my father was leading in the hotly contested race, but lost at the end. He was accused of being a communist spy, simply because he used to be a friend and mentor of Kim Il Sung. In my father's book, *A Short History of the Overseas Korean Revolutionary Movement* (two vols., published in 1945 and 1946), he had written a rather flattering description of Kim Il Sung, praising his accomplishments as an independence movement fighter, a fact which no one could dispute.

The Korean War broke out on June 25, 1950. Two days later, on June 27th, the plenary session of the National Assembly passed a resolution saying, "Along with one million citizens, we will defend Seoul, our capital city, to our death." Only half of the 210 congressmen had attended the session. Surprisingly, both Mr. Sin Ik-hui, the speaker, and Mr. Cho Bong-am, the vice speaker of the National Assembly, took the resolution to President Syngman Rhee at Gyeongmudae, the presidential palace. To their consternation, President Rhee had already fled the city without even notifying the chairmen of the national assembly.

The second national assembly and the entire population of Seoul collapsed into unimaginable turmoil. Approximately twenty-four national assemblymen were captured and taken to the north. Most South Korean politicians had already fled Seoul or

Choi Hyungwoo with his four children from first two marriages. From left to right: Chuljoo, Seokjoo, Dongjoo, father, and Youngjoo, circa 1940.

were in the process of escaping as quickly as possible. The whole city was turned upside down in chaos. Many people didn't know where to go or what to do. The People's Army had already gained tight control over the city

When the Korean War broke out, my mother was six months pregnant. I was eight years old, Myungjoo five, and Hyunjoo, two. Within a matter of a few weeks, Seokjoo, Chuljoo, and Dongjoo were forcibly conscripted by the People's Army of North Korea. My eldest sister Youngjoo and her husband were also captured by the People's Army soldiers and disappeared. I can't imagine how my mother and father coped with the terrible blow of losing five children from their lives overnight. During this volatile time, my mother encouraged my father to flee Seoul with the others. He was faced with a dilemma, as he had borrowed heavily to finance his campaign for the election. In order to pay off this debt, he quickly sold our beautiful house in Yaksoo-dong and moved our family to a small humble house in Chunghyeon-dong—just two days after the war broke out. Financially ruined, and with a pregnant wife and three young children, he refused my mother's plea for him to escape. He did not have the heart to abandon his wife and children. For him, it was a very clear choice. He decided to stay in Seoul with his family and let destiny decide his fate.

—⟿—

CHAPTER 4

NAMSAN MOUNTAIN

The bright moon is like our heart, undivided and true.
—from *Aegukga* (national anthem)

Three months later, on the 21st of September, while the war was still raging all over the country and the People's Army was in full control of the city, my father had to venture out to secure more food and other essentials for his very pregnant wife and three children. The baby was due to be born in about two weeks. Alas, the North Korean soldiers captured him on the street and locked him in a prison cell where one of his best friends, Choi Seungjo, was already imprisoned.

On September 27th, the day before the Allied forces recaptured Seoul, my father, Choi Seungjo, and several other prisoners were taken up to Namsan Mountain, located in the heart of Seoul. They were going to be executed. Loosely roped together, they were forced to climb steep hills through thick shrubs and pine trees. Along the way, my father gave strong hand signals to his friend Choi Seungjo to escape. It was well past midnight, but the sky was clear and bright with moonlight, making it dangerous for prisoners to flee. As they were nearing a remote point that seemed a perfect place for the soldiers to execute their prisoners, Choi Seungjo couldn't wait any longer. With a final glance at my father, Choi Seungjo cut loose his rope and sprinted down the hill. He ran with all his might, stumbling and nearly falling, when he heard the submachine guns (Russian ppsh-41) firing at him.

Awaking the next morning, he found himself lying alone in a small ditch and realized that he must have fainted. He barely made it to his house, having fainted again on the way from exhaustion. When he was awakened by his worried wife some hours later, she told him the news that Seoul had been recaptured by the Allied Forces. That same day, in the late afternoon, despite his wife's objection, Choi Seungjo decided to visit my father's house to find out if he had succeeded in fleeing the soldiers and returned home safely. My father wasn't there.

When she heard Seungjo's story, my mother realized what had happened to my father after he left the house seven days before. Her heart sank and she couldn't think or move. Choi Seungjo tried to explain their ordeal in detail to my mother and expressed his hope that my father had escaped and fled. But none of it registered in her mind. Without her husband's presence, nothing mattered, and no words of consolation could assuage her tormented mind and soul.

The next day, on September 29th, Choi Seungjo and my mother hired a few men to search all over the mountain to see if they could find any corpses or traces of the execution. It was to no avail. There was no evidence to be found. My mother and the search crew assumed that my father had been taken to North Korea after he was arrested. The question of whether he was executed or still alive would continue to haunt my family. Was he executed by the North or South Koreans? Was he viewed as a communist sympathizer or a patriot?

On October 3rd, twelve days after my father had left the house to get more food for our family, my youngest brother Sungjoo was born with the help of our neighbor. According to my mother's memoir, my father had a premonition before he was captured and had taken the time to name the unborn baby. Sungjoo was the best-looking boy, my mother often said in later years.

My mother decided it was no longer safe for our family to stay in Seoul, and wanted us to escape as soon as possible. She decided to take my three younger siblings and me to her parent's house in Incheon. My mother didn't know whether her parents were still in Incheon or had already left town to avoid the war, but she thought it would be safer for us there than in Seoul.

—ⵚ—

CHAPTER 5

THE OX CART

It was January 4, 1951. The highway to Incheon was completely covered with snow and it was painfully beautiful and tranquil. The Chinese People's Volunteer Army had crossed the Yalu River in North Korea and were fast advancing to the South along with the People's Army of North Korea. The United Nation's forces and Korean Armies had already evacuated from Seoul.

Without any means of transportation available, my mother had gone out to the marketplace early that morning and somehow managed to get an ox cart, but without an ox, of course. We loaded the bare minimum of essentials, including some roasted wheat and water, into the cart, and put my younger sisters Myungjoo and Hyunjoo on top. Three-month-old Sungjoo, bundled in a blanket, rode on my mother's back.

My mother started pulling the cart and I pushed from behind. The distance between Seoul and my grandparents' house in Incheon was approximately thirty miles. The retreating Korean soldiers had destroyed the steel bridge across the Han River to stop the fast advancing Chinese and North Korean soldiers, and hurriedly built a temporary wooden bridge on top of hundreds of military rubber boats bound together. The river was over two thousand feet wide. After miraculously crossing this perilous bridge, we headed down the road to Incheon. There was hardly any traffic on the highway, with occasional refugees hurrying down toward the south.

We were able to advance only about ten miles that day before it started getting dark. My mother was completely soaked with sweat and had lost all her energy. I was relieved when she stopped pulling the cart. I couldn't push the heavy cart any longer. Many times, I had fallen so far behind that my mother had to wait a long time for me to catch up with her. My legs felt like lead and I almost didn't care if I died on the highway. Totally exhausted, my mother and I sat down on the side of the road. We couldn't go one step further.

The temperature was dropping fast. For a second, I thought maybe we would all freeze to death. I looked at my mother. But she was calm, without showing any sign of fear or concern. Then, all of a sudden, she sprang up quickly and ran toward two young men who were walking down the highway. They had backpacks but carried nothing in their hands. My mother and the young men were discussing something, but I couldn't hear what they were talking about. I got up and walked over to listen to them. My mother was negotiating with the young men and pleaded with them to pull the cart for us. She offered to give them all the money she had. But they refused to lend their hands. They said the money she offered was not enough and just took off down the road.

As we walked back to tend my two sisters, feeling discouraged and not knowing what to do, we noticed there was an elderly gentleman, perhaps in his sixties, with a white beard standing right next to our cart. He said to us, "Hmm. Men came first before the money not the money before men. Let me help you."

He didn't even ask my mother how much money she had. He simply started pulling the cart right away. He said we might be lucky and find an empty house nearby where we could stay overnight. Indeed, he was right. Before long, we found a house, but it was already crowded with other people who had escaped from Seoul. When they saw the young mother with her baby and three young children, the people in the room quickly made room for us. The floor was heated, but the room was so small we couldn't find enough space to properly lie down. Nonetheless, my mother and I felt immense peace from the love and kindness extended to us by our fellow refugees.

The next morning, with the old man pulling and my mother and I pushing the cart from behind, we reached our grandparents' house safely by nightfall. Luckily, my grandparents were still there. They said they were waiting to see if one of their five children and their families would come before leaving town. They were planning to take a boat from Incheon to Dangjin, Chungcheongnam-do, located about fifty miles further south, where they thought it would be safer.

As soon as we arrived at our grandparents' house, my mother asked her parents to take good care of the gentleman who had helped us. Then she collapsed and couldn't get up for two days. To this day, I am amazed when I think about what happened. It was a miracle that we survived. I firmly believe the elderly gentleman who helped us was an angel sent by God.

When my mother finally awoke from two straight days of sleep, she still was in no condition physically to travel to Dangjin with her parents. Our grandparents decided to wait and give my mother more time to recover. Ten days later, together with our grandparents, we went to the Incheon pier and managed to get on a small fishing boat that took us to Dangjin, where our grandparents' older brother had a huge house with room for all of us.

Life in the remote country village of Dangjin was much more peaceful than in Seoul or Incheon. Occasionally, we saw soldiers of the People's Army patrolling around the town, but they never bothered us. Several months passed by quickly. As soon as my mother heard news that the Allied Forces were winning and the North Korean armies were in retreat, she decided to take us back to our old house in Chunghyeon-dong and prepared us for the journey. However, when we reached the Han River at Yeongdeungpo, we were blocked by South Korean soldiers who would not allow us to cross. We were told that the war was still not over and that it was too risky to go back to Seoul.

CHAPTER 6

NO PLACE FOR CHILDREN

We were now stuck in the village of Yeongdeungpo, which was only six miles south of Seoul, but on the opposite side of the river. Somehow, my mother managed to find an empty house for us. There was a horse stable attached to the house, where she spent an entire day cleaning out the horse manure to start a business. A U.S. Army barracks was stationed right across from the house, and she had noticed many Korean women waiting underneath the wire fence to receive bags of laundry from the U.S. soldiers on the other side. Apparently, the army barracks did not have a laundry facility and the soldiers either had to wash their own clothes or pay these Korean women a small fee to do their laundry.

My mother quickly learned the trade and started working day and night. Just as she was gaining a good reputation with the soldiers and her income was increasing, she was stricken with another misfortune. My eight-month-old brother Sungjoo contracted smallpox and died in a matter of a few days. The loss of Sungjoo was devastating for my mother. Due to the chaotic situation of the war, she had forgotten to have Sungjoo vaccinated. She couldn't blame God for this tragedy and was seized with remorse. After she sent Sungjoo away to heaven, she was determined to pay even more attention to her three remaining kids.

Surprisingly, my mother's laundry business started gaining

traction and her volume increased substantially. She hired three women to help her. Now that she didn't have to handwash the mountains of clothes herself, she could concentrate on ironing them, often working past midnight. In order to communicate better with her GI customers, she found an old Japanese-English dictionary and memorized many English words essential for her trade.

Although she was making enough income to support our family, the surrounding neighborhood was turning into a brothel. Day and night, many prostitutes strolled down the streets with half-naked GIs. This was not the place to raise her children, she quickly realized. After praying and pondering over the situation, she decided to apply for a job at the U.S. Army barracks across the street.

As it happened, they were looking for a personal assistant to a U.S. Army head nurse. She was scheduled to be relocated to Yanggu, Gangwon-do, approximately sixty miles north of Seoul, close to the war zone. Somehow, my mother passed the rigorous tests, and incredibly, the head nurse said she would allow my mother to take my younger sisters Myungjoo and Hyunjoo, who were seven and four years old, with her to work. This nurse was yet another angel in the lives of our family as far as I was concerned. That was February 15, 1952, according to my mother's memoir.

Before my mother left for her job as a nurse's assistant in Yanggu, Gangwon-do, she arranged to put me under the care of her three women employees at the laundry shop. I badly wanted to go with my mother and my sisters, too, but I was not allowed. The American head nurse had gone through a lot of red tape to convince her commanding officer to hire my mother, and they would only permit her to bring her two daughters.

I was ten years old at the time and enrolled in the public school near our house. There was a boy in our neighborhood two or three years older than me. His name was Jinsoo. He had lost his parents during the war and was now living with his aunt, who was in the laundry business like my mother. Jinsoo was very nice to me and we spent a lot of time together.

One day, he asked me if I would like to eat some American chocolate. I said, of course, I would love some right now. He didn't have any, but he said he knew how to get it. Without saying anything further, he asked me to follow him. It was bitterly cold that day, probably toward the end of February. We stopped in front of a small general store. Before we went inside, Jinsoo instructed me to go into the store first and pretend that I was just looking and find out where the chocolates and candy were located. He said he would follow me into the store and start making some noise to distract the owner's attention. While the owner was looking the other way, he said I should grab as much chocolate as I could and run out of the store. He said it would be very easy and I didn't have to worry about anything because he would be the one who would get caught first if things went wrong.

Before I even opened the door of the store, my heart started pounding and my legs felt shaky and rubbery. Jinsoo pushed me through the door and, seconds later, I found myself inside. He followed right behind me. Thankfully, there was nobody in the store, including the owner. I looked around nervously and waited a few seconds to see if the owner might come back in, but still no one was in sight.

Jinsoo gave me hand signals to quickly grab something. Frantically, I looked around for the chocolate. It must have been right under my nose, but I couldn't see it because I was so nervous. Instead of chocolate, I found some white sugar cubes piled up in a little box. I grabbed a few of them in my small hand and shoved them into my pocket. At that very moment, the owner jumped through the door behind the counter and ran over and grabbed my neck. I was frozen to the spot, but Jinsoo managed to run away without getting caught. The owner was an elderly man but very strong. He frisked my pockets to retrieve the sugar cubes, and then slapped my cheeks a few times.

I had to tell him everything, including the story of how I got involved in this robbery scheme. He said he already knew about Jinsoo and his notorious reputation as a petty thief and asked me to never get mixed up with him again in future. He demanded to know my parents' names and where we lived. When the store owner learned that my mother was not in town, he took me over to my school and reported the whole incident to the principal. Once again, I got chewed out badly, both by my principal and my classroom teacher. My classmates gave me a bad time too, when they heard about what had happened, and called me a thief for the next couple of months.

Jinsoo came over to my house a few more times after that incident and asked me to hang out with him again. I never caved in. The shock treatment I had received from the store owner, the principal, my teacher, and my classmates was so powerful that the thought of stealing anything from anybody never came into my mind for the rest of my life. Thank God, it was a failed robbery of only three small cubes of sugar that had taught me this life-changing lesson.

After a month or so, when my mother returned home for a break from work at the army base, her employee friends immediately told her about my stealing incident. I was quietly reprimanded, but she never beat me. I saw tears in her eyes, and she looked distraught, not knowing what to do for her dear child and only son. Leaving me in the care of the three women was no longer an option, and she couldn't possibly take me to her job. The next thing I knew, I was being sent to live in Yongsan, Seoul, with my Uncle Taewook and his family, where I would stay for the next ten months.

Due to the worsening war situation in the north, my mother thought it was no longer safe to keep her daughters with her in Yanggu. She decided to quit her job and make another attempt to return to our old house in Seoul. By this time, the war was at somewhat of a standstill; truce negotiations between the Allied Forces and the People's Army were being conducted at Panmunjeom. One afternoon, my mother and my sisters came to pick me up at my uncle's house in Yongsan, north of the Han River and close to where we lived in Yeongdeungpo. That same day my mother decided to return to our old house.

Kookjoo standing in front of mother's laundry shop; two women employees in background. The boy on the left is Jinsoo, who taught me how to steal chocolates. Our first heist was a miserable failure. Yeongdeungpo, Seoul, Korea, 1952.

Hyunjoo and Myungjoo (author's sisters); girl on right unknown. U.S. Army barracks in Yanggu, Gangwon-do, Korea, 1952, where Yoo Taejung served as head nurse's assistant.

—∿—

CHAPTER 7

THE NOODLE HOUSE

As expected, when we got back to Chunghyeon-dong, our house was half-destroyed like the rest of the houses in our neighborhood. All the doors and windows were broken, and it was filled with dust and cobwebs. My mother had such sad memories of this miserable place where she had lived with her husband and three stepsons before they were captured by the North Koreans. This place must be cursed, she thought. She sold the house without any regrets, and we moved to a small two-story house in a shanty town on the bank of the Cheonggye Stream.

With extra cash from the proceeds of the house sale, my mother opened a business selling noodles and mung-bean pancakes on the first floor, and we used the upstairs for our family dwelling. After her success with the laundry business in Yeongdeungpo, she thought running a small restaurant business would be easy. She overestimated her ability, and after six months' time, the noodle shop was still failing miserably.

One day, Uncle Taewook visited us at the restaurant and learned about the dilemma my mother was facing. Immediately, he suggested for my mother and family to move the restaurant to his house in Yongsan. He owned a two-room place right next to his own house that he said could easily be converted into a small restaurant. We could use the spare room for our dwelling. My mother hesitated initially, because she felt it would be too much for her brother and his wife to accommodate our family on top of their own five children. But Uncle Taewook was a very generous man, and he had a very strong and persuasive personality. He insisted that my mother accept his offer, adding that she needed to have a man around who could protect her in case of an emergency or any unexpected events. My mother was lucky to have such a caring brother. Since she had no other option, she reluctantly agreed, and we packed up and moved our family to the little house in Yongsan.

As the saying goes for business, it all depends on location, location, location. Our restaurant was less than five-hundred yards from the Yongsan Train Station. After the initial trial and error period, my mother's new noodle house business started picking up. She had many regular customers who worked for the train station, as well as employees from the nearby offices that housed a large communications company. Finally, she started to feel comfortable that she was making a decent living at this business and assured that her family would be free from hunger. She was making enough money to hire a private tutor to prepare me for the middle-school entrance examination the following year. She realized that my elementary education had been seriously disrupted by the war and having to move our family so many times over the past few years due to our unfortunate circumstances.

All was going well until, one day, she received a notice from the county office in the mail. The notice stated that she must close the restaurant business immediately. It was illegal to run a business without a license issued by the proper authority. Obviously, both my mother and uncle had ignored the issue, either intentionally or unintentionally. They were short-sighted. It probably was intentional, as they would have to pay out lots of grease money to get the license. For some unknown reason—at least, to me, instead of applying for the business license, my mother decided to close the restaurant for good.

Not long after that, she managed to find a well-paying job

as a housemaid and cook for an American political attaché, Mr. Curtis, at the American Embassy compound located in Anguk-dong. Our family moved once again—this time, to a lodging house located in Sajik-dong, which was only twenty minutes walking distance from her new job. At last, our family could settle down. My mother and my sisters Myungjoo and Hyunjoo and I would live at this new place for many years.

CHAPTER 8

THE LESSON

While raising us children in Seoul in the 1950s, my mother stressed the importance of our education. She constantly encouraged us to develop our intellect and fulfill our dreams. I couldn't count the times she told us how much she longed for a higher education. I was enrolled at the Paichai Middle and High School. It was the first private Christian school in Korea, established in 1886 by Dr. H.G. Appenzeller, an American Methodist missionary. My sister Myungjoo attended the Ewha Women's Middle and High School. We were diligent students, but we didn't appreciate the value of education the way our mother did.

Since my mother was born into a well-to-do Korean family in the 1920s, her parents did not encourage her to receive much formal education. She was being groomed to marry well and fulfill the duties of a wife and mother. My mother received a junior high school education at Pai Wha Girls' Middle School, the second oldest girls' school in Korea, founded by the American Methodist missionary Josephine Campbell in 1898. By the time she started formal education, she was one of the oldest students in her class and felt shy and awkward, but she didn't care. Gaining new knowledge taught by the missionaries and their Korean assistants was a refreshing challenge. "Faith, Hope, and Love" was the school motto. She accepted Jesus Christ as her savior and her faith in God was deeply embedded at this time. She felt like she was born again.

On the threshold of this metamorphosis, much to my mother's dismay, her mother refused to allow her to complete the full school curriculum. My grandmother's conservative generation was behind the times.

"Women don't need a higher education. You have had enough," she insisted.

To support the needs of their large family household—which included her three brothers and sister, and a staff of servants to attend to their many guests, her mother needed all the help she could muster. As the eldest daughter, she could not escape from these traditional domestic duties. She was trapped.

My grandmother scolded my mother whenever she lodged complaints and expressed a desire to continue her education. She would not budge. However, within a matter of few years, as the new reform movement started slowly spreading in Korea, my grandmother also changed and allowed my mother's younger sister Taeshin to finish high school at Jin Myung Women's High School. Of course, by then my mother had already missed her chance. She was married to her first husband and had children of her own.

It was not funny how often we heard my mother express jealousy of her younger sister Taeshin while we were growing up. "Although your aunt received her high school diploma, she never read literary books as much as I did," she would say. One time after a visit from her sister, she blurted out, "She is so ignorant and stupid!" Notwithstanding the hidden jealousy between the two sisters, they remained best friends until they departed this world in their nineties.

Indeed, my mother was very literate. She was especially fond of Japanese translations of Western classics. Her favorites were *War and Peace, Crime and Punishment,* and the books of Confucius, Sun Yat-Sen, Lin Yutang, and the author Natsume Soseki. She enjoyed classical music as well. My mother's grasp of world events and human relations was also impressive. I sometimes wondered if the education she had received in middle school was superior to my own education. Perhaps it was because she had read so much literature—or perhaps God had just endowed her with much wisdom.

Raising us, my mother had to wear two hats, as both father and mother. She demonstrated strict discipline with my sisters and me. She rarely reprimanded us for small matters. However, that didn't mean that she ignored or forgot the many transgressions we committed. Once they piled up and reached critical mass, she would explode. It was like multiple volcano eruptions. She was loud and menacing. We had no place to hide but quickly had to ask for her forgiveness. Once the storm passed, she would find her cigarettes and light one up. A few deep puffs usually restored her to her gentle self, and she would make up by way of preparing special treats or side dishes for lunch or dinner.

I thought she was especially harsh on me because I was a son. She constantly reminded me. "Unless you want to be called a fatherless son of a whore, you better watch out and behave properly. Always."

One day when I returned home from school, my mother was waiting for me at the door. She used to work until late in the afternoon at the American Embassy as a housemaid and cook. I thought it strange that she was home early, but I didn't attach much meaning to it. Boy, was I wrong! No sooner had I put down my school bag on the floor than she practically grabbed me and demanded an answer.

"Did you steal the money that I hid inside the chest?"

The large chest was used to store mattresses and quilts and other junk. It was located in the corner of our only room in the rental space that housed all four of us.

"No, I did not," I replied, puzzled.

"Don't you dare lie to me! You better speak up now.

Otherwise—"

Even before I noticed the long stick in her hand, I felt a harsh pain sting my back. She struck me again and again. I started screaming, not knowing why I was being struck. I had never seen my mother so angry and upset with me. I thought I was being punished for something I had done in the past. But I couldn't remember anything I did to deserve such punishment. Never had I been beaten like this. I thought she was going crazy.

After a few more blows, which hardly inflicted any more pain, she finally sat down with the stick still in her hand. She was completely exhausted. By that time, our whole neighborhood had heard my screaming and her yelling. A woman from next door rushed into the room, grabbed my mother's arm, and took the stick away from her.

"Calm down, calm down, Mrs. Yoo. You are going to kill your own son. By the way, what is the matter with your son? What did he do to deserve such harsh punishment from you?"

She didn't answer. She had no energy left to speak and started crying.

The next morning, hardly anyone spoke. It looked like my mother was deep in thought. Something was still bothering her, but she would not say what it was. My two sisters and I were still scared that she might blow up and punish me again. Without a word, she fixed us a breakfast of barley rice and pickle, then left for work. We children went to school as if nothing had happened. I was relieved that she had not blown up at me again.

On my way home from school, I was still very worried about my mother and wondered why she was so upset with me for something I never did. Then I shuddered, suddenly remembering the time when I had stolen the sugar cubes from the shop owner. Now, I understood why she was so angry with me and why she was so quick to accuse me, though she hadn't mentioned anything about it.

Did a thief come in and steal the money? I wondered how

much money was taken. I was racking my brain to figure out if it was really stolen, as she claimed, or she had put it somewhere. For my own self-defense, I needed to come up with a darned good solution, lest I get into trouble again. My brain went blank.

Surprisingly, she was home early again. My heart started pounding. She was in the kitchen alcove preparing some food. I had smelled something nice cooking when I opened our door from the yard, and I wondered if we were having guests to dinner. I was apprehensive but managed to say a perfunctory greeting to her. She only gave me a nod, with a sheepish smile.

I smelled bulgogi (marinated slices of meat) grilling on the brazier. No way! I thought. I couldn't believe the smell was coming out of our own kitchen and not from the neighbor's. We hadn't had bulgogi for months. We couldn't afford it. At that moment, I completely forgot what had happened the day before. The pain on my back seemed to have disappeared, too. I was really hungry, though I wouldn't dare say anything.

When I looked over at our dining table, I saw that a very nice meal had already been placed there. The dishes were covered with cloth to keep out the flies and dirt in the air. My mother quietly came in and sat down at the table. She asked me to sit down on a cushion beside her. She pulled out a hot bowl of rice from underneath the blanket covering the ondol floor (heated by a 19-hole briquet) and put it on my side of the table. She had kept it under the blanket to keep the rice warm for her son. She opened the lid. There in the bowl was shiny white rice with its soft feathery steam spiraling gently upward. I couldn't believe my eyes. We could never afford to have 100% white rice!

"Kookjoo, I must apologize to you," my mother said. "I thought I hid the money inside the chest. I was wrong. Today I remembered I hid it underneath the cupboard. I am terribly sorry."

I didn't know what to say and kept silent.

"Will you forgive me for not trusting you from the beginning? I know you have always been honest—just like your father."

All of a sudden, I wanted to cry, and I struggled to hold back my tears.

"It was such a substantial amount of money I borrowed from one of our relatives. I momentarily lost my mind and doubted you." Her voice was trembling and barely audible. "Will you forgive me?"

I quietly stared down at my plate. I could not speak or look into her eyes, but I felt immense love flowing between us.

I knew my mother was a very strong woman who did not apologize easily to anyone. But she asked me again for my forgiveness, and her tears overflowed from deep remorse and love for her son. I still didn't know what to say. Since she had said nothing about the sugar cube incident, I decided not to bring it up either. I was just upset with the whole hullabaloo. Now the pain on my back returned. I started crying, too. Not because of the physical pain, but from the pain of watching my dear mother in such agony with her heart broken. It made me feel sick to my stomach. I wasn't even happy that I had been vindicated—possibly, because I knew I hadn't stolen the money. Nor was I bothered by her anger and the unwarranted punishment. I was just sad to see my mother, who was such a strong-minded woman, even bother to apologize to me. I didn't feel hungry any more. I had lost my appetite completely. Somewhere deep inside, I felt as if this punishment was justified because she hadn't struck me when I stole the sugar cubes.

Ever since this episode, I was treated like a king in our household. Whatever I did my mother supported me one hundred percent. My portion of delicacies on the table was always larger than that given to my siblings. Precious fried eggs were given to me first. My younger sisters were jealous and fumed internally over my being favored. They still complain about how Mom treated them unfairly by favoring me all the time.

In later years, I came to realize the huge impact that little incident had on my life. When you receive unconditional love and trust from someone, it's not easy to go against that trust. It keeps you acting straight and honest without even trying. It becomes second nature to you, a habit. The psychological trauma from pain inflicted on you can last for a very long time. The physical pain becomes an unforgettable memory, too. However, the reward for that pain was immeasurable. I felt proud of my honesty.

Knowing that the force of my mother's trust was always with me gave me self-confidence that would help me in all aspects of my life. My relationship with my mother grew stronger and never wavered as the years went by. I always tried my best to match her unconditional love and trust in me with the same respect, love, and admiration for her. I was determined to never disappoint her with any wrongdoings. In fact, I don't recall that I ever disobeyed her or turned down her requests, no matter how difficult or awkward the circumstance might have been, until the day she departed from this world.

Growing up, my sisters and I felt that our mother reprimanded us more than necessary, lest her fatherless children become victims of misfortune. Nevertheless, we always thought we had the best mother in the world. She urged us to be generous with others and never get involved in petty matters. Most important of all, she constantly reminded us to become good human beings and live our lives with honor and integrity.

My mother was very considerate of others and had such a giving heart. No beggars were ever turned away from our door without receiving something from her. My grandmother told me a story that she had to scold my mother on numerous occasions as a child for being too generous to beggars. One time she gave too much rice to a beggar. She almost got kicked out of the house by our grandmother. Years later, it was my mother, not her other four siblings, who would take care of my grandmother until she passed away in war-torn, poverty-stricken South Korea.

I remember one time when my younger sister Yuni (Myungjoo's nickname) lodged a strong protest against our mother for saving meat and delicacies for our grandmother rather than feeding the food to her own children. My mother's answer was simple. "You young children will have many opportunities to eat meat and good food in the future, but grandmother is old and sick, and her days in this world are numbered."

Her strong faith in God and her giving heart certainly influenced me. It became my practice to ask God for answers whenever I found myself in a difficult situation. And God never failed me.

CHAPTER 9

STORM CLOUDS

On April 19, 1960, The April Revolution, a popular uprising led by labor and student groups, broke out in Korea. I was a senior in high school at this time. President Syngman Rhee was forced to resign and quickly exiled to Hawaii. Temporarily, Mr. Yun Posun was installed as the interim president. Both he and the Prime Minister, Mr. Chang Myon, were weak and incapable of performing the tasks for which they were responsible. Daily strikes and demonstrations were rampant all over the country. Slogans of the people on the streets said, "We Are Hungry," and "Let's Change the Government."

Out of nowhere, on May 16, 1961, one year later, the military coup led by Major General Park Chung-hee broke out. The corrupt politicians and heads of large corporations were rounded up, detained, and imprisoned. Martial law was declared with a twenty-four-hour curfew and the street demonstrations and strikes finally ceased. The bickering between the opposing politicians also came to an end. Many newspapers and book companies publishing propaganda were forced to close their doors.

People were still very apprehensive about the newly self-appointed supreme commander, Major General Park Chung-hee, except that his immediate political and economic agenda was impressive and refreshing for people who had been exploited and misled by their leader's false promises for so long. Korea at this time was the second poorest country in the world with a per capita income of $69. The Republic of Congo had the honor of being the poorest.

Looking back, I don't recall how the first semester of my freshman year of college began and ended. I was enrolled as a student at Korea University, one of the top private universities in South Korea. Most of the classes were either cancelled or suspended due to the number of students who were participating in the various strikes and street demonstrations. Military soldiers and KCIA agents were stationed on the college campuses watching every move of the student activists. While the country was going through this radical revolution, I was busy taking care of my mother and two younger sisters. I had little time to pay attention to what was happening to our country. I felt sad that I couldn't participate with the other students. By that summer, things had settled down again on campus.

One summer morning, I was sitting at the table preparing the registration forms to enroll in my second semester at Korea University. Somehow, my mother had saved enough money for my tuition to make sure I would continue my college education. I had been accepted to study in the department of Political Science and Economy.

"Kookjoo, let's have a talk," said my mother. She sounded grim and serious.

I suddenly noticed she had visibly lost weight. She looked pale and unwell. I knew something was wrong, but I couldn't imagine what it could be.

My mother had been working as a housemaid and cook for the American Embassy employees for the past several years. It was a hard-earned job for her. She got the job because she was able to communicate in English, even though it was pidgin English, acquired while working in Yanggu.

"What is it mother?" I felt a chill go through me. Myungjoo and Hyunjoo came over and stood beside us.

"I went to see a doctor today. The doctor said I have uterus cancer."

Immediately, my sisters started to cry. I wanted to cry too but held back my tears.

"Don't worry," she said. "Maybe his diagnosis could be mistaken. I will get a second opinion."

"Can you take me to another hospital next week?" she asked. "I already made the appointment at the Seoul National University Hospital." She looked distraught but refused to show her deep concern.

My heart sank. Cancer was considered a death sentence for patients in those days. Was she going to die? What would happen to my sisters and me? My panicky thoughts were rushing all over the place. Soon my mother couldn't hold back her tears either. We all cried for a while.

Finally, she stopped sobbing and dried her tears. Then she told us in the most determined manner: "Listen, it is true that cancer is a terrible disease and may be incurable. But it doesn't mean I will die tomorrow or next week, right? I could live a few more months or years if I am lucky and take good care of myself. So, don't worry too much for now. Let's get a second consultation first, and then I can tell you what we can do next."

She sounded confident and showed no fear whatsoever, which reassured my sisters and me. I was proud of her.

The following week, I took my mother to the Seoul National University Hospital clinic located in Wonnam-dong. It was the best hospital in Korea. Their doctors had a great reputation and the clinic's excellent treatment of patients was well known. After the examination, the oncologist asked me to come in and sit with my mother.

"Your mother has cancer of uterus," he said. "The cancer is between stage 3 and 4. It has already spread to other areas, so it is too late for surgery. The only other option is to treat her with radiation, but we don't have the radiation equipment yet in this hospital. Without the surgery or treatment, she still could live another year or so. I would recommend you take good care of your mother until her passing at home."

My mother and I were dumbstuck by the death sentence given by the doctor. It was such a cruel prognosis for her. The doctor made sure I clearly understood the exact condition of my mother's cancer. His prognosis sounded so convincing and clear-cut that it left no room to ask any more questions. After all, he was the best doctor at the most prominent hospital in Korea.

Walking with my mother down the gentle slope from the hospital, I felt weak and frightened. The sky looked yellow—or was it black? I can't remember now. I was nineteen and my younger sisters, Myungjoo and Hyunjoo, were sixteen and thirteen. It seemed as if our future was doomed. My mother had been the sole provider, the breadwinner all these years. But I didn't have the luxury to dwell on this matter too long. I had to deal with my mother's cure at any cost. *No, no, she can't die yet!* my inner voice screamed.

"Mother, don't you worry now. I will find some other way. We will find a good doctor who can cure you." I wondered if I knew what I was talking about. I felt reckless. I had no choice but to give her all the comforting words I could think of. How I wished that my father was still alive to help us during this trying time.

On the way home, my mother didn't say a word. She just kept walking with her hands tightly clinging to my arm. The day was hot and humid, and the stifling summer temperature was unbearable. It was a long, arduous walk back from the University Hospital to our home in Sajik-dong where we lived. I say "home," but actually we were renting just one small room from a landlord. In other words, we were lodgers. When we arrived home, my two sisters were waiting for us. They immediately sensed that the outcome of our visit to the doctor's office was not good. I told them the truth. I also announced that I was not planning to go back to college for the second semester, but would use the money for mother's medical expenses, hoping this would put everybody's mind at ease.

My mother instantly objected to the idea and scolded me, "Don't you ever entertain the idea of discontinuing your education again."

I said that I would only be missing one semester. She didn't believe me, but I had already made up my mind. I knew that I must take care of our mother no matter what. She had suffered enough and sacrificed her entire life for us. It was my turn to pay her back.

CHAPTER 10

PULLING STRINGS

Out of desperation, I went to see my friend Yoon Byungkwon the next day. He was working as a clerk's assistant for the county administrations department, which had jurisdiction over many public clinics and hospitals in the city. I explained to him about my mother's medical condition and our dire financial situation. I was not a personal friend of his, but he had always liked my mother and our family. He listened carefully and told me to go home and wait for a few days. He said that he was close to his boss and would discuss the matter with him.

Byungkwon was my only hope now. He came to our house the next day. I was surprised to see him so soon. He said there was hope. A new National Medical Center had been founded in Seoul three years ago. It was established with a fund donated by Denmark, Norway, and Sweden, three foreign countries that had participated in the Korean War. It was a first-class hospital with modern medical equipment, as good as the Seoul National University Hospital, if not better, he said. The only catch was that you could only be treated or hospitalized there if you were either super rich or extremely poor. He knew we were not rich, but we were not extremely poor either, according to the established regulations. Extremely poor for them meant the people who had no dwelling or any assets whatsoever. We were not going to be qualified. Besides, it was going to cost us some "grease money," he said.

The following morning, I went to the National Medical Center and picked up the application forms anyway. The clerk at the reception desk looked at me and showed me the pile of applications stacked on his desk. He said my application would go to the bottom. The normal waiting period was one to two years. "Sometimes, you never get called," he said. Obviously, he was telling me there was not much hope to get accepted into the "extremely poor" category of applications. Even so, I decided to go ahead and prepare the application forms. Byungkwon somehow managed to pull some strings and made my application qualify for extremely poor status. As Byungkwon forewarned me, he would need money to convince his boss and other people to make our application status qualified. It was illegal, but I had no choice but to spend a substantial amount of money from my college fund to cover the under-the-table expenses. Of course, I couldn't tell any of this to my mother—at least, not yet.

After filing mother's application forms, along with the thick pile of qualifying documents issued by the county administrations department at the hospital, I returned home with a sense of huge accomplishment. Maybe I was not as incompetent as I had thought. My small ego was chuckling inside of me. One big hurdle was over, but what could I do next to expedite the process? I told the whole story to my mother. She was impressed at what I had done so far. She looked pale and weak from continuing loss of blood. Her condition was noticeably getting worse.

"Kookjoo, let's try this. This is our last hope. I am not sure if he will listen to my plea, but I have to give it a try."

She was referring to her former employer, Gregory Henderson, who was a cultural attaché at the U.S. Embassy in Seoul. She had worked for Mr. and Mrs. Henderson as a housemaid and cook for three years before quitting her job due to conflicts with Mr. Henderson. He was a brilliant, Harvard educated man who spoke both Japanese and Korean fluently. His hobby was collecting Korean antiques, especially ceramics, and he spent an enormous amount of money amassing invaluable Korean treasures. (Many of these vessels were on display in "First Under Heaven: The Henderson Collection of Korean Ceramics" at the Arthur M. Sackler Museum at Harvard University. Maria donated the collection to the Sackler Museum after her husband's death.)

"Why don't you visit Mr. and Mrs. Henderson and explain about my illness and the difficult circumstances we are under at the National Medical Center," my mother said. "He is a very influential man with many friends in the Korean government. Maybe he can do something about our application and help us getting accepted fast. Even though we had our differences, I know he still has some respect for me as a woman who is sacrificing her life for her children's education."

Gregory Henderson's view on education was different from my mother's but quite practical. His view was to go to college only when you could financially afford it. He objected to my mother breaking her back to secure college funds for her son. I remember my mother saying she had told Mr. Henderson, "I will support my children's education until the day my eyes are filled with dirt."

I followed my mother's instruction and visited him that same week. He was very businesslike and told me he would see what he could do. He said in Korean that he couldn't promise me anything but asked me to come back and see him again the following week. We couldn't afford to have a private telephone line in those days.

By now, the beans were spilled regarding my tuition. My mother couldn't believe what I was willing to do for her. She repeatedly asked me to never give up on completing college, assuring me that she would find a way to make up the lost tuition money. For me, my college education was secondary at this time. My priority was to save my dear mother from the terrible cancer. I also had to worry about the future of my two younger sisters, as they were at such a tender age. I thought the situation must be doubly hard for them, and I couldn't fathom how they were able to handle their own personal trauma so well. I was determined to do everything within my power to help my mother and sisters.

When I visited the Hendersons, he wasn't at home, but his beautiful wife Maria von Magnus Henderson greeted me with a smile and expressed concern for my mother's health. She was always very kind to my mother and us children and treated our family with great sympathy and love. Maria was a sculptor who taught at the Seoul National University. She had created a number of award-winning sculptures with the assistance of my mother; among them were fourteen pieces in a bronze series representing the Stations of the Cross for St. Benedict Church, or Hyehwa-dong Catholic Church, in Seoul. It had taken Maria two years to complete the project. During this time Maria and my mother became good friends.

Maria was a German-American who had come from an aristocratic banking family. She had shared stories with my mother about her miserable experiences in Germany during the Second World War. She had suffered as many ordeals and hardships as we had during the Korean War—maybe more. I couldn't begin to imagine how difficult it must have been to live as citizens of a defeated nation like Nazi Germany.

"Kookjoo, I have good news for you today," Maria Henderson said. "Please go visit Dr. Koller at the National Medical Center. He is a Norwegian doctor. I think perhaps he can help your mother."

She gave me a little envelope containing a letter addressed to Dr. Koller. I don't recall whether I remembered to thank Maria properly. I practically ran all the way back home to give the good news to my mother. She was very happy to hear it of course.

Although we had the letter for Dr. Koller, the terrible prognosis we had received from the oncologist at Seoul National University Hospital was still ringing in my ears, and I was not sure that Dr. Koller would be able to help.

I did not want to waste any time, so I decided to visit Dr.

Koller that same day. By then, it was late in the afternoon. Dr. Koller had already left the clinic and gone home. Luckily, I learned where his residence was located; it was inside the same compound as the medical facility. The security guard called Dr. Koller, and then let me inside the gate. I found his residence and knocked on the door. Dr. Koller appeared. He was a tall, handsome man with grey hair, a kind looking gentleman. I told him the purpose of my visit in broken English and gave him the envelope from Greg Henderson. He said he had already received a call from him earlier that morning.

"Please bring your mother tomorrow morning to the clinic. I already ordered my nurse to bring me your mother's application," he said with a warm smile.

I had often thought that Americans were the nicest looking people. Henry Fonda, James Stewart, Alan Ladd, Burt Lancaster, John Wayne—these actors were all young Korean men's idols when I was growing up. Dr. Koller was the handsomest of all, I was sure of it.

CHAPTER 11

LEARNING TO PRAY

My mother and I had a light breakfast of mixed barley and white rice, with pickle and bean sprout soup, and then headed out to the National Medical Center. It was a warm summer morning. The cicadas had already started their chorus. I am sure my mother was nervous as hell, but she tried not to show it as we walked down the sidewalk together. I was happy and proud that I could help to give my mother a second chance at saving her life. I felt like I was dreaming. Knowing full well that her prognosis was terrible, it seemed strange that I wasn't feeling more nervous at the time.

Upon our arrival at the hospital, we were led to Dr. Koller's office. He took my mother into his office and asked me to wait outside. Before long, Dr. Koller and his resident staff appeared, and he said, "Although, your mother's cancer is already far advanced, we will give it a try and operate on her. There is no guarantee that she will survive—you understand that, don't you?"

I nodded, dumbstruck by the news that he would operate.

Then Dr. Koller said, "I will do my job as best I can. But God has to help us." He pointed his index finger up towards heaven.

How could it be possible that this doctor from Norway was going to operate on my mother? Was I hearing his words correctly? Didn't the doctor at the Seoul National University Hospital refuse to do the surgery, blaming the late stage of the cancer? I had a strange feeling that maybe my mother was going to overcome the odds and survive, even though there was no guarantee.

That night, alone, I climbed to the top of Namsan Mountain to get a view overlooking the National Medical Center where my mother was hospitalized. My mother would go through the surgical procedure the next morning. I prayed and prayed for her and the doctor. I had never prayed to God that long and that seriously before.

The next morning, before my mother's scheduled surgery at 9:00, Dr. Koller came out to meet me in the hallway. He assured me, once again, that he would do his best, but the rest was up to God. I thanked him again and again. He looked like a god to me.

The surgery took almost five hours. Dr. Koller came out of surgery looking tired, but I noticed the hint of a smile on his face. He tried to use very simple English for me and explained that he'd had to remove the entire womb from my mother's body. The metastasis of her cancer was not as bad as the initial examination had indicated. He said that she couldn't have any more babies even if she had wanted to. I didn't know whether he was joking or not, but I could tell the surgery was a success. She was going to live, providing there was no recurrence of the cancer. She would have to remain in the hospital a few more days for observation.

I needed to get back home fast and share this wonderful news with my sisters. But I couldn't walk. I felt so weak that my legs refused to cooperate. I sat down in the sparsely occupied waiting area. I was totally spent—exhausted. I closed my eyes and prayed silently.

"Thank you, God, you saved my mother." I also thanked Dr. Koller and the entire medical staff. It seemed as if my mind and brain had been emptied clean.

Praying to God was somewhat new to me, as I had only been a Christian since my junior high school days when I attended the Paichai Middle and High School. I wondered how often I had sincerely prayed to God and thanked him for all the blessings given to my family and me over the years. Honestly, I couldn't remember one single time. Why did I only give thanks to God after going through terrible trials? And doing so, only after having a good outcome. What if my mother's surgery had turned out to be a disaster and she had died? Would I have thanked God for that, too? Or blamed Him? Did I really know who God was? I was puzzled about my ambivalent attitude toward God. I felt ashamed, and I didn't feel that I could call myself a true Christian—a believer in God and Jesus Christ like my mother.

Suddenly, I realized that I hadn't eaten lunch. But I wasn't hungry at all. Even if I had been hungry, I didn't have enough money to buy a decent meal. I decided to buy some grilled flat buns filled with little bit of sugar on my way home and share them with my two sisters. I kicked myself for wasting so much time at the hospital. I was eager to get home and share the wonderful news with my sisters.

"How did it go with Mom's surgery?" Hyunjoo asked, jumping out of the room when my sisters heard me coming up the stairs.

"It went well, according to Dr. Koller. He said Mom is like a man now. She has no womb. But he said we don't need to worry about the cancer now. We need to make sure she takes the medications Dr. Koller prescribed regularly and let her eat well and rest a lot."

We all cried with joy.

At the time, Myungjoo was a sophomore at Ewha Women's High School and Hyunjoo was in Soongui Junior High. Myungjoo was the brightest among the three of us. She always excelled at school and got good grades, which made our mother happy and proud. Hyunjoo was our mother's favorite daughter though. She had such an angelic heart and was always very caring for our mother and others. She never put up any fight against her older siblings, even though we treated her unfairly at times. Our only concern was that she was physically weak and often got sick. She also cried easily. We gave her the nickname "Woolbo," meaning cry baby.

That evening, I made my sisters go to bed early. Together, we were going to visit our mother at the hospital the next day. I tried to get a good night's sleep, too, but I just couldn't fall asleep with so much going through my head.

If our mother couldn't work anymore, how were we going to support ourselves from now on? I asked myself. What can I do? What kind of job can I find? So far, my part-time job experience had been limited to house cleaning and serving cocktails at the big parties Mr. and Mrs. Henderson frequently gave at their house.

Maybe I could find a job as a bartender's assistant and become a bartender myself for better pay later on. I was proud that I was able to come up with this idea on my own. I didn't realize it would soon get me into big trouble with my mother. When she learned about my intention, she became really angry with me.

"Is that the big idea you came up with? Just to become a bartender? Can't you dream of something better which could be useful for your future?"

I assured her it was just a part-time job; I didn't plan to make it into a career. She refused to hear what I was saying.

"I will recover quickly and get a job before too long. So, don't you worry about getting a job now. Just concentrate on your college registration. You still have a couple of weeks until the deadline, don't you?"

Apparently, she didn't know that all the tuition money she had given me was already spent on her medical and other living expenses. How could she come up with that kind of money? I wondered. What about all of our living expenses? I was slowly waking up to the fact that I was about to become the head of a household, with the huge responsibility attached to the title. But, for now, I was happy that my mother was recovering from her surgery rather well. She had even started to regain some weight. We all got our lives back from a living hell. For the first time in a long while, my whole family felt at peace and believed that our mother was going to be with us for the time being.

—∿—

CHAPTER 12

SALVATION ARMY PASTOR

We had a long rainy season that summer. Everyone was glad when the rain finally ended in late August. A brief span of cool weather was a welcome break. My mother had started moving around a lot better, albeit quite gingerly. She even began to go out and visit her mother, who was sick and living alone in a rented room not too far from us. Her brothers and sister did not provide much help for their mother. They were all dirt poor, too. It was my ailing mother who provided food and other daily necessities for my grandmother.

For a few weeks, I had not attended church, the Salvation Army Seodaemun Corps, located in Jung-dong next to the American Embassy compound in Seoul. My high school buddy Lee Jungil's father was the pastor there. One day I had a surprise visit from Jungil at home. He wondered why I had not been attending the Sunday services. Jungil was quite concerned when he heard about my mother's cancer surgery and our dire financial situation. I told him that I was planning to skip the next semester of college because I had already spent the tuition money for my mother's medical expenses.

He had a soft heart and encouraged me not to give up easily on my college education. I told him that I intended to resume my studies as soon as I could save enough money to register again. But he and I both knew how difficult it would be to return to college once I skipped a semester or two. Making money in Korea was not easy for a college dropout.

Jungil came by to see me again the next day. He said he had discussed my family situation with his father, Pastor Lee Hwankwon, who subsequently visited an American missionary, Captain Fred Ruth, of the Salvation Army Headquarters at the same location as our church. Capt. Ruth was interested in seeing me to find out how he could help.

Without expecting much, I went to see him the next day. We prayed together briefly. He was a very handsome man. I learned he was single and had arrived in Seoul not too long ago. To my surprise, he spoke almost perfect Korean. I explained my family situation as best as I could. After a few minutes, he asked me what the tuition was for the semester. It was approximately two hundred dollars per semester (the equivalent of about two thousand dollars today). He asked me what I was majoring in and what I planned to do after graduating from college. I told him my plan was to go into the Foreign Service and become a diplomat. He then asked if I would be interested in enrolling in the Salvation Army College in London. He said he would be happy to sponsor me. I couldn't believe what he was offering to me. How much does he know about me? I wondered. Why was he being so generous? I thought that perhaps Jungil's father, Pastor Lee, who knew me rather well, must have given him a good reference about my family and me.

Studying abroad was the dream of every college student in Korea. I had a vague idea of going to the United States to continue my education after I obtained my college degree in Korea. For now, I was not even certain that I could finish my degree in Korea.

"I don't think I could accept your kind offer of sponsoring me to attend the Salvation Army College in London," I told him, all the while suppressing my inner desire to say yes. "My mother and my two younger sisters need me here in Korea."

I couldn't imagine leaving them for the next four years. I expressed my sincere thanks for his generosity, and then I said, "Besides, I am not sure that I have received the calling from God to become a Salvation Army pastor."

I knew my faith in Jesus Christ was still on very shaky ground. I believed in God, but I struggled with the teaching that Jesus Christ was the only way to salvation. I was not a devout Christian by any means. I attended church because I loved the friendship and singing in the choir every Sunday. The men's quartet that Jungil and I had formed was very popular at our church and we frequently got invited to sing at the neighboring churches.

"It's okay. You don't have to go to the Salvation Army College in London. I can appreciate your family situation. Your thoughtfulness and care for your mother and two sisters is commendable," he said. "But I can still pay for your college tuition until you graduate."

I paused for a while. I wasn't sure that I had heard him correctly. Once again, he stated that he would be happy to help me and my family out. Suddenly, I understood what he was offering me—tuition at Korea University. Immediately, I thought about how happy my mother would be when she heard this good news.

Walking back home from the church, I felt as if I was walking on a cloud. The heavy load on my back seemed to have been taken off my shoulders. I asked God, what did I do to deserve this amazing gift? I admitted to Him that I was not even a good Christian. Did He not know that?

Who was this Captain Fred Ruth? I wondered. All I knew about him was that he was a pastor from the United States of America. Most of the Salvation Army pastors were married. They always wore their Army uniform and were good-looking people. Rarely did I see a Salvation Army officer without a smile. Most of them were also musically talented, playing at least one instrument. Otherwise, they are all great singers. Their faces radiated warmth and made you feel comfortable whenever you were with them. I thought of them as model Christians. I still have the utmost admiration for the Salvation Army and their officers for their unselfish efforts to help the poor and destitute people of the world.

I realized back then that the average salary of the Salvation Army pastor was considerably lower than the pastors of other denominations. I knew that because I had seen Pastor Lee's humble family life. Whenever I was invited to join my friend Jungil and his family for lunch or dinner, the meal on their table was always very simple, with lots of vegetables and hardly any meat. Their life was both humble and pure.

With Captain Ruth's low salary, I wondered how he could possibly afford to pay $400 for my tuition every year? He was willing to help others even though his income was hardly enough to support himself. He must be an angel, I concluded. His generosity impressed me deeply. I told him I would like to pay him back someday in the future.

He said, "You don't need to feel obliged to pay me back. But extend your willing hands to others whenever you can."

I promised myself I would keep his wishes in my heart for the rest of my life.

When I got home, my mother and sisters were happy to hear the good news. They also wondered how something like this could happen to our family. Being a devout Christian, my mother immediately wanted to give thanks to God, and we all prayed silently together.

I managed to register for the second semester the day before the deadline. It was hard to believe that I had almost given up the hope of returning to college. How in the world could one's fate change so quickly? Who makes these decisions? I knew it didn't happen because of my own strength or determination. I believed in God. I had never doubted His existence. I simply couldn't cope with the idea of a monotheistic God and the exclusiveness of a religion that treats non-Christians or non-Muslims as heathens or devils.

Although, the problem of my tuition was now solved, I had to earn money for other school expenses, such as books and other necessities. I also had to remind myself I was the head of our household and had to be more responsible in financial matters, too. I needed to continue working as a houseboy and part-time waiter whenever I could. I also managed to get a part-time job as a tutor for middle and high school kids. For a while, I wasn't sure what the top priority of my life was. I needed to bring home more income for our family. I could not afford to pass up any opportunity to work and accepted any part-time jobs made available.

Because of the heavy pressure on me, I couldn't concentrate on my college courses. It was almost impossible for me to work and study effectively. I had never been physically healthy, nor was I very strong. As a sophomore in high school, I had contracted tuberculosis and had to go through extensive treatment for over a year. The initial shock from the illness was devastating. I thought for sure I was going to die within a few years. The advanced medicine for treating tuberculosis was not readily available back in those days. Miraculously, however, I recovered from the disease, except for many calcification scars in my lungs. Besides my physical challenges, I knew that I was not endowed with the smartest brain; I was an average student. Something had to give.

I decided to quit all my part-time jobs except for the tutoring. One of the families I worked for asked me to move in with them and tutor their son, who was preparing for the college entrance examination the following year, and I accepted the job. My mother was happy about my decision, as it gave me more time to study and took the pressure off of me.

Ironically, due to my pre-existing medical condition, I was not able to apply to my first-choice university, which was a public university, where the tuition would have been much lower than at Korea University. Public universities mandatorily screened all applicants for tuberculosis and dropped anyone who showed symptoms of the disease. It was unusual that the private university to which I applied did not require applicants to have an x-ray examination. Once again, I was puzzled and amazed by the fate determined by God.

—∞—

CHAPTER 13

FAILED SOLDIER

While dealing with my mother's uterine cancer and her medical complications, during my college years from 1961 to 1965, I also struggled with my own issues recovering from tuberculosis while working at part-time jobs to supplement our family income. Consequently, my grades in college were not outstanding, but I managed to successfully graduate with a BA degree in Political Science and Diplomacy. I yearned to become a diplomat and work at the United Nations someday.

During the second semester of my senior year at Korea University, while sitting at the campus stadium looking down the track and soccer field, I started thinking about my future career. Ever since the military coup in 1961, the government had been tightly controlled by the colonels and generals. I had learned that the retired generals filled most of the important posts in foreign embassies. There weren't many professional diplomats. Besides, to qualify as a diplomat, I would have to take another rigorous test, the Civil Service Examination, which is equivalent to a Bar Examination and extremely difficult to pass. It would take another few years for me to prepare for the exam and qualify for a position. I simply didn't have the luxury to extend my education. Right then, I gave up the hope of becoming a diplomat. Instead, I decided to pursue business and start making money right away. I wanted to apply for a job at an international trading company.

In order to get a decent job, you not only needed a college degree, but it was also mandatory to serve three years in the military without exception. There was no time for me to fool around and delay the military service. After consulting with my mother, with her blessing, I voluntarily enlisted into the army. Immediately, I was sent to the Korea Army Training Center located in Nonsan, Chungcheongnam-do, Korea.

As soon as we arrived there, they put the enlisted men in the different barracks and gave us brief orientations for the next few days. I loved the rigorous discipline enforced by the sergeants. I was also pleasantly surprised that I didn't dislike the food they served, despite the notorious reputation it had back home. The army food was sometimes even better than what I was used to eating at home. After the orientation period was over, the enlisted men were given the physical and medical tests, which included x-rays, to get qualified for the regular military training over the next three years.

Although, I had been diagnosed as completely healed from tuberculosis by the doctors in Seoul, I knew the calcified scars were still there. But I felt healthy and strong and had no doubt I could handle the rigorous training. The x-ray test results came back a week later. I was disqualified, which meant I was exempt from military service. "I flunked out," was how it felt. Psychologically, I was bruised and felt like a total failure in life for not being able to fulfill this honorable duty.

When I returned home, less than two weeks after I had left, my mother and my sisters were shocked to see me. Recognizing the state of my mind, my mother quickly offered encouraging words of comfort, reassuring me that I was already completely healed from the terrible disease and I shouldn't worry about it. Initially, I was in denial and didn't want to believe my mother's reassurance or the doctor's report given to me earlier. I firmly believed the military doctors were as competent as the civilian doctors, and I feared they had detected something in my x-rays that had forced them to remove me from the training camp, due to concerns about possible contagion.

After recovering from the shock of my failure to become a soldier, I managed to regain my strength and returned to my usual self. Through the grapevine, I learned that an American company called Evans Products Company, based in Portland, Oregon, had an office in Seoul. They were looking for an assistant to an American manager whose name was Fred Jenkins. Evans Products was the largest importer of Korean plywood, and Jenkins was an inspector in charge of quality control over the many suppliers in Korea. Despite my insufficient ability in English, I was hired immediately. I had now become a legitimate employee of the largest importer of Korean plywood. I worked hard at my job, accompanying Mr. Jenkins on trips to visit the different mills scattered throughout the country for the next two years. I learned about the business and the importance of quality control very quickly. Fred Jenkins was a nice gentleman who loved to drink, but when it came to the quality of the products he was buying, he was strict and did not allow any mistakes on the part of the suppliers.

In late fall of 1967, I received a phone call from Mr. Kim Junghan, the general manager of Korea Plywood Manufacturing Company in Seoul. He asked to meet with me. Their company had a plywood manufacturing mill in Gunsan, Korea, which I knew rather well, after making many trips down there with Fred Jenkins for quality inspection of the products we ordered. Over lunch, Mr. Kim asked if I would be willing to come to work for him and his company as an assistant to the export manager, Chung Ilsoo, with whom I had already become acquainted at trade conferences. He said they needed someone who spoke English to assist him and his boss, Mr. Ko Pannam, the owner of the company, to negotiate with foreign buyers.

Immediately, I thought about my future with the Evans Products Company. It was a foreign company and its future was totally dependent on the market condition. In other words, they could potentially close the Korean office if they no longer saw the merit of having a representative in Korea. My future with Evans Products didn't seem too promising, although I knew my salary was much higher than that of their Korean counterparts. Sensing my hesitation, Mr. Kim quickly said he would match my current salary and assured my advancement in the company as long as my performance warranted it. I told him I would seriously consider his offer and return to him within two days.

That evening after dinner, I told my mother what had happened at the meeting with Mr. Kim and asked her opinion about the job offer from Korea Plywood Mfg. Company. Initially, she was skeptical about working for a tight-knit, family-oriented company like Korea Plywood. Indeed, nepotism was more prevalent there than at the other large plywood manufacturers in Korea. Everyone seemed to be related to the owner. Even Kim Junghan and Chung Ilsoo were considered outsiders, though they never expressed any negative comments about it.

When I met Kim Junghan the following week, he offered me a position as a deputy export manager, which I graciously accepted. Immediately, I turned in my resignation to my boss Mr. Jenkins, who was rather surprised but congratulated me and asked for my cooperation in future dealings with his company. The move to Korea Plywood was a win-win for both Evans Products and Korea Plywood. Due to my favorable relationship with Fred Jenkins, more orders from Evans came through to Korea Plywood and the owner Ko Pannam was delighted. Although my title was deputy manager in the export department, I was allowed to handle almost all the export-related business, including the meetings and entertaining the buyers from overseas. My workload was heavy, but I was extremely happy with my job and worked like a dog day and night for the company.

Soon we learned that our export volume had doubled. Ko Pannam's company was recommended to receive the Korean President's Award from the government for their excellent performance and huge contribution to Korean export growth. The military government, led by retired General Park Chunghee, was pouring out its efforts to encourage the exporters to expand their businesses. Along with the award for his company's excellent export performance, the government allowed Ko Pannam to purchase any foreign cars he liked. Until then, the import of foreign automobiles was strictly prohibited in order to protect the fledgling domestic car manufacturer Hyundai. Mr. Ko bought a large, luxurious Chevrolet once used by a U.S. military general in Seoul. He was proud of this car, and everyone in the office dreamed of being invited to ride with him someday.

As the plywood business quickly expanded, Ko Pannam started diversifying his business. At the same time, he showed interest in Korean politics and decided to run for a seat at the National Assembly. As soon as he got elected, his only son, Ko Byungok, took over the helm and Korea Plywood began a new era under his young leadership. During this transitional period, my boss Ko Pannam asked me to accompany his son Byungok on an extended business trip overseas that would eventually take us to the West Coast of the U.S. I gladly obliged, and immediately began thinking what a perfect opportunity this could be to study in the United States. After sweating for many days and nights, worrying about how to approach my boss with the idea, I decided to be totally honest and open about my dream.

One morning, I went to Mr. Ko's office and asked if he would allow me to remain in the United States after his son Byungok and I completed our business in the United States. Amazingly, his first reaction was, "What about your mother and your family? Who is going to take care of them?" By this time, my sister Yuni had become a stewardess for Cathay Pacific Airlines based in Hong Kong, and my mother was working part-time as a party chef for the expat community in Seoul. I assured my boss that my family was financially comfortable without my income. With that, he said he would allow me to leave the company if I would find a competent replacement. I couldn't believe what a generous and caring person he was. He could easily have fired me on the spot and hired a replacement of his choice without any problem.

I went to see Mr. Kwon, managing director of Global Enterprise in Seoul, who was a family friend. He referred me to his assistant, Cho Youngjin, who in turn recommended his best friend, Kim Heejoong. My boss Ko Pannam was extremely happy because Kim Heejoong was a graduate of a top university in Seoul. Besides which, he was born in the Jeolla Provinces like Mr. Ko. People born and raised in these provinces tend to have great affinity for each other and like to stick together. I was happy that, once again, I had managed to create a win-win situation for everybody when making a career move.

Yuni (Myungjoo) and Yoo Taejung at Kimpo
International Airport, Seoul, Korea, 1968. Yuni
leaving for Hong Kong to start work as a stewardess for Cathay Pacific Airlines. My mother was so
proud of her daughter, I rarely saw such a happy
smile.

CHAPTER 14

FAREWELL

On a very crisp, cold day in early February 1969, I stood on the tarmac of Kimpo International Airport with my boss, Ko Byungok. As deputy export manager of Korea Plywood Manufacturing Company, I was accompanying him for an extended business trip. We were on our way to Manila in the Philippines to visit our suppliers of Lauan mahogany logs.

I looked back at the terminal, where my mother, my sister Hyunjoo, and friends from the office were waving farewell. It was a bittersweet moment. Everybody knew that my eventual destination on this business trip was the United States, but no one, including myself, knew how soon I would be able to return to Korea.

The bone penetrating cold was unbearable as we boarded the plane. Winter in Korea is known for its intensity. Briefly, I was reminded of the day when my mother and I trudged down the snowy highway to Incheon with my little sisters riding in the ox cart. I'll never forget the man who pulled the cart for us and guided us to shelter that night. He saved our lives.

Before leaving for Tokyo, Hong Kong, and Manila, my boss Mr. Ko Pannam and I had thoroughly discussed my plan to stay in the United States. He was an extremely generous gentleman, and willingly gave me his blessing and wished me well. I was lucky

Yoo Taejung, Kookjoo, and Hyunjoo at Kimpo International Airport, Seoul, Korea, 1969. The author was on his way to the United States for the first time via Tokyo, Hong Kong, and Manila.

that I had such a generous boss who was willing to invest in an ambitious young man. It was no coincidence that when he later acquired a newsprint manufacturing plant in Gunsan, Korea, he asked my help in supplying the raw material for his mill. Not only did I gladly oblige his request, but I also became one of his most loyal suppliers for many years, even after his passing in 1998.

We stopped at Tokyo briefly and met with Matsushita Lumber Mfg. Co. Ltd., our supplier of machinery parts. They subtly discouraged us from increasing our plywood production capacity. We suspected they were fearful that the Korean plywood industries would soon challenge the Japanese export market in the

United States. Their fear soon materialized, as the Korean plywood manufacturing companies kept increasing their production capacity to become the world's largest exporters to the United States.

We proceeded to Hong Kong and spent two days there before heading to Manila. My younger sister Yuni, a stewardess for Cathay Pacific Airlines, happened to be in Hong Kong that week. Before becoming a stewardess, she had worked for KBS Television Broadcasting Company as an actress. She was one of a handful of actresses who had passed the rigorous audition process. She became famous quickly, but soon realized how corrupt and crude the entertainment industry was. Consequently, she resigned from KBS and decided to work for Cathay Pacific Airlines. She truly looked beautiful donned in her uniform. I was proud of her.

We were happy to see each other in a foreign land. Learning about my intention and goal to continue my education in the United States, she gladly gave me a hundred dollars out of her own savings. I was pleasantly surprised by her generosity. It was quite a large sum in those days. I now had two-hundred and fifty dollars in my pocket. I felt rich.

After visiting Manila, my boss Byungok and I arrived in Honolulu, Hawaii, in mid-February. We then flew to Los Angeles. Our largest plywood import customer, Evans Products Company, was located in Corona, approximately fifty miles east of LA. The traffic even back then was heavy, and it seemed to take forever to reach our destination. I saw with my own eyes that the United States of America truly was a large and blessed country.

PART TWO

LAND OF THE FREE

Kookjoo and Myungki at Multnomah Falls, Columbia River Gorge, Oregon. Late summer, 1969.

CHAPTER 15

OPPORTUNITY KNOCKS

When I arrived in Portland, Oregon, in March of 1969, I was twenty-seven years old and single, with a three-month business visa and only two-hundred and fifty dollars. My English was pathetic, but passable. I had decided to come to Portland because I had an American friend, Will Bone, with whom I had become acquainted while working as a deputy export manager for Korea Plywood Manufacturing Company in Seoul. He had come over to Korea to promote American industrial products for plywood mills. He owned and operated a small export brokerage company that handled a variety of industrial goods and exported to Asia. I was one of his first customers in Korea and he had been grateful for the business. Will invited me to visit him whenever I came to Portland. I planned to give him a call. My first priority was to get enrolled in the MBA program at Portland State University.

I stayed at the YMCA hostel in downtown Portland for a few days. Although the hostel rate was inexpensive, I knew full well that to save money I would need to move to an apartment as soon as possible.

The day after my arrival, I went to the admissions office at Portland State University to check my eligibility for the MBA program. Unfortunately, my hope of enrolling that semester quickly evaporated. I had missed the deadline by one week. I also learned that to qualify for the program, I would need to take additional business-related classes.

The school recommended the University of Oregon in Eugene or Oregon State University in Corvallis, but the schools were too far away from Portland and I had only limited financial resources for public transportation. Not to mention having to deal with the uncertainties of living in this new country, which was overwhelming enough. At least in Portland, I had a friend who might help me to get started in America.

Feeling desperate, I called Will Bone to get his advice. When he learned about my predicament, he suggested that I get a full-time job. I knew it would be illegal to seek employment with the temporary three-month business visa given by the Honolulu Immigration office. However, I had no choice but to take a chance, with full realization of getting deported if I got caught.

Will kindly gave me a part-time job painting his house while I looked for suitable employment. He immediately referred me to his friend Pat Connolly, owner of the Connolly International Sales Company in Portland. I mailed my resume to his attention and soon had an interview with Pat Connolly, who called me back for a second interview.

Connolly said he liked my background, especially my experience in plywood sales and export. He said he needed somebody with my experience who could help his company to expand its business by importing Lauan plywood from Korea. The company was already importing prefinished plywood from Yuasa Trading Company in Japan. However, he said their sales were stagnant due to the depressed housing market. He asked me if I could start working right away.

Naturally, I was overjoyed, but I had to tell him about my three-month business visa status that prevented me from seeking long-term employment in the United States. He asked me to wait a moment, then picked up the phone and called his company attorney.

The next morning, I met the lawyer and learned that it was possible for me to start working immediately as long as my work permit application had been accepted by the U.S. Labor Department. Pat Connolly was happy to hear the news and introduced me to his entire staff. My work permit was issued within a month. I couldn't believe how fast they processed my application. With work permit in hand, I was now qualified to apply for a green card or alien registration card. I was now a legal resident. I no longer had to worry about getting kicked out of the country.

It was now time to move out of the YMCA hostel. I found an ad for a rental in the Sunday *Oregonian* newspaper. It was located at the corner of 21st and NW Lovejoy Street, only about thirty minutes walking distance from my office at Connolly International Sales. The ad said it had one bed, a refrigerator, a small stove, and a sofa, with a shared bathroom in the hallway. Most important, it had a black and white TV in the room. The rent was forty-five dollars a month, plus first and last month's rent as a deposit. After a week at the hostel, I didn't have enough money left to cover the deposit, but I decided to visit the rental place anyway.

The house was a large two-story structure about thirty years old. An attractive, elderly lady met me at the door and offered to show me the rental. We climbed the stairs to an attic room that was converted into an apartment for students or single professionals. It was clean and neat like the landlady herself. I explained my financial situation and offered to pay one month's rent in advance but asked if she would forgive the first and last month's deposit. After reflecting a moment, she said she could wait a few months, assuming I would pay it as soon as possible. I thanked her profusely and immediately moved into the apartment, proud to have found my first home in the States. Although I didn't yet own a car, walking back and forth between my apartment and the office would give me excellent exercise.

The day when I had learned it wasn't possible to enroll in the MBA program at Portland State University, I decided to ask the foreign student advisor for a list of the Korean students currently enrolled at the university. I desperately needed more information about the school and its enrollment process. There were only six students listed, including two with telephone numbers. One was Paik Okhee and the other was Hahn Myungki. Clearly, Okhee was a girl's name, but I wasn't sure whether Myungki was a boy or a girl. I decided to give Myungki a call, assuming he was a boy. I presumed I could communicate more openly with a boy student than a girl.

"Hello, this is Litton's residence, may I help you?"

Momentarily, I thought I had misdialed the number, as the lady on the other end of the line said it was the Litton residence. However, I quickly noted that her English accent was clearly that of a Korean and surmised that she might be Mr. Litton's wife.

"May I speak to Mr. Hahn Myungki?" I asked.

She seemed a bit taken aback and hesitated before saying in Korean that Hahn Myungki was her name, and that Mr. Litton was her brother-in-law to whom her eldest sister Sue was married. I quickly explained the reason why I was calling and asked if she or any other Korean students enrolled at Portland State University could meet and give me some information about the admission process. She agreed to meet the following week.

Myungki brought another graduate student, Lee Moowoong, along with her when we met at the school cafeteria. I soon learned that Myungki was quick-witted and intelligent. She had arrived in Portland six months earlier and was a graduate student majoring in general music education. I learned that she was the younger sister of my high school alum Hahn Sungki at Paichai High School. Her father Hahn Byungchul was a famous physical education professor at the Sungkyunkwan University in Korea. Immediately, I felt attracted to her, but at the time, I could not afford to think of anything but how to get accepted by a university in Portland to pursue my education in the evenings. With the exception of farewell or welcoming parties for students leaving or coming, we rarely saw each other for a couple of months.

With my dream job at Connolly International Sales secured, and my living situation squared away, there was nothing I was afraid of now. Without the cloud of anxiety hovering over me, I began to see the immense freedom I could enjoy in this land of opportunity. It had been only a few months since I first arrived in Portland. Thanks to my friend Will Bone's good advice and my boss Pat Connolly's guidance, I felt like I had already become a good citizen of this great country. Though now I missed my mother and sister more than ever.

—ɷ—

CHAPTER 16

SERENDIPITY

The first car I purchased with savings from my new job at
Connolly International was a 1965 Ford Mustang. It had 50,000
plus miles on it and the color was cobalt blue. As soon as I learned
how to drive the car, I had an urge to show it off to someone.
Since I was busy working, I hadn't had a chance to make any
friends, and there weren't too many Korean students in Portland
at that time. I remembered Hahn Myungki and decided to give
her a call.

On a rainy Saturday morning in April, I called Myungki to
see if she would like to go out for a drive. Her sister, Sue Litton,
came on the line and said Myungki had moved out of her house
and was now living in an apartment in downtown Portland.
Myungki had no telephone, but her sister was nice enough to give
me her address. Although I now had her address, I did not have
the courage to visit her unannounced. I had only met her a couple
of times, and I was not mentally prepared to ask any girl out for a
date. After all, I had only been in Portland for a few months, and
my life was just beginning to settle into place with my new job
and studying in the evenings. All I wanted was to give somebody
a ride to show off my beautiful car. And yet I couldn't resist the
urge to drive over and see her.

Her apartment was located very close to the University campus downtown. Not yet having the courage to park, I circled the

apartment block at least three times. What would I say if she comes out and meets me? Wouldn't I look stupid if I said I came over just to give her a ride? I knew I was not ready to ask her out for a date. However, asking a girl to go for a drive meant a lot according to Korean customs.

After circling the block two more times, I managed to stop and parked my car on the side street. I walked to the front of the apartment building and stepped inside the foyer. I saw the address panel with the names of all the residents with a receiver attached. There was her name, clearly written beside her apartment number, but I hesitated before I finally pushed the button. No answer. I pushed again. Still, no answer. When I was about to push a third time, I noticed a lady standing behind me. She asked if I was looking for Myungki. She was the manager of the apartment and told me that Myungki had moved out about a week ago, though she didn't know where. My heart sank and I was filled with indescribable disappointment. I couldn't help but feel a little embarrassed, too. I wondered whether I had certain feelings towards Myungki after all.

The morning rain turned into a steady drizzle. Disheartened and dejected, I decided to drive out to the beach in Seaside, Oregon. I needed to shake off the anxiety that had been building up in my mind all morning. Slowly driving up Clay Street toward the Sunset Freeway, I noticed two young women dressed in typical Asian style, with black umbrellas, walking down the gentle hill. When they were about fifty yards away, where a historic old church was standing, I realized that one of the girls was Myungki. I didn't know who the other girl was. I couldn't believe this was happening. Now, I wouldn't have to give her any excuse or tell her that I had been looking for her. I slowly approached and stopped my car on the street right next to them and honked. They were startled. Keeping a straight face, I rolled down my window and asked where they were going and offered to give them a ride.

Myungki smiled and quickly introduced her friend, a former

classmate at the Ewha Girls School in Korea, who was majoring in Sociology at Portland State University. She was a quick-witted girl too, and gracefully said goodbye to Myungki and me. To this sudden change in the situation, Myungki reacted as if she had been duped, but she quickly recovered and asked if I could give her a ride to a large grocery store located nearby on Northwest Burnside Street. She explained that she had recently moved to a new apartment and had been doing her grocery shopping at the convenience stores where prices were much higher. Of course, I didn't tell her I had been to her old apartment looking for her earlier. I gladly obliged her request.

When we got to the grocery store, I followed her inside and offered to push the shopping cart for her. I didn't need any groceries, but I decided that I might as well be a good gentleman. Unlike me, she took her time shopping, as if she had all the time in the world. She was very careful selecting fruits and various produce. Soon over an hour had passed. Hmmm, I thought. This was taking a bit too long. And yet, I couldn't quite complain.

Myungki noticed me looking at my watch and apologized for the inconvenience she was causing me. She added, "I never had the luxury of shopping at a large grocery store like Fred Meyer and I wanted to take advantage of your kindness."

By the time she was done shopping, the cart was loaded with three large bags snuggly sitting together. Almost an hour and a half had passed. It was well beyond lunchtime. I felt hungry, but I didn't feel like offering to buy lunch for her. Rather, I was hoping she would offer to buy lunch for me.

We arrived at her apartment and I unloaded all three grocery bags in front of the door, but she didn't invite me in for lunch. All she said was, "Thank you very much. I hope to reciprocate you sometime." She was very courteous but cool. I was miffed. At least she could have invited me in for a cup of tea. Maybe she doesn't like me, I surmised. I said a polite goodbye, then turned around and walked briskly to my car, hopped in, and drove away.

I thought about stopping at McDonald's for a burger but decided to head home. It was too late to go to the beach now. I returned to my apartment with a feeling of emptiness in my heart. The only consolation for the day's adventure was that my inner feelings for Myungki had not been exposed or detected. What a bittersweet day! The bowl of cold cereal for late lunch tasted like eating sand.

—ᴍ—

CHAPTER 17

ONE AT HEART

It was late May and summer was fast approaching. One day a friend of mine, Ko Byungwook, the cousin of my old boss Ko Byungok, called from San Antonio, Texas. He was doing graduate work at the University of Texas. He said he wanted to visit me as soon as the semester was over. He asked me if I had a Korean girlfriend in Portland. He wanted to visit the Oregon coast and thought it would be nice if my girlfriend could bring along a friend. It was an excellent idea but alas, so far, I didn't have one, I confessed. He was disappointed to hear it, but said he intended to come and visit me anyway.

One Saturday, a Korean elder and successful businessman invited all the Korean students in town to his house for dinner. He and his wife were very generous with the students, and they frequently gave dinner parties for us, knowing we were always hungry and missed authentic Korean food like kimchi and bulgogi.

When I arrived at their house in Beaverton, I found Myungki in their fenced back yard playing volleyball with other students. I joined them, and soon found that Myungki was very athletic. She had an outgoing personality and got along well with other students. I was hoping she would comment on the help I gave her that day at the Fred Meyer store, but she had either forgotten about it or was simply ignoring me. Surprisingly, I no longer had any ill feelings toward her; instead, I found myself strangely attracted to her aloofness. Knowing my friend Byungwook was hoping for a double date to the beach when he visited me in July, I decided to approach Myungki to see if she and a friend could join us.

Toward the end of the party, we managed to exchange some pleasantries. Naturally, we had much in common, since her father had been my physical education teacher and her brothers had attended my high school. I felt totally comfortable with her. Of course, I still couldn't forget the heart-throbbing adventure when I accidentally met her on the street in April. Without hesitation, she gave me a positive answer when I told her about the upcoming vacation plan with Byungwook. We exchanged telephone numbers. Now I was convinced that she at least didn't dislike me.

The month of June in Portland felt like heaven. The number of rainy days was greatly reduced, and flowers of all varieties were blooming everywhere. The pure fresh air made me feel truly alive. The streets of Portland were decorated with hanging plants and the city and its residents were getting ready to celebrate the world-famous Rose Festival. July was just around the corner, and I hadn't seen Myungki since the party at Mr. Paik's house. I decided to give her a call. I invited her out for lunch that Saturday. I made a reservation at the Benihana of Tokyo in downtown Portland, one of the best Japanese restaurants in town.

Myungki was about fifteen minutes late, but I didn't mind waiting. I had arrived early, as usual, and was already sitting at our table. I liked to be at least five minutes early for my appointments. This had been a habit of mine for so long that I couldn't change even if I had wanted to. I couldn't understand why some people were habitually late; it seemed discourteous. I was hoping that Myungki was not that type of person. Minutes later, Myungki walked into the restaurant. She was wearing a dress, with high heels and makeup. She looked dramatically different from the student Myungki I knew. She was beautiful. I was dressed in one of the suits and ties I wore to the office every day.

Myungki sat down across from me, and we immediately fell into conversation. She admitted that she had felt jealous the day we met on the street and she saw that I already had my own car, even though I had only arrived recently. She was curious to know how I had landed my first job with an American company so quickly, and she wondered how I was also managing to take classes in the evening. Myungki didn't say it, but I knew she was impressed with me. I didn't bother to tell her that I had been an export manager in Korea for two years before coming to Portland. Actually, I was a legitimate and semi-polished businessman, not a student like herself.

After lunch, we drove to Washington Park, overlooking peaceful downtown Portland. It was beautiful that time of year, with many colorful varieties of roses planted everywhere. We sat down on a park bench and watched people strolling by, and lovers walking hand in hand. We talked about our families and our future plans. I learned more about Myungki's large family, with four brothers and four sisters. Her father had retired from teaching at Sungkyunkwan University. Two of her brothers were doctoral candidates, one at Ohio State University, and the eldest brother at the University of California, Riverside. Her brother Sungki, my high school classmate, was a Professor of Physical Education at Kukmin University in Korea. Myungki was majoring in music education and planned to become a music teacher in the United States. She said she had no plans to return to Korea at the moment.

I told her more about my family as well, and my plan to pursue a career in business. I explained that I intended to get my MBA degree, but my number one priority was to have a solid career as a businessman and achieve financial freedom as soon as possible. This was the reason why I had come to the United States. She didn't seem impressed with my goal. I wondered if perhaps she was hoping for a boyfriend who was either a graduate student or already had a doctoral degree and a secure job at a college or research institution. To change the subject, I suggested we take a walk.

Right away, I saw young lovers sitting on the grass, hugging and kissing each other. I felt jealous. Obviously, Myungki saw them, too, but she pretended she was not watching. Slowly, I reached out and grabbed her hand in mine. I wasn't thinking about what I would do if she rejected my hand. I just took the chance. She didn't resist. Her hand was small and warm. I felt like I had just conquered a mountain.

While walking with our hands held together, I started humming a few tunes. Being a music student, I was sure that Myungki would recognize them. I loved music, too, and I knew a lot of hymns and sacred songs by heart. Then Myungki and I began to sing. She had a fantastic alto voice and our harmony was out of this world. I fell in love with her that very moment. Music touched our soul and spirit. I knew we were one at heart.

We met a few more times during that summer. Myungki and I were both convinced that we loved each other. The day after a farewell party for one of our mutual friends, I invited her out for a drink and proposed to her. I told her that I might not be the most ideal candidate for her, but I was confident I would never allow any hardships to befall her as long as we were together. She smiled at me and said yes. But the little tear I had expected to see in her eyes never showed.

The first thing we needed to do was to write letters to our parents in Korea and request their permission for us to get married. This was a formality, but we agreed it was absolutely necessary. We came into this world through our parents. Paying tribute and respect to them was like acknowledging and thanking God for His grace. Without our parents, we would not have been born in this world.

We received their positive replies in no time. The next step was to advise her sister Sue Litton and her husband Jim about our plan. They also welcomed our decision. Everything was happening fast, but we knew we had to concentrate on our daily responsibilities at school and work. All the same, we saw no reason to delay our wedding. We decided to get engaged in October, followed by a wedding in November. Sue checked with the pastor of her church, who said that November 21st would be open for our wedding at the church. We grabbed the date.

CHAPTER 18

THE WEDDING RING

As soon as I started working for Connolly International Sales as a salesman, I enrolled in evening business classes in the continuing education program at Portland State University to qualify for the MBA program. I was working a nine-to-five day at the office, while also attending evening classes. By the time I got home, it was usually past midnight. But one way or another, I had to find a part-time job to give me some extra income. I had not been able to save enough to buy a ring for Myungki.

While perusing the want ads for employment opportunities in the Sunday *Oregonian*, I found a small ad for a newspaper deliveryman. "Starts at 4:00 AM and ends at 6:00 AM $100 per month." They would pay me a hundred dollars for a mere two hours of work every day for a month. This was a gift from heaven, I thought. I figured I could save three hundred if I worked there for three months. That would be enough to buy the ring I had found for Myungki at a local jewelry store. It was a white- gold band with a small diamond; the price was two-hundred and seventy-five dollars. I called the newspaper delivery depot and talked to the manager the next day. He gladly hired me.

Boy, oh boy, did I misjudge the logistics of newspaper delivery. I had to get up at three in the morning and go to the central depot to prepare the delivery for the day. I had approximately eighty houses in my delivery route. By the time the delivery was completed, it was close to six-thirty in the morning. I would go home, freshen up, have a quick bite to eat, and then walk thirty minutes to my office on 12th and S.W. Morrison Street in downtown Portland. I slept an average of three or four hours a day. It was brutal. I couldn't catch up on sleep because there were no holidays for delivering newspapers. I knew I couldn't continue this routine much longer.

One rainy Sunday morning while on my delivery route, a huge black dog barked ferociously at me and almost jumped over the fence trying to attack me. It scared me so much that I intentionally skipped the newspaper delivery for that house. I was expecting a complaint from my manager, but he never called. To this day, I still get scared whenever I see a big black dog on the street.

By the end of the third month, I had made three hundred dollars, enough to buy the ring. My manager was surprised that I wanted to quit the job so soon. I told him about my predicament of working eight-hour days and attending evening classes. I had never missed a day delivering papers, and he appreciated that. Some delivery boys were not reliable, and it was the manager's responsibility to complete the delivery himself. He told me that if I ever wanted to come back to work, he would give me the job. It was reassuring to know I had something to fall back on.

By now, I had grown to like Portland. I thought it was a beautiful city, especially when it wasn't raining. The streets were clean, and the people were exceptionally friendly. Since the day I first arrived in Portland, I had never encountered any kind of racial discrimination or bad treatment from anybody. The only complaint I had, from a business standpoint, was that the city was too small, with a population of only about 350,000 including the suburbs. Compared with the large metropolitan city of Seoul where I had grown up, the potential for business growth in Portland looked seriously limited. I was already having thoughts about how to start a business to support my future family.

One day, I called Myungki, who was living with her sister in

Milwaukie, and invited her out for lunch. We met at the Benihana Japanese Restaurant in downtown Portland. It was her favorite restaurant because this was where we'd had our first date six months before. I proudly flashed a white envelope in front of her. She quickly grabbed it and opened the envelope. She was surprised to see the money inside.

"What's it for?" she asked.

"It's for your wedding ring," I said, grinning.

Strangely, she didn't smile back. She said, "I am embarrassed that I don't have any money to buy a wedding band for you."

I assured her that it wasn't important. We had agreed to skip the formalities of engagement and had not exchanged rings or necklaces. We simply didn't have the money for it. Both Myungki and I were totally unconventional in that sense. The most important thing going for us was that we were truly in love and enjoyed each other's trust and friendship.

"I am not sure it's wise to spend a lot of money for rings at this time," she said. "It's going to cost quite a bit for the wedding, and we will also have to purchase essentials to start our new life together."

Myungki was right. But my male ego told her not to worry about the money. I took her to the jewelry store and showed her the ring I had reserved for her. She said she really liked the ring. Since I still had twenty-five dollars left, after paying for the ring, I asked the manager of the jewelry store if I could buy a gold wedding band for myself for twenty-five dollars. He smiled at us and said the lowest price he could offer was forty-five. Myungki quickly said she would chip in twenty dollars. Now we were ready for our wedding. We were not going to allow any material concerns to interfere with our relationship. We looked at each other and exchanged confident smiles.

For the past few months, I had been working so hard that I had forgotten all about my green card application, until one day, I found the green card in the mail. I was so happy when I opened the envelope; it felt as if my dream had come true. Everything had gone so smoothly with the application. I shared the news with my fiancée, Myungki. She was ecstatic and jumped up and down with joy. Now she wouldn't have to worry about her own legal status any more either.

Wedding of Kookjoo and Myungki at Oak Hills Presbyterian Church, Milwaukie, Oregon, November 1969. We had no fears about the future and were excited about our new life together in America.

CHAPTER 19

HONEYMOON

Our wedding day was only about a week away. I had just picked up my Mustang from the garage. I wanted to have my car well-tuned up before the long trip to San Diego. We planned to visit her eldest brother Youngki, who was in the doctoral program at the University of California, Riverside. I needed to visit Myungki at her sister's house in Milwaukie that morning. Once again, the weather was gray and drizzling. As I was approaching a small curving tunnel near the Marquam Bridge on Powell Street, my car spun and hit the concrete side wall. I didn't think I was driving very fast, but there was no excuse for it. Luckily, no cars were following behind me. My car got banged up from the impact, but I wasn't injured. Soon a police car arrived, and the officer ordered a tow truck for me.

I thought our honeymoon was over now. Maybe it was better not to make a long trip to Southern California, after all. I called Myungki and explained the situation. Level-headed as always, she said, "It's completely okay if we can't take the honeymoon trip right now. We could always make time for our honeymoon in the future." I agreed.

The next morning at the office, my boss Pat Connolly learned about my accident.

"Ken, don't worry about your car. You can have my car and make the trip to San Diego." Pat was the one who had given me my American name "Ken." He thought the name Kookjoo was inappropriate for a salesman. Also, it wasn't easy to pronounce, he said.

I couldn't thank my boss enough for his generous offer. His car was a huge new Chevy Impala.

Our wedding was held on November 21, 1969, at the Oak Hills Presbyterian Church in Milwaukie, Oregon. Myungki's eldest sister Sue Litton and her husband Jim were members of this church. It was a small and humble wedding. Rev. Alfred Marquam officiated the wedding. Besides the Littons, my sister Yuni, and Pat Connolly and his wife attended. Neither Myungki's parents nor my mother and Hyunjoo were able to attend the wedding, since they lived in Seoul and could not afford to make the trip. It didn't matter terribly to us, as I had a full-time job and was a legal resident now, and Myungki was a full-time graduate student. Although we had no savings and didn't own a house, we felt rich and were not afraid of anything. We had our youth and our health. Our new life had just begun in the Land of Opportunity.

We decided to take the scenic route on Highway 101 instead of taking the Interstate toward the south. We had never known how rugged and beautiful the Oregon Coast was. Its natural beauty was out of this world. All the way down to San Francisco, Myungki and I sang every song we could think of—hymns, sacred music, Negro spirituals, and even Korean children's songs. We were so happy together. We had finally met our soul mates. For the first time, I felt truly grateful to have found a wife who was going to be a music teacher.

Driving through the seventeen-mile Monterey Peninsula that hugs the Pacific coastline, the views were breathtaking. We stopped many times to take photos. I had never seen Myungki so happy and content. Myungki's eldest brother Youngki and his wife Sue welcomed us at their humble apartment in Riverside, California. Youngki was very close to getting his doctoral degree. I was envious and wondered if I would ever complete my MBA degree.

Since I was meeting my brother-in-law for the first time, he asked me many questions about my parents and family. He had heard rumors that I used to be a rice dealer back in Korea. I assured him that it was not true, and went on to explain my background in detail. He expressed his discomfort that I was not a full-time student and encouraged me to continue my education at all costs. I agreed with him. But I didn't tell him that I was in survival mode and wanted to obtain financial freedom as soon as possible. Getting a higher degree didn't seem important to me unless someone wanted to pursue teaching or a research occupation. I had no inclination for either.

After our visit to the world-famous San Diego Zoo, we returned home safely to Portland and started our new married life together. Myungki moved in with me at the apartment on Northwest 23rd and Oak Street. As soon as she moved in, the first thing she wanted was a small upright piano for her music study. Since it was an old apartment complex, there was hardly any insulation between the floors and adjoining rooms to soundproof our apartment. After negotiating with the manager, Myungki was allowed to practice certain hours every day. We were happy with the arrangement and bought an old used piano without delay.

Myungki had only three quarters left to complete her master's degree in music. Ever since we first started dating, I had supported her by covering school tuition and other expenses. She tried to help by getting a part-time job as a dishwasher in a restaurant. I couldn't bear to see her doing that tough job. Whenever she returned home from work, her clothes were soaked in sweat and smelled of stale food. She was always tired and couldn't find time to study.

After Myungki had worked at the restaurant for a week, I asked her to quit her job so she could concentrate on her studies. She gladly obliged my suggestion. She was always quick to assess a situation and didn't like to dwell on the negatives. She seemed to know when something sounded like a good idea, even though it might not have seemed fair for me to shoulder the burden of our finances. Her attitude about life was always positive and she had no fear when it came to practical matters. I was glad that she trusted me to make the right decisions.

—⚂—

CHAPTER 20

BLINDSIDED

In October of 1970, a year after Myungki and I were married, we moved to Scappoose, Oregon, where Myungki started her first job as a music teacher. Back then, Scappoose was a small town with a population of about two thousand people, and most of them were in farming, dairies, and logging. We rented a small two-bedroom apartment close to the Otto Peterson Elementary School where Myungki was teaching. It was a forty-minute commute to my job at Connolly Sales in Portland, twenty miles away.

One day in late November, my boss Pat Connolly called me into his office. He asked me to accompany Mr. Murata of Yuasa Trading Company in Japan to a warehouse in Longview, Washington. We imported prefinished plywood from Yuasa Trading on a D/A (Documents Against Acceptance) 90-day basis, but had not paid them, despite the fact that our payment terms had expired months ago. (D/A is an arrangement whereby an importer will not receive documents giving them ownership of the goods until they accept and promise to pay the bill of exchange.)

Mr. Murata had come over from Japan to confirm whether the goods were still in the warehouse or we had sold the material and were withholding payment. Obviously, he detected something suspicious. He and I drove out to the Longview warehouse together, where he carefully counted all the crates containing the prefinished plywood. Unfortunately, the number of crates was far less than the book showed. It was obvious that there was a huge problem.

Behind closed doors, Mr. Murata and Mr. Connolly had a heated argument. Mr. Murata demanded immediate payment for all the plywood, especially that which had already been sold. The company had no cash on hand, nor any receivables on the books. Mr. Murata threatened to sue the company and returned to Tokyo in a rage.

It had been only about a year and half since I first started working for the company. I was beginning to understand the business and the logistics of marketing. However, I had no way of knowing the company's financial situation. My experience as an export manager in Korea was not very useful in this situation. We always sold our plywood to foreign buyers strictly on "at sight letter of credit" basis and never had to worry about the collection of the money. The next thing I learned was that Mr. Connolly had declared bankruptcy even before Yuasa Trading Company had filed a suit against us in the federal court. I was now out of a job. Unemployed!

Mr. Connolly was quite sad that his business had to end this way. He apologized to all the employees and wished everyone well in seeking new employment. I didn't have much to pack and left the office around noon. I didn't have the guts to go straight home. Obviously, Myungki would be terribly upset and disappointed. I was sure she would worry about our financial future.

On my way home, I decided to stop at the Sauvie Island recreation area off Hwy 30 west, the largest island along the Columbia River with 26,000 acres. It was a popular place for picking pumpkins, with great fishing, and duck and goose hunting. I wished that I had a fishing pole with me. I found a park bench overlooking the river and sat there for a long time, pondering what to do next, and wondering what kind of destiny lay ahead for me.

Being unemployed for the first time in my life was very unsettling. Somehow, I felt as if I had contributed to the bankruptcy due to my ineptitude, though I knew that wasn't the case. Pat Connolly had helped with my legal status, trained me, and taught me everything about marketing the imported goods to wholesalers and customers on the West Coast. Many times, he and his wife had invited Myungki and me to their house and served us delicious Italian meals. Pat Connolly's wife Jo was Italian American. They treated us like members of their family. I felt helpless and regretted that I couldn't do anything to help Pat and his company survive.

I returned to our apartment around six o'clock, pretending as if nothing unusual had happened that day. Myungki was already home and dinner was almost ready. Kongdori, our toy poodle, was jumping up and down, happy to see me. Myungki was happy to see me, too, and gave me a big hug. She loved her new job at the elementary school. Her master's degree in education was overkill for teaching at this age level, but it didn't matter to her. She was excited to be working with the children.

After dinner, I told Myungki that I was out of a job. I explained to her what had happened with the trading company in Japan and why Pat Connolly was forced to declare bankruptcy. To my surprise, she didn't seem to be terribly concerned, nor was she interested in learning more details.

"You can get another job right away, can't you?" she asked. "You are a legal resident now and you shouldn't have any problem, right?"

She was right in what she was saying, but I was not so confident that I could get a job that easily. I hadn't attended college in the States and my English was still very poor. I couldn't get rid of the heaviness in my heart, but I was relieved a little by Myungki's naive optimism and total confidence in me.

"At any rate, don't worry too much, but take some time off and plan what you want to do next. My salary is more than enough to support both of us. Thank God, we don't have any debt."

She was a fast thinker and never seemed to show any fear

regarding uncertainties. Suddenly, I remembered Sandy, the office secretary, tipping me off before I left the office that I was qualified to file an unemployment claim with the State of Oregon because I had worked for the company more than eighteen months. My immediate thought was, No, I had better not file the claim. It was too embarrassing. I'd had great jobs in Korea and in Portland. I was too proud to say anything about this to Myungki. I decided to find another job fast.

A few days later, without telling Myungki where I was going, I drove to the Oregon State Unemployment Department in downtown Portland. There was a long line when I walked in the building. I felt embarrassed and looked around to see if any Koreans I knew were standing in line. None, thank God. Soon it was my turn to submit my application. The clerk on the other side of the window perused the application, then asked a few questions to verify my ID and employment history. She approved my application and told me my first unemployment check would arrive in a few weeks. Once I started receiving benefits, I would have to report back every month to prove that I was actively looking for a new job.

Filing the unemployment claim was my backup plan, knowing the chance of getting another job like my previous one was slim. I wanted to go into the import and export business on my own—except that I didn't have the money to start a business. All we had was a thousand-dollar emergency fund in our savings account. Even with a steady job for over a year and half, we had not been able to save any money. As the sole breadwinner, I had been paying for Myungki's tuition and other college expenses before she got her teaching job. In addition, I had been remitting a hundred dollars a month to my mother and little sister Hyunjoo in Korea.

While I was searching for a job and trying to figure out what to do next, Myungki never showed any concern whatsoever about our future. She simply kept encouraging me and made sure I didn't lose hope and get depressed. She clearly had more confidence in my ability than I. For the first time, I wondered if maybe I had been underestimating myself all these years.

—𝕞—

CHAPTER 21

BREAKING INTO BUSINESS

One morning, out of the blue, I received a call from a college friend of mine in Los Angeles. I learned that he was working for his brother, who had a highly successful business importing and distributing wigs and toupees from Korea. I explained to him about my recent layoff from the company and said I was considering going into business on my own. He already knew about my past experience in international trade in Korea. Without hesitation, he asked me if I would entertain the idea of becoming a distributor for his company in Oregon. I told him I didn't have any funds to purchase the merchandise.

He paused a second, and then said, "Let me talk to my brother first. I will call you back tomorrow."

As promised, my friend called back the next day. He said that his brother Kim Seemyun, president and owner of the highly successful See's Trading International Inc., was willing to give me merchandise on a consignment basis. He said they had never before extended these sales terms to anyone or any company in the United States. His brother was willing to give it a try on one condition. He had to meet with me first.

The next day, I flew down to Los Angeles to meet with Mr. Kim. I rented a small Hertz rental car and drove out to his home. It was a grand Spanish colonial-style house built high on a hill. The enormous house was beautifully decorated with expensive furniture. When I walked out to the garden behind the house, Mr. Kim was watering the fruit trees. Briefly, I imagined owning a house like that myself someday. He was one of the largest importers of wigs in the United States. He said that he'd had a difficult time, too, when he first started his own business. Mr. Kim assured me I would become successful if I would give it 100% of my effort. His only concern was that the demand for wigs in Oregon might not be very high. We liked each other from the get-go. He was soft spoken, with a genteel appearance. But I could tell he had been through a lot, and had willpower made of steel. He agreed to extend me a credit line of twenty-thousand dollars worth of women's wigs on consignment. He asked for no guarantee or collateral of any kind. He trusted me.

Upon returning from the trip to LA the next day, I told Myungki about my plan of setting up my own company. I had already selected a company name, Global International Sales Co., and registered it with the State of Oregon. Myungki was excited to hear about my plan. She joked that she could now call me "President Choi" like all the Koreans and Japanese do.

The next step was to find an office space with a storefront where I could display the wigs and use the back office as a warehouse. I couldn't afford to lease an office space in downtown Portland, so I found a place on Northeast Sandy Blvd. on 52nd Street.

For the next six months, I tried everything possible to sell the wigs. First, I approached all the wholesale and retail stores. Most of them had lined up their suppliers a long time ago and didn't want to make the switch to mine. I tried door-to-door sales to all the beauty salons, but without much success. Most of the salon owners were women, and I found it difficult to deal with them. Out of desperation, I foolishly decided to try selling the wigs at flea markets on weekends. Still, I had no success. There was no hope in sight. I concluded that either the Oregon market was too small or there was a flaw in my marketing strategy. I didn't know what to do next. Belatedly, I realized the fatal mistake I made by selecting a sales item that had limited market exposure and would require time and investment to penetrate the well-established market chain. I ran out of ideas and had no money left to try anything different.

One afternoon, I had a rather unexpected visitor from Korea. He was a tall good-looking guy. I vaguely remembered him. He was the managing director of a Korean firm and the son-in-law of the company owner. People I knew in Korea had told me he was a great businessman with a strong reputation and high integrity.

"Don't you remember me? My name is Park Youngju from Kwang-Myung Lumber Company in Korea."

Now I remembered that I had met him a couple of times at the business receptions sponsored by major American importers in Seoul. He had represented his company and I had attended as a representative of Korea Plywood Manufacturing Co., Ltd.

"What in the world are you doing here? Selling wigs?"

He couldn't believe I was selling women's wigs. He said he was visiting Portland to meet with some of his American customers over the next few days. He asked me if I could join him for breakfast the following morning. He was staying at the historic Benson Hotel in downtown Portland, known for its elegant European design. Many U.S. Presidents and CEOs have made the Benson Hotel their home away from home since it was first built in the early twentieth century. I thought Park Youngju had great taste to choose this excellent hotel.

After listening to what I had been up to since arriving in Portland, Youngju asked me if I was serious about my wig business. I told him that I honestly didn't see any future in this line of business. Besides, I didn't appreciate the nature of this business, and I simply had no desire to continue selling wigs. Then he asked me if I would be willing to come back into the plywood business. An American friend of his, Bill Wilprud, who used to be an import manager of a large American company in Portland, now had his own company and was interested in importing plywood from Korea. He was willing to introduce me to Bill Wilprud and his company, called Mark Thomas International.

Without hesitation, I told him I would be very interested in coming back to an international trading business. This was the kind of business I truly wanted to get involved in again. He arranged an interview with Bill Wilprud for the next day. Youngju kindly accompanied me to the interview and introduced me to him personally. Bill Wilprud was not an easy man to impress, by any means. He thoroughly reviewed my resume and asked what I did at Connolly International Sales and what had happened to the company.

Mark Thomas International was importing kitchen cabinet doors from the Matsushita Lumber in Hokkaido Japan. The company was selling the doors to the kitchen cabinet manufacturer, Diamond Industries in Medford, Oregon. He was interested in importing plywood from Korea and was looking for a reliable supplier. Park Youngju needed a buyer who could extend the Red Clause L/C, to his company. This type of letter of credit is an instrument that permits the beneficiary to draw the funds in advance against an undertaking to the bankers. Beneficiaries who act as purchasing agents for buyers in another country commonly use these types of LCs.

It was not difficult for me to foresee the potential business opportunity the three of us could develop down the road. I was the perfect guy, someone who could oversee the entire process and the paperwork to ensure that all the transactions went through without a hitch from beginning to end. Besides, I already had complete knowledge about the import and export business. Now I understood why Park Youngju had wanted to introduce me to Bill Wilprud, who was a smart businessman himself. He quickly offered me the job. I didn't need to think twice about his offer. I gladly accepted the job on the spot.

Park Youngju congratulated me on the new job. He asked me

to pay special attention to all the paperwork related to the business. Everything was settled within a matter of days.

—ɱ—

CHAPTER 22

ENTREPRENEUR

Myungki was ecstatic about my new job as import manager for Mark Thomas International. We would no longer have to rely on unemployment checks to supplement our income. I immediately notified the Oregon State Unemployment Insurance Department that I was now employed full-time. Being unemployed had been an invaluable experience for me, because I learned how miserable it felt to get in that long line of unemployed people to file the application. Drawing unemployment checks made me feel like a loser, someone who was incapable of supporting myself and dependent on government subsidy. I didn't come to this country to become a loser like that, I told myself. I would never put myself in that position again in the future. This painful experience is engraved deeply in my mind.

The next thing I needed to take care of was to notify See's Trading Company in Los Angeles that Global International Sales was closing. They were not too surprised to hear the news and agreed with my decision. They even congratulated me on my new employment with an American company. As I recall, due to the extreme financial difficulties I was under, I was not able to pay the unpaid balance that I owed to See's Trading on time. However, Mr. Kim, the owner of See's Trading, was very patient and generous and waited for a long time until everything was settled. Mr. Kim was a true gentleman and I owe him a great deal.

Mark Thomas International Inc. was located in an attractive five-story concrete building in a shopping mall close to Beaverton. Our office was on the third floor, with four private offices and one spacious reception area. I was assigned to a private 10 x 10-foot office space, with just enough room for a desk and a chair. The company was very small, with only four employees including the owner, Bill Wilprud. There was a bookkeeper, a receptionist, and Bill's wife Gloria, who stopped by the office to help out once in a while. From the standpoint of the number of employees, this company was even smaller than my previous employer, Connolly International Sales. I was taken aback initially because of its size and worried whether this company was financially secure and profitable in business.

It didn't take long to figure out what kind of business Mark Thomas was involved in. Bill had an exclusive marketing agreement with the Matsushita Lumber Company in Japan. Matsushita Lumber manufactured kitchen cabinet doors made of Ash wood grown on Hokkaido Island; the company containerized the product and shipped it to Mark Thomas in Portland. Bill's company had only one customer, Diamond Industries, in Medford, Oregon. It was one of the largest kitchen cabinet manufacturers on the West Coast. The business volume was not great, but the profit margin was good. Apparently, Bill was quite content with this business.

The plywood business with Kwang Myung started immediately and it was quite lucrative for Mark Thomas. The paperwork was not complicated, and it didn't take too much time to complete my day's work. One day, sitting alone in my office, and with plenty of free time on my hands, I started getting a little bored. Strangely, Bill didn't spend much time in his office, and I noticed that he usually left the office around eleven o'clock and didn't return the rest of the day. Before long, I learned that he owned a couple of small airplanes. He had his pilot's license and loved flying. He also was engaged in buying and selling small and medium-sized aircraft. I didn't think that wood products and air-craft were a good product mix. I felt uneasy about it, but I was in no position to voice my opinion.

Not knowing what Bill's business plan was for the future, I felt my time with Mark Thomas was not being utilized to its full po-tential. One Monday morning, I dropped by Bill's office. He was reading *The Oregonian*. He must have wondered what I was up to, but he offered me a chair. Bill was always somewhat aloof, unlike Pat Connolly, who was warm and kind-hearted. But I didn't take it personally. Not wanting to waste any of our time, I got straight to the point. I told him I was getting a little bored with the lack of work, and especially in the absence of more guidance or training from him. He was surprised, and asked me, with a slight smirk on his face, "Do you have any good ideas?"

Ever since I first joined Mark Thomas International, I had made up my mind that I would do everything possible to en-sure the success of the company. I was determined that I would never put myself into a helpless position and let the company I worked for fail or go out of business. The memory of the Connolly International Sales bankruptcy was still very fresh and painful. I had been making mental notes about the strengths and weakness-es of the Mark Thomas company and what we could do to with-stand an unexpected turnaround of the market and economy.

I told Bill that we needed a business plan. Not only did we need to have our short-term, mid-term, and long-term goals care-fully defined, but we also needed to review the product lines we could handle year after year. The Mark Thomas company was an importer. But it was one of the many wholesale intermediaries whose fate was totally dependent on the whims of the suppliers and the customers. For now, we only had two items, kitchen cab-inet doors and plywood, thanks to the exclusive agreements we had with Park Youngju of Kwang Myung Lumber. I told him our exposure to market risks was way too big, making us vulnerable.

I told him we were too dependent on import. We needed to

develop some items that we could export to foreign countries to balance our trade. More than anything else, I stressed that we needed to draw up a master business plan without further delay. Now was an especially good time to do so, when the market was stable and our current business model was working smoothly.

Bill kept silent and acted as though he wanted to hear more from me. I told him I didn't yet have a specific business plan for the company in mind, and added that I hoped I had not offended him.

After a few moments, he broke into a smile and said, "Okay, you are in charge of our import and export department. Feel free to go out and research any items we could export."

He also asked me to prepare a business plan for the company. At first, I thought he was joking. I didn't quite expect him to ask me to draw up a business plan. He was a seasoned businessman himself and he should have thought about this a long time ago. I asked him if he was serious about his request. He said, "Yes, I am."

For the first time since I had joined the company, he offered to buy me lunch. We went downstairs to the famous Shaw's Hamburger on the first floor. They had the best hamburgers in that part of town.

I had no experience drawing up business plans in any of my previous jobs. But I remembered the importance of having a business plan from one of my evening marketing courses at Portland State University. It was my understanding that the owners of the company drafted a plan with the help of their consultants and accountants. The only knowledge I had for writing a business plan was based on common sense and some business acumen I never knew I had. After toiling many days and nights, I finally came up with a five-page plan. It was more of a quick marketing plan than a full-fledged business plan.

My plan was simple and straightforward. To balance our import, we needed to aggressively develop commodities to export.

Even then, the United States was known for its import and never was keen on exporting American products overseas. The problem with international trade imbalance was that not many companies were paying attention to this issue. It seemed as if everybody was importing and all the American buyers were hooked on cheap foreign goods. I was confident that we would have many opportunities. It was a crude, but bold plan and I was pleased with it. I put the plan on Bill's desk for his review and approval. It took a few days before I received his nod. At first, I was puzzled regarding his slow action. I imagined that he wasn't satisfied with it, but he was my boss and I had to wait.

One day, I recalled that the previous company I worked for, Connolly International Sales, used to import prefinished plywood from Japan. Prefinished plywood is made of thin veneers of hardwood logs, with wood such as American Black Walnut and Red and White Oak, pressed on top of the Lauan veneer substrates. The beautiful plywood is used for interior walls for residential and commercial buildings. The Korean plywood industry was thriving, and they were the largest exporters to the United States at that time. But the plywood being exported to the United States was unfinished and did not have any added value compared with the Japanese product. My brain clicked. That was it! We could export American hardwood logs to the Korean plywood mills and have them manufacture the prefinished plywood using genuine hardwood veneer and export back to the United States. I told Bill what we needed to do right away. Bill liked my idea and gave me the go ahead.

After doing some research, I found a number of hardwood log producers in the country. They were mainly located in the midwestern states like Iowa, Kansas, and Nebraska. There were a handful of producers in Oregon, but the quality of the White Oak in Oregon was not as good. Bill was now very excited about the prospect of the potential new business. Together, Bill and I made a whirlwind trip to the Midwest. Our trip was a success.

We learned how the logs were harvested and who were the largest producers with the highest quality control systems in place.

Next, I needed to locate customers in Korea. By this time, many of my old friends in the Korean plywood industries were already in key positions and extended their willing hands to me. First, they liked the idea of producing the prefinished plywood using genuine hardwood logs instead of inexpensive preprinted vinyl. In fact, some of the plywood manufacturers were already producing the cheap vinyl prefinished plywood.

It didn't take long before we received our first order of American Black Walnut logs from Tong Myung Plywood in Busan. They were the largest plywood producer in the world.

—w—

CHAPTER 23

SUCCESS

Now that I was more comfortable as an import and export manager at Mark Thomas, I decided to invite my mother and little sister Hyunjoo to move to Oregon as soon as possible. Myungki agreed that it would be wonderful to have them join us. I knew from my mother's letters that they had opened a small gift shop at the Kimpo International Airport, but their business was not profitable in that highly competitive environment. I wanted to help them get rid of their hardships in Korea once and for all.

Without further delay, I called Mr. Arenz, the attorney who had helped me to obtain my green card. I asked him whether it would be possible to invite my mother and sister to come live with me despite the fact that I was not yet a naturalized citizen. After a few days, Mr. Arenz called back and said I could invite them without much problem, as the immigration policy had changed drastically in recent years, and the U.S. Government was allowing a great number of people to emigrate to the United States from Asian countries.

It was November of 1972 when my mother and my sister Hyunjoo arrived. I picked them up at the Portland International Airport. Almost four years had passed since I had left Korea in February 1969. It was an emotion-filled reunion. We embraced each other for a long time.

Myungki and I were still living in our two-bedroom apartment close to the elementary school where she worked. It wasn't much room for us all, but Myungki and I were eager to welcome my mother and sister into our home. Understandably, my mother was disappointed with our living circumstances and the small size of the community. She had envisioned both Myungki and me as highly successful and living in a spacious house in the big city of Portland. Compared to a metropolitan city like Seoul, in the eyes of my mother and sister, life in Scappoose offered no opportunity or future for them. For some reason, after all her years of hard work, I thought my mother wouldn't care to seek employment. She had suffered so much and worked hard her entire life. She looked old and fragile to me, and she knew I was happy to take care of her financially. But she was only fifty-four years old, and, by golly, she was still ambitious and wanted to be independent.

Less than a month after their arrival, my mother and my sister grew restless and decided they wanted to move out and live in downtown Portland near Yuni, my younger sister, who had emigrated six months earlier. Yuni was majoring in Fine Art at the Museum Art School and lived in an apartment near the school. Yuni would earn her bachelor's degree in Fine Art and a master's degree in Philosophy at Portland State University, and later became an art teacher at the Wilson Middle School.

Everyone agreed that their move downtown was a great idea. As soon as my mother and Hyunjoo had settled into an apartment in the same building as my sister Yuni, they started looking for jobs. It wasn't long before my mother managed to get an assembly-line job at Tektronix Inc. in Beaverton, an electronics manufacturer with thousands of employees, where she would work until her retirement at age sixty-five.

My sister Hyunjoo enrolled in the dental program at North Pacific College, and waitressed in the evenings. After graduating, Hyunjoo worked as a dental technician for eleven years, and then set up and managed her own dental lab. Four years later, she sold her business to a friend and acquired a hamburger chain, which was highly successful for Hyunjoo and her husband Mike Caravatta, whom she met while she was managing the dental lab. He worked as a production management consultant for Tektronix.

Looking back, I am still amazed at how easily my mother and sister handled the challenges of starting their new lives in America. Their success seemed like a miracle to my entire family. They adapted to their new country with grace. My mother later wrote to her fellow Korean Americans, "Even though we are aging and old, as immigrants in this country, we must try our best to adapt ourselves to a new culture, new social mores, and have respect for the American people who made this country great and beautiful."

CHAPTER 24

DOUBLE BLESSING

Time flew by, and I hadn't yet realized that I had become a classic workaholic. I was always the first person in the office in the morning and the last to leave. The number of trips to Korea and Japan were increasing. It seemed like I was always traveling. If I wasn't flying to Asia, I was on the road. Frequent trips to the Midwest for inspection and sourcing the hardwood logs made my absence from home a routine. I was young and fully charged up. I worked as if I owned the company and hadn't forgotten the painful memory of the bankruptcy of Connolly International Sales. I wasn't even paying attention to how much money I was making. I always gave the paycheck to Myungki and let her handle the finances at home. I was giving 100% of my energy and effort to the success of the company. I was determined to grow with the company and planned to retire there.

Our first daughter, Jennifer, was born on July 2, 1974. Myungki had miscarried our first child in 1969 and wasn't able to conceive another child for five years. We were not worried, but our parents were giving us pressure all the time to have children. This baby girl was a blessing to our family. We were doubly excited when I learned that I had just been promoted to vice-president from the position of export manager. That morning, I was surprised to find a box of business cards printed with my new title on my desk.

Bill had never said anything about this promotion face to face, and when I got to my office he was already gone for the day. While his behavior seemed odd, I knew he was an astute businessman. He was very thorough in details and didn't tolerate even small mistakes to be made by his employees. My first impression of him had been that he was a tough-minded Jewish boss, but I soon learned he was of Norwegian descent. I liked his toughness, because I knew I could learn a lot from him and strengthen my own resiliency at the same time. My family, especially my mother, perceived me as too soft and weak. I knew this promotion would help me to build more nerve and gumption.

The workload in the office compounded by leaps and bounds. We had to hire another clerk to handle the documents for export and import. We also decided to hire another salesman who could handle the plywood sales. Bill now gave me another responsibility and asked me to visit Japan and handle all the business between the two companies. Whenever I went to Japan, I usually had to extend my trip to Kitami, Hokkaido, where the plant making kitchen cabinet doors was located. I had to inspect the quality of the kitchen cabinet doors. The Matsushita Kitami plant was located about 275 miles north of Sapporo, which usually took well over four hours by train. It was a long trip, but I always enjoyed the visit there. The plant in Kitami was impeccably run and the management was first class. They were humble and always courteous. Our customers rarely rejected their excellent products.

One of the side benefits of visiting Kitami was the pleasure of eating sashimi and sushi prepared from the fresh fish caught off Hokkaido Island. The fish was really fresh and literally melted in my mouth. My Japanese counterpart told me that if I wanted to enjoy the true sashimi and sushi taste, I was not supposed to have miso soup or use wasabi or any other condiments. Also, he said to pick up the sushi with my fingers rather than using chopsticks, and only to use soy sauce if I must, but drink green tea rather than cold water. I followed his advice at the time, but I still prefer soy sauce mixed with wasabi on my sushi.

After a few trips to Japan, Matsushita's Tokyo managers start-ed treating me like one of their own family members. I became close to one of the managers called Tony. He spoke fairly good English. He took me to many different restaurants and we often drank sake together until we couldn't handle any more. One day, while we were discussing various subjects, I asked Tony what he and his company could do for our company other than selling their products to us. He was surprised by my question. I pointed out that Japan's economy was booming primarily because of ex-port to the United States. The U.S. trade imbalance was a seri-ous problem for the United States, and conflicts between the two countries were growing every year. I asked him if he could spend some time researching products their company could import from the United States. Tony listened to me with intense interest. He agreed with me 100%. He even admitted to their shortsightedness and agreed that they had been trained to follow the leader and never paid attention to anything outside of their job.

When I met Tony again in Tokyo the following year, he invit-ed me to a sporting goods store located on the outskirts of Tokyo. It was like the typical sporting goods stores in the United States, except for its size, which was very small—mom-and-pop style. They also had a small back yard with a few straw-bale targets for shooting bows and arrows. A young couple was enjoying target practice and it looked like fun. Tony asked me if I would be in-terested in shooting some arrows. We each picked up a bow and arrows and spent about half an hour trying to hit the target. It wasn't easy, but I thoroughly enjoyed it.

After the shooting practice, we sat down inside the store and ordered some ice coffee, which was really sweet but delicious.

Tony looked at me and said, "Ken-Sang, we are interested in importing bows from the United States. Do you think you could help us?" ("Ken-Sang" was like calling me "Mr. Ken," but in an endearing way). "You asked me to find items we could import from the U.S. I think bows may work."

I smiled at him encouragingly.

"As you know, Japan is a very small country compared to the U.S.A. We have a population of only a hundred million people on four islands which are smaller than the size of California. Because of the tightness of the land space, the majority of the people cannot afford to enjoy outdoor sports like golf and tennis as the Americans do. According to our own market research, the indoor or outdoor bow and arrow target practice business has huge potential. We have already contacted many sporting goods stores and their response was positive."

I thought the idea was excellent. The sheer number of wooden bows we could sell to Japan was exciting to consider. At the same time, I had concerns as to whether it would be possible to price the American bows competitively, because the cost of labor would be much higher in the United States. I asked Tony about this potential problem. He said most of the Japanese manufacturers were making bows for target practice, unlike in the United States, where the bows were manufactured in massive volumes for both target practice and hunting. Besides which, there were not many Japanese makers and their products were expensive. He wanted to know whether I could find some reliable American bow manufacturers that could offer competitive pricing.

The long return flight from Tokyo back home didn't seem tiring at all. I couldn't sleep even if I had tried, as I was so excited about the prospect of the new business. I couldn't wait to tell my boss Bill about the whole trip. I wondered how he would react to my new business idea. He was a very cool and calculating guy. He never seemed to get excited about anything. But his quick insight and judgment were always impressive.

As expected, his response was swift and lukewarm. After carefully listening to my presentation, he allowed me to proceed with my marketing idea. It wasn't difficult to locate several reputable bow manufacturers in the United States. Out of the many companies available, we chose to deal with one manufacturer, Martin

Archery, located in Walla Walla, Washington. Once again, Bill's skill at flying airplanes came in handy. We were able to visit the maker and return to our office in the same afternoon. It was so convenient and easy, I actually thought about getting a pilot's license myself.

After many months of negotiations, sample testing, and umpteen numbers of trips to the Martin Archery, the first trial order of one 20-foot container load of Target Bows was received from Tokyo. The profit margin was very low, but both Bill and I were extremely happy because our sights were fixed on the future, and we believed the larger orders would bring us enough profit to solidify the new business.

About three months later, we received two more 20-foot containers. The shipment was way off the initial order projection we were given. We were expecting to receive orders of at least six 20-foot container loads. They blamed it on the pricing and said that the bow and arrow target practice business was not spreading as fast as they had expected. Lack of space for target practice in the existing sporting goods stores was the real culprit.

A few more orders trickled in, but my initial enthusiasm about this new business had waned considerably. It looked like a nickel-and-dime business compared to the other business we were handling. Bill was no longer interested, and he left everything up to me. Bill and I had very different personalities, but we were both somewhat impatient. There were some rather complicated quality claims issues I had to deal with that drove me crazy. Our other businesses were doing great. The hardwood log exporting business was extremely profitable, and the volume grew substantially. Compared to these ongoing businesses, the bow exporting business seemed like a toy. Serious doubts sprang up in my mind. Maybe I had chosen the wrong product. It went against my original plan of creating a product mix of an industrial or commodity nature that was not too glamorous or sensitive to the whims of the market, and that would yield repeat orders on a regular basis.

I was blindsided and easily convinced about the potentially huge volume I thought the bow import business could generate.

Once I had this doubt in my mind, I could no longer push my Tokyo counterpart for more orders. I decided to let the Japanese market take care of our future course of action. I had an urge to drop the business right away, but the investment in time, energy, and money was too big to make a hasty decision.

The author (second from right) with Tony and staff of Matsushita Lumber at a sporting goods store; the store owner is inspecting an American made bow. Tokyo, 1973.

—~~~—

CHAPTER 25

ANOTHER MAN'S TREASURE

One Sunday at around four o'clock in the morning, I received a telephone call from Korea. It was my old boss Ko Pannam, president of the Korea Plywood Manufacturing Company. I was surprised to hear from him, and my first reaction was that I feared he was going to order me to return to Korea immediately and help him in the export department. Thankfully, my gut instinct was wrong.

Ko Pannam was an astute businessman and he didn't waste any time but got straight to the point. "Kookjoo, can you find a supplier of waste paper for me and my company? We recently acquired a newsprint manufacturing plant and we need lots of waste paper to make the newsprint." (Later, I learned that the name of the newsprint mill was Korea Newsprint Manufacturing Company, established in 1940. Subsequently, he changed the name to Sedai Newsprint.)

I quickly realized that he was referring to old recycled newspaper, not garbage. He said it was urgent and needed to import a rather large volume, a minimum of 1,000 metric tons per month, as soon as possible. Without hesitation, I said I would be honored to help him.

The telephone call from Ko Pannam was a wakeup call for me. I had long since forgotten about Mr. Ko. But I would never forget the special favor he had extended me as his employee and the generous financial support he gave me when I left Korea. This was a great opportunity for me to return his favor. I was determined to do a good job for him.

Up until that time, I had no idea that there was such a commodity as waste paper, and that it was being used to make newsprint, Kraft Liner Board, tissue paper, and all kinds of other specialty papers. Also, I couldn't help but think that the waste paper business was like a garbage business, and I didn't like the connotation of the word. At this time, the concept of recycling waste paper and other materials, such as plastics and metals, was still very new to most people's minds.

As I was not fully convinced about this potential new business, I decided to keep my telephone conversation with my old boss confidential and not mention it to Bill right away. Instead, I frantically started researching into the nature of the business and the possible suppliers scattered around the country. The first item I found under the commodity category of "Waste Paper" in the library of the Portland Chamber of Commerce was "Used IBM Tabulating Cards, 50 metric tons" exported to Korea. It opened my eyes. Wow! Even used IBM tabulating cards were being exported. Although the volume was small, I saw the immense potential of the business. More research showed that only a handful of exporters on the West Coast were exporting Old Newspaper (ONP) and Old Corrugated Containers (OCC) to Korea and other Asian countries. I also learned that all the exports of these recycled papers were being shipped in break-bulk, not in containers. The container vessels had barely been introduced in the world market and were not readily available on the West Coast ports of the United States at this time.

Further research and investigation of the paper industry revealed the enormous potential of this recycling business. First of all, Korea had virtually no forest resources, and thereby had to rely on almost 100% imported chemical pulp to produce and meet the demand for finished paper products. The technology of de-inking the old newspapers was brand new, but the processing technology was improving at a rapid pace. My heart started pounding hard with excitement. I don't recall exactly when or why it first began, but I had noticed that whenever I came across a wonderful new idea unexpectedly, my heart started pounding. But I had to remind myself that I had the same reaction to the idea of exporting bows to Japan. I would have to be more careful this time, and not be overly optimistic. And yet, timing was of the essence—I had the responsibility to quickly advise Ko Pannam in Korea whether we could supply the Old Newspapers to his company. I couldn't hold back my excitement any longer and decided to share this new idea with Bill without further delay.

As usual, I had prepared a five-page marketing plan for the waste paper business and presented it to Bill the following Monday morning. This time, he read my report while I was still sitting in his office.

"Waste paper? You mean, *garbage* business"? he asked, grimacing, and looked at me to make sure I was serious about this business.

By this time, I knew he trusted me and my business acumen more than ever. I explained about the telephone conversation from my ex-boss in Korea and his request to supply 1000 metric tons of old newspapers. My business plan elaborated the potential size of this industry, which was huge and comprised exports to many countries in Asia. True, it was not very glamorous, and it was low key, but this was a raw material supplying business, not a garbage business.

Not surprisingly, Bill did not show any enthusiasm or excitement about the prospect of this new business. He said, "Ken, I will be honest. I don't like the nature of this business. But go ahead and see what you can do."

By "nature," I knew Bill was alluding to the negative association of waste management with the mafia. This was a clean operation—recycled waste products, not garbage. But I was glad that he did not reject this plan, since he had never rejected any of my new ideas in the past.

It didn't take too long for me to find suppliers in Southern California. I also found a couple of medium-sized waste-paper recycling plants in Portland that collected waste paper, then segregated old newspapers, old corrugated containers, and other specialty grade papers from the waste stream and turned it into bales bound by strong wire suitable for stowage in oceangoing break-bulk vessels.

The next thing I did was to call my ex-boss Mr. Ko in Korea and tell him I was ready to supply him a minimum of 500 metric tons immediately. I could have offered him 1000 metric tons, but I wanted to be cautious and start slowly at the beginning. He then turned me over to his assistant to wrap up the details. We issued our formal offer along with our pro forma invoice, which was quickly accepted with their counter signature. The payment term was at sight Letter of Credit in our favor basis and it was opened quickly.

In the meantime, I went out to our two Portland suppliers and promptly secured 500 metric tons (M/T). I quickly made a booking on a break-bulk vessel with the American President Lines, which had a berth at the Port of Portland Terminal #2 to carry 500 metric tons to Inchon, Korea, the following month.

Mark Thomas International was now in the waste paper exporting business! We had successfully added another commodity to our export lines. I knew the potential of this business was great, but I never anticipated the explosiveness of the volume and profit it would soon generate. The word about our company supplying old newspapers to the Sedai Newsprint Mill spread fast in Korea. In essence, we were the broker between the customers and the suppliers. The difference in our case was that we were not merely a commission-based middleman. We physically took possession of the goods and shipped them under our own title and name. Although, the letters of credit opened by our buyers guaranteed our payments, we needed a minimum of forty-five to sixty days to finance the goods purchased until we shipped them out and the original ocean bills of lading were issued for us. We then had to present the shipping documents to our bank and receive the payment, providing we met all the terms and conditions stipulated in the letter of credit issued by the buyer. It required our company to lay out a substantial amount of capital to finance the inventory for at least forty-five days, and sometimes longer.

I felt good that the first order from my former boss Ko Pannam went through without any problem. The follow-up order of another 500 M/T was quickly confirmed, and we tentatively agreed to supply Sedai Paper a minimum of 1000 M/T every month. It was not a written long-term contract, but more of a gentlemen's agreement. I found a few more suppliers in Southern California, especially in Los Angeles, Orange County, and Pomona.

The average gross profit margin was about 15% of the invoice value. It was not great, but not bad at all, considering the potential volume of business we were going to generate in future. My initial projection was to supply approximately 10,000 M/T of different grades of recycled fiber to Korea every month. At this time, Korean Paper Mills were importing approximately 50,000 M/Ts monthly and the import volume was increasing rapidly. I couldn't believe what a great opportunity we had ahead of us.

Bill didn't hide his distaste for the waste paper business, but he finally was convinced that we had found a new export item, one that looked unbelievably promising. Other paper mills and different agents in Korea inundated us with their telex messages inquiring whether we could supply many other different grades of waste papers. I had to learn about this new business of secondary fibers very quickly. It was not very complicated, but I learned the importance of the quality control. Most of the American suppliers who owned their packing plants throughout the country had started their businesses as garbage collectors in one form or another. Most of them were rough and not sophisticated. Not only did these companies lack understanding about the importance of strict quality control, but they were also unethical and insensitive toward their customers and their needs on the other side of the ocean. The East Coast suppliers were especially notorious, as some of them were rumored to be associated with the mafia or other suspicious organizations.

Because we didn't have many competitors, our business quickly expanded to other grades and the monthly export volume increased on average to 3000 M/T. Naturally, we encountered many logistical problems of shipping the goods in break bulk instead of by containers. The bales bound by weak wires broke loose at the loading and unloading ports, creating massive mountains of loose waste paper at the piers on both sides of the ocean, and the frequent material shortage claims by the buyers became a huge headache for us. My trips to Korea every two or three months had become a ritual. I also had to visit and develop new suppliers on both the West and the East Coasts, especially in Los Angeles, New York, and New Jersey.

Bill was very happy with our expanding business and its profitability, but he never showed any interest or volunteered to make trips to LA or New York to develop new suppliers with me. The only time he visited a recycling plant with me was for our first order of Old Newspapers out of the Resource Recovery Recycling Plant in Portland, Oregon, several months before. I'll never forget Bill's reaction when we received our first quality claim from a paper mill in Korea. It was a moisture claim. The average content of the moisture in any paper products is approximately 8-10%. The customer was claiming the moisture content was close to 40%. In other words, they claimed they had paid for 30% water. Bill thought the claim by the buyer was greatly exaggerated and he absolutely refused to pay for it. I agreed with him, but I told him we needed to negotiate and try our best to reduce the claim size while we turned around and filed the same claim against our suppliers. In the end, we were able to settle the claim amicably with both the customer and the suppliers. However, I noticed that Bill's distaste for the waste paper business only grew, and his attitude never changed, despite the mounting profits for the company.

By now, my monthly salary was raised substantially, and Bill gave year-end Christmas bonuses to all the employees. One day—as it happened, the day when I learned that Myungki was pregnant with our second daughter, Christine—Bill stopped by at my office and invited me out for lunch. He was smiling, so I knew our meeting was going to be a pleasant one. We went downstairs to our favorite restaurant, Shaw's Hamburger.

For the first time, Bill lavishly praised me on my accomplishments at the company. He appreciated that our business was thriving and was now well balanced between the import and export business. Our export business that I had developed was actually doing much better in terms of volume and profitability than the imports. To my surprise, Bill said he was talking to his company lawyer to see if he could sell me some company stocks at the book value. He didn't say how much, but I didn't care at that time. I was overwhelmed by the fact that he now trusted me and was willing to share the ownership of the company with me.

This was exactly what I had wanted. When I first arrived in the United States, I read some advice in a business magazine that had stuck with me. There were three ways to become successful in business. One way was to invest in real estate. Historically, real estate value always appreciates; you rarely see news about investors who have lost money. The second idea was to invest in the stock market. The third way was to become a lifetime corporate man or start your own business. Now Bill was offering me a chance to become a minority shareholder of his company. What a great opportunity! After all, I had been working diligently as if Mark Thomas was my own company from day one. I had already made up my mind to retire from this company a long time ago, with or without the ownership of the company.

I thanked him for trusting me and giving me free rein to go out and develop new products for our export business.

—ᵐ—

CHAPTER 26

CHANGE OF FORTUNE

With Bill's offer to make me a shareholder in the company, my future at Mark Thomas looked more than promising—it was assured. Myunki and I were grateful that our growing family would be financially secure. At thirty-two, I was the proud father of our daughter Jennifer, almost one year old, and Myungki and I were soon to be blessed with a second daughter.

We thought it would be a good time to move to a bigger house where we could raise our children in a more spacious environment. Our first house in southwest Portland was a little over 950 square feet, with three small bedrooms and one bathroom. The price we paid for this house purchased two years earlier was $25,000. Meanwhile, its value had appreciated substantially. We soon found a perfect house in Northwest Beaverton in the popular Oak Hills area. It was a modern California-style 2400-sq.-ft. home, with a beautiful atrium at the entrance, three bedrooms, two full baths, and underfloor heating throughout the house.

We moved into our new home in mid-August of 1975. On October 24th, our second daughter, Christine, was born. Myungki had experienced hardly any side effects from her pregnancy, and the baby came into this world after only thirty minutes of labor at St. Vincent Hospital. I was amazed that Myungki was able to have our two daughters without any complications from childbirth whatsoever. Myungki said that her own mother had not suffered much during pregnancy and giving birth to her eight children.

At my encouragement, Myungki had stopped teaching when she became pregnant with our first child, Jennifer, and we had managed to make ends meet over the years despite the ups and downs in my business ventures. But for the first time in a long while, I felt financially secure and had peace of mind about my ability to support my family.

Meanwhile, although our export business was going strong, our bow export business to Japan was stagnant and the outlook was dim. Out of the blue, another new idea popped into my head. I had learned that bow manufacturing was quite labor intensive and required high-level skill and experience. Although the process looked simple, in reality, it took many hours to produce good quality bows. The United States had the biggest market in the world for hunting and target practicing bows. So, I thought, why don't I import the bows from Korea and sell them in the U.S.? Actually, this idea had occurred to me a while back. My heart had started pounding with excitement, but I ignored the sign, due to the pressing issues involved with our export and import business. Day and night, all I was thinking about was the development of more products for the overseas markets.

At first, I thought about introducing the new idea to Matsushita Lumber Company in Japan. I had no doubt they could do a good job. Then I changed my mind and decided to find a bow manufacturer in Korea. While I had no concern about getting competitive pricing, my primary concern was whether the Korean maker could match the quality of the bows the American buyers would demand. Besides, my Korean DNA and patriotic spirit convinced me I needed to give this great idea to a Korean manufacturer instead of a Japanese company. As far as I knew, no one else in the United States was importing bows from Korea at that time.

Naturally, I thought about Korea first because I was absolutely certain that their pricing would be a lot more competitive than Japan. Besides, their bow manufacturing technique should be as good as that of the Japanese. The Korean archers were winning all the medals in the Olympics and the World Championship games. How could you not have confidence in them manufacturing the best bows in the world? Actually, I was badly misled by this poor assumption on my part.

Although this idea of importing wooden bows from Korea sounded good and made sense, I knew I had to be more careful and do some thorough market research before I presented the idea to Bill. On my next trip to Korea, I sat down with our Korean sales agent, Cho Youngjin, of Hanjoo Trading Co., in Seoul. He was acting as our exclusive sales agent for the waste paper business and was allowed to make offers to the paper mills in Korea on our behalf. I asked him to quietly research the bow manufacturing industries in Korea and recommend one or two reliable bow makers for us as soon as possible. Cho Youngjin was a very smart guy. He was the one who had recommended his best friend as my replacement when I resigned from the Korea Plywood Company. His report came within a matter of few weeks. Of the two makers he presented, the company called Hwagok Industries looked more solid and reliable. They had never exported their products to customers overseas, but with our help and assistance, they were willing to try to export to the United States.

I thought the timing was about right for me to present this brand-new marketing idea to Bill. My typical five-page marketing plan to Bill was quickly approved. Like me, Bill also saw the huge potential of the bow importing business. I won't elaborate on what we had to go through to convince Martin Archery to place sample orders with us, not to mention all the trips I had to make to Seoul to visit the Hwagok bow manufacturing facility to inspect the quality of the bows. It was an incredibly arduous journey and required a painstaking effort on my part. Frankly, with only lukewarm support from Bill, I couldn't believe what I had managed to accomplish single-handedly in a few short years.

Despite the approval of the initial samples presented to

Martin Archery, the actual sample order of one 20-foot container had many defects in the bows. The quality issues were quickly resolved, and a second order was placed; however, the same quality issues persisted. Our customer Martin Archery was adamant that they did not want to import any more Korean bows. Meanwhile, I was preparing to make a trip to visit Bear Archery in Evansville, Indiana, to introduce Korean bows. They were the largest bow manufacturers in the United States.

While having lunch with Bill one day, I told him I could no longer handle quality issues with the Korean bows. I was sick and tired of the bows and hated making constant trips to Korea for quality inspections and other matters. Besides, our bow exporting business to Japan was also struggling and was going nowhere. I told Bill I had no more energy left to visit our new prospective customer, the renowned Bear Archery in Indiana. Thankfully, Bill understood and agreed with me wholeheartedly. Without hesitation, we decided to discontinue the bow import and export business. Just like that. Being a small company, our decision-making process had to be quick and drastic.

Our sales agent Youngjin of Hanjoo Trading and Hwagok Industries were terribly disappointed to hear that we had decided to discontinue the bow importing business. They acknowledged the problem with their quality control system, but I could appreciate their disappointment and knew it was not a small matter for them. About a year later, I heard from Youngjin that he had personally made a substantial investment of his own money in the new bow manufacturing plant and had started exporting bows to customers in Europe. I wished him well.

Once we got rid of the bow business, my life became more normal and manageable. In fact, I couldn't believe how fast our secondary fiber export business was expanding. The number of quality claims had also increased, but we considered them a necessary evil and couldn't possibly avoid them completely. Since Bill was rarely involved in the export business, he was pretty much free from responsibilities such as obtaining orders, securing the material for exports, and handling the logistics involved in booking the container space with many different shipping companies, while constantly monitoring the quality of our shipments prior to loading into the containers. Somehow, I was able to manage all of this by myself without losing my mind—only my hair.

*

One day it dawned on me that almost a year had passed since Bill and I had the conversation when he offered to sell me a certain percentage of the company. I was surprised how fast time had flown by. That night, I couldn't sleep very well. I wondered why Bill had not brought up the subject again. Had he forgotten about it? Bill knew how busy I was. Because he did not want to get involved in the details of running the business, he practically allowed me to run it myself. His habit of leaving the office in the late morning and not returning until the next day hadn't changed much, even with the expanded business. He had all the time in the world. He could not possibly have forgotten about his offer to sell me company stocks at book value. It seemed unfair and I decided to confront him the next morning.

As usual, I was the first one in the office. I made coffee and was enjoying the first cup, with cream and sugar, while rehearsing how I would broach the subject to Bill about the company stock offer he mentioned a year ago. One by one, all the employees showed up on time. Bill was a bit late that morning, and I waited until he settled down in his office. I noticed my mind was racing fast, and I felt very nervous about asking Bill for something he might not want to be reminded about. I recalled that I had never had to ask Bill for a raise or a bonus over the past five years. And it was Bill who had offered the company stocks to me. I never asked him for it. I decided to play it cool and went to Bill's office.

"Good morning Bill, may I come in? I have something to discuss with you."

I got straight to the point. I asked Bill if he'd had a chance to review the stock-sharing plan with his lawyer and was ready to offer the shares to me. He said that he had, but that he had changed his mind about it because he wanted to bring his only son Mark into the company and let him take over someday. I couldn't believe what I was hearing. Mark was only eighteen years old, a senior in high school. He had never been trained in the business, and as far as I knew, he was starting college at Oregon State University the following year. Bill was an alumnus of the college. Bill said his decision didn't mean that he wouldn't eventually sell company stocks to me but for now, I would just have to wait.

It was such a shocking revelation that I momentarily went completely blank. I didn't know what to say. I didn't want to argue with him. It was his company and he didn't want to sell it now. How could I respond to that? I had worked so hard for the company over the past five years. I had poured my heart and soul into my work for the sake of the growth of the company, especially from the day he said he would sell me company stocks. I sat in his office for a moment without saying anything, and then I got up and walked out.

I returned to my office and sat there for a while thinking about what Bill had told me. Was it okay for Bill to just flip his palm like that? All my life I was taught that a man's word was as good as gold, and he never goes back on his word. Once you promise something to someone, you must keep it with your life. Bill had destroyed my dream and shattered my trust in him. I couldn't concentrate and was unable to sit in my office any longer. I desperately needed some fresh air. I told my secretary Jeannette I would be out for the rest of the afternoon and left the office.

—ɯ—

CHAPTER 27

BY WAY OF THE RIVER

It was mid-October in Oregon. The sun-soaked fir trees along Interstate-84 eastbound toward The Dalles looked rich and healthy. There was hardly any traffic. The mighty Columbia River on the left side of the highway was calm that day and flowed lazily along, as if it had no concern in the world. I felt jealous. I was raging inside, like water boiling in the kettle on a hot stove. Why can't my mind be more like the river? I thought. I didn't understand what had prompted me to drive out to visit the Columbia River. I just knew I had to go somewhere quiet in nature and cool my head. I have always preferred the river and the ocean to the mountains. They are like a mother, reaching out to welcome me with an open heart and soul.

Although the peak shad fishing season was over in October, I noticed there still were quite a few people fishing for the famous Oregon shad downstream from the Bonneville Dam. I had never been very drawn to fishing as a hobby, but I had come out this way a few times to fish for salmon and shad. I pulled into a small park adjacent to the river. Since I didn't have my fishing gear, I found a bench where I could watch people fishing and look at the river and the mountain ridges under the blue sky. I was glad that I had stopped by a deli in town and picked up my favorite tunafish sandwich and orange juice for lunch.

Eating lunch alone out in nature made me feel truly alive. I tried not to think about anything, not even my own family. I simply wanted to empty myself of any thoughts. I was surprised at how fast my mind was able to go from churning water into a calm river.

I decided to put myself in Bill's shoes and revisit my conversation with him earlier that morning. From many years of my observation of Bill's behavior, he clearly was not the most ideal type of businessman. He never demonstrated any passion for his work nor showed much interest in his employees, customers, and suppliers. He was a very private individual. It seemed the only hobby he had was flying his airplanes and going to remote places for fishing. But I had no doubt that he had become a multi-millionaire by now, thanks to our success in the export business I had developed over the past five years. He was financially secure and could retire anytime if he wanted to.

In most any business venture, there are hidden risks and pitfalls. I recalled the time when our company was sued by a Japanese shipping company due to the cancellation of a charter contract I inadvertently signed when negotiating a large-volume sale of American softwood logs with a buyer in Korea. The buyer claimed they had already negotiated a very attractive freight rate with the shipping company, and all we needed to worry about was to prepare good quality logs for shipment from the Port of Astoria in Oregon. Due to some Korean foreign currency law related to the freight and other reasons negotiated between the shipping company and the buyer, they asked me to sign the charter contract on their behalf. The buyer was going to open the Letter of Credit on C&F Basis, meaning the sales price would include the cost of the logs and the ocean freight, and then the shipper would pay the freight to the shipping company directly.

While negotiating this contract with the buyer in Korea, I was staying at the Chosun Hotel, located in downtown Seoul. I called a friend who was an executive at a local shipping company and asked his advice about the potential risks of signing the charter contract. He explained that as long as the buyer opens the Letter of Credit as promised, and we were confident about the cargo we were preparing in Oregon, I should have nothing to worry about. Since I was in charge of all the export business for Mark Thomas, I didn't see any reason to get Bill's approval for this contract. The buyer promised they would open the L/C the next day, and he asked me to sign the charter contract immediately, due to the fluctuating charter market. The shipping company was threatening to raise the freight rate any time now. I caved in and signed the contract. This order would indeed put our company in a different league, and we could become major exporters of both American hardwood logs and softwood logs. But I was too gung-ho; I wanted to play the hero for Bill and the company.

Unfortunately, the buyer failed to open the L/C as promised; he blamed the quick market turnaround, and we were hooked to the charter contract that I was not familiar with at all. I frantically visited the shipping company and tried to cancel the contract, but they refused to budge. I even flew to Tokyo and visited the main headquarters of the shipping company, where I met with their executives and pleaded our predicament to no avail. By now, I had to advise Bill what had happened and confess the terrible blunder I had committed by signing the charter contract. Bill was beside himself; he chewed me out on the telephone and in telex messages.

My return flight from Seoul to Portland was like a plane ride to hell. I felt like I had gone from hero to villain overnight. For this legal problem, Bill handled everything with his lawyer and did not want me to get involved. We never had to go to court. I wasn't informed how it was settled or how much damage was done to the company, but I knew the mistake I had made was a costly one. And the valuable lessons I learned from this transaction stayed with me.

Other than this one major catastrophe, we experienced no further problems, except for the ongoing small claims from the overseas customers. However, I could see that Bill was annoyed and nervous all the time. Perhaps because he never poked his nose into the details of the business, to him the concerns and unknown risks looked larger than reality. I wondered whether he wanted to retire. Then why bother to sell company stocks to me or to anyone? His excuse of wanting to turn over the company to his son Mark seemed like a random spur of the moment decision on his part. Okay, I got it, Bill. I fully realized where Bill was coming from. Even so, I couldn't forgive him for betraying my trust in him. He hadn't been honest with me, nor had he the courage to inform me sooner about his intention not to sell the company stocks while continuing to dangle the false hope in front of me.

While sitting beside the river that day, my mind gradually cleared completely. I was no longer angry with Bill, although I had lost respect for my boss. There was no future for me with Mark Thomas International. Losing trust in somebody is one of the most unbearable experiences. Rather than face that person, you want to stay as far away from them as possible.

—ɯ—

CHAPTER 28

ON MY OWN AGAIN

Surprisingly, my return drive home from the magnificent Columbia River Gorge was pleasant and I felt completely rejuvenated. I had not yet decided whether I should resign immediately or wait until later. But I was certain that I would leave the company. Myungki was at home tending our beautiful daughters— Jennifer, now two years old, and Christine, whose first birthday was approaching in a few days. Myungki was happy raising our daughters. She especially enjoyed them as soon as they started smiling back and making noises in response to their mother's encouragement.

After dinner and with the babies in bed, I told Myungki what had transpired at the office earlier that day. As expected, her reaction was very quick—she asked me to resign from the company immediately. She said she would do the same. She also questioned Bill's character, as she thought he seemed callous and not very trustworthy. By this time, maybe she assumed that I would have no problem getting a job with another company. I enjoyed listening to Myungki's agitated remarks about Bill and his character. She was speaking my mind for me.

Since I had never thought about resigning from the company so soon, we hadn't saved much money. We had built up enough emergency funds to live on for a while, but not enough to start a new business. The idea of starting my own company now seemed an improbable quest, knowing how much it would cost to finance and run a business like Mark Thomas International. I got scared when I recalled how my first company, Global International Sales Co., Ltd., had ended in such miserable failure. However, since I had already made up my mind to resign from the company, I decided not to think about the new company for now. My gut instinct was telling me not to even bother to go back to the office but to quit immediately. Soon, the better side of me took over. I decided to tender my resignation to Bill with a month's notice. I would take care of all the pending claims, complete the outstanding orders to our customers, pay the bills owed to our suppliers, and notify our overseas agents as well as our suppliers about my decision to leave the company. During this time, I also wanted to train the person who Bill might hire as my replacement.

The next morning, I walked into Bill's office and put the envelop with my typewritten resignation on his desk. He glanced at the envelope but didn't open it or ask me for an explanation. Instead, he simply asked me some questions regarding the pending business issues, then said he would be gone for the rest of the day as usual. I quietly left his office, hoping he would come to my office to discuss my resignation. He never did. Looking back, I am almost certain that he didn't believe I would actually quit and hoped I would change my mind.

The month passed quickly. I took care of all the necessary business, including giving Harriet Clothier, our long-time accountant and office manager, a list of instructions to handle any loose ends I may have overlooked. She said she was really sorry that I had decided to resign and asked me to reconsider my decision. She had told Bill to try to stop me. I smiled at her but said that my decision was final. She gave me a big hug and wished me good luck.

About a week after my resignation, Bill's wife Gloria came to our house unannounced. Myungki and I were surprised to see her and invited her into our living room. She said that Bill had not asked her to visit me, but she was certain he must be regretting his decision not to ask me to stay. She asked me to reconsider my resignation. I told her I would think it over, knowing full well that my resignation was final.

It was a rainy November afternoon when I left the office for the last time. The Thanksgiving holiday was just around the corner. Winter temperature in Oregon is somewhat unpredictable, but I remember it was quite mild that day. I got into my Volkswagen Dasher, put on my seat belt, and turned on the engine. Where to now? Momentarily, I forgot I had just quit my job and was now unemployed. The thought of filing another unemployment claim never entered my mind. I had enough savings and I felt confident about meeting any challenges that lay ahead of me. I knew I was not the same clueless guy who didn't know what to do to support himself and his family.

I decided to go hit some balls at the driving range at the Progress Downs Golf Course (currently RedTail Golf Center), located in Beaverton, only ten minutes from the office. I purchased a large bucket of balls and spent about an hour at the range. I had no goal for my swing practice that day. I just kept hitting the balls one after another, letting out all the stress and frustration built up over the past five years. I hit one last ball, and then went into the coffee shop at the driving range.

After I ordered my lunch, I looked out the window at the beautiful fairway sheltered by tall fir trees. I decided to mentally summarize the game plan I had been working on since I made the decision to leave Mark Thomas and start my own company.

Despite the strained relationship between Bill and me, I always thought of him as a shrewd businessman. He was very thorough and detail-oriented in all matters of business. Of the many lessons he taught me, there were a couple I could never forget.

One was to never assume anything; always double check and triple check. The other was to pay attention to details. "Details, details," his voice is still ringing in my ears.

Several years after my departure from Mark Thomas International, Bill visited me in my new office one day. He said he had closed his company and was now looking for a job to utilize his knowledge and experience in international trade. I was happy to see him again, but shocked to learn that he wouldn't mind working for my company and me. Something like this would never happen in Korea. Koreans would think it too embarrassing to go to a former employee and ask for a job. However, I was immensely impressed with Bill's openness and his practical mind. I wondered if this was the true meaning of American pragmatism.

Another lesson I learned from Bill was not to take his criticism too personally. He was right. Like all Koreans, or Japanese for that matter, saving face is of the utmost importance, and I simply couldn't stomach the thought of doing anything wrong. I always acted as if I knew what I was doing, often forgetting how inexperienced I was. Bill was twelve years older than me. He was a great teacher for business, and I owe him dearly for my success with the business I started after I left his company.

—◊—

CHAPTER 29

K-C INTERNATIONAL, LTD.

The new company name was K-C International Ltd. The "K" and "C" came from the initials of my first and last name. I had checked out the availability of the name with the Oregon Business Bureau to officially register it. There were many things to take care of without delay. I needed to lease an office space, buy office furniture, order the telephone, and so forth. I also needed to inform all my suppliers and customers, especially my Korean sales agent Cho Youngjin at Hanjoo Trading, and Park Youngju at Kwang Myung Lumber in Korea, about my resignation from Mark Thomas, and let them know about my new company. But most important of all, I would need to find a banker willing to extend my company a credit line. My mind was now crystal clear. I knew I didn't have enough capital to start a fresh new business, but I was confident that my credibility and business reputation built over the past five years would be a great asset.

The Bank of California in downtown Portland seemed the logical choice, as it was the main banker for Mark Thomas. The bank knew our business rather well and also had the best international department and a knowledgeable staff. I made an appointment with Perry Holland, the branch manager, who had handled all the negotiation papers for our letters of credit. I had met with him many times in the past and I thought he had a good impression of me.

When I met Mr. Holland in his office, I presented my five-year business plan and also submitted my personal financial statement. I knew beforehand what would be required from the bank to determine the credit worthiness of my company. The first thing he asked me was why I had resigned from Mark Thomas International. I simply stated that Bill and I had a different vision for the business. He smiled and said that he knew Bill rather well, not surprised that I had left. Then he told me he could extend me a line of credit on the condition that all future negotiation documents would be handled through the Bank of California. I was surprised by his offer because my personal financial statement showed hardly any assets.

He extended his hand and said, "Ken, I know you successfully generated much new business for Bill, and I have no doubt that you will also succeed in your new venture." Then he said, "For now, $150,000 is all I could offer you. It might not be enough for your line of business, but we would be willing to review the line of credit and increase the amount as your company grows."

Although I knew I had a remote chance of getting a line of credit from the bank, I honestly didn't expect to be extended that much off the bat. There have been many angels in my life, and Perry Holland was definitely an angel sent to me by God. Without his assistance and bold commitment, K-C International could never have gotten off the ground.

K-C International was officially registered with the state of Oregon in December 1976. I found a perfect office space in Portland located at the junction of Hwy 217 and Sunset Freeway. The address was 9999 SW Wilshire Street; number 9999 was a good omen for me. The office on the second floor of the Wilshire Professional Building was only 250 square feet—enough space for two desks, chairs, a telex machine, and a copier. It was truly a humble beginning, but I was proud of my company and ready to embrace the world on my own. Although it was a small two-story office building with 10,000 sq. ft. of rental space, I told myself that

I would become the owner of this building one day. I eventually did become its owner, free and clear.

One by one, I started making calls to our overseas agents, suppliers, and the customers. They all congratulated me and promised me their support. One large waste paper supplier in Southern California, with whom I had been dealing for the past few years, offered me rather generous payment terms to help me out. They gave my company net 60-day payment terms until our cashflow improved, and then net 30-day terms thereafter. Typically, most suppliers' payment terms were net 10-day (payment within ten days from the invoice date). It was like receiving another credit line from the bank.

With the sufficient lines of credit with our bank and one of our largest suppliers in Los Angeles successfully arranged, it was time to start generating some new business as quickly as possible. I had already worked up my business plan and everything was clear in my head. Fortunately, the world economy was coming out of a long recession and there were plenty of secondary fiber orders available. Most of the Korean paper mills were running at full capacity and they demanded much raw material. The payment terms were strictly at sight L/C basis, which meant we would collect our money from the bank as soon as we presented our shipping documents to the bank.

Even before the new year had begun, we already had plenty of orders confirmed and all the materials had been secured back to back. More orders followed from our Taiwanese customers as well. My first-year sales goal was $1,000,000 gross revenue. As stipulated in my business plan, we were going to handle the three core items of secondary fiber, hardwood logs, and plywood for the first few years. My long-term plan was to diversify our product lines into various industrial products for both import and export and then eventually grow into a medium-size trading house like Daewoo International of Korea. Daewoo had become a successful conglomerate. The owner and CEO of Daewoo, Kim

Woo-choong, who was a legend in Korea, had started his company very humbly like I did. My vision for short, medium, and long-term goals was very clear at this time.

Surprisingly, my first-year sales goal was easily met and even exceeded the projected revenue amount. I was certainly over-worked, but happy to have eliminated most of my concerns about starting a new business, including the possibility of failing in the first year. The domestic suppliers and the overseas customers in Korea and Taiwan no longer treated us like a newcomer. As all of our L/Cs from foreign customers were advised through the Bank of California, Perry Holland and his staff were fully aware of our progress in export business. Naturally, Mr. Holland was very happy and gladly increased the credit line substantially. In our second year, revenue tripled; it would double again in the third year.

❦

On the strength of K-C International's early success, Myungki and I decided it was time to build the home of our dreams. We found a half-acre lot in Portland's sought-after Hartung Farms neighborhood, close to my office in Cedar Hills, and built our house in 1978. It was a four-bedroom 3400-sq.-ft. house with a den and a sauna room. Myungki and I considered this would be our last house. It was the ideal place to raise our daughters Jenny and Christy, then four and five years old; our third daughter, Didi, would be born in 1981. Our spacious living room was perfect for the baby grand piano that I purchased for Myungki and our daughters. Music was a big part of our lives.

Once we settled into the Hartung Farms house, it became a regular gathering place for all of our family members, including both sides of Myungki's and my extended families that had emigrated to Portland. On Thanksgiving and Christmas holidays, our house was jam packed with family members, numbering about fifty, including the children. We served roast turkey or

Myungki at piano accompanying her mother-in-law, Yoo Taejung, who loved to sing. Yuni front left. Hartung Farms house, Portland, Oregon, early 1980s.

Kookjoo and Myungki with daughters Jennifer, DeAnna, and Christine in front of Hartung Farms house in Portland, Oregon. Easter Sunday, 1982.

ham, along with many Korean dishes, such as bulgogi, galbi, pan-fried fish filets, and kimchi, of course. As head of the household, my mother always asked me to say grace for the meal and the wellbeing of our family. After dessert, we enjoyed some singing and music, with Myungki at the piano, and our girls and the rest of us joining in. Then all the adults would gather in the living room and kitchen to share stories about our life as immigrants, especially the difficulties and frustrations of getting established in the land of opportunity. But, in the end, we all agreed that our life in the United States was much better than living in Korea, and we gave thanks to God.

One day, Harriet Clothier, the office manager at Mark Thomas, called and asked me if we had an opening for an accounting position in my company. By this time, our staff of three was over-worked, and John Bopp, a CPA with an office in the building, was helping us with the bookkeeping. We also needed more office space and had acquired another 500 square feet next door. Without hesitation, I hired Harriet as our accountant and office manager. With her wonderful outgoing personality, I knew she would be a great asset for my company. Most importantly, she and I worked really well together as a team. The morale of the whole office was uplifted by her presence and everyone seemed happy with their role in the business.

Our business continued growing rapidly, and so did our reputation all over in Asia, especially in Korea, Taiwan, and Indonesia. Our product mixes expanded to include other industrial products; we even exported spare parts for the power plants in Korea. Naturally, more salesmen and sales engineers, along with additional supporting staff were hired to handle the fast-expanding business. My goal to become a true trading house appeared to be well on its course. In my original long-term business plan, I had identified three commodity groups that we would focus on and develop: forest products, such as plywood, hard and softwood logs, and secondary fiber; industrial products of U.S. manufacturers for overseas markets; and agricultural commodities. Like the fluctuating economy, the condition of the international markets constantly changed and evolved. Our plywood import business was soon to become the first victim of the market. Since our other export items were flourishing, we discontinued it without hesitation.

During Jimmy Carter's tenure as president, from 1977-1981, the administration faced many political and economic problems. On the economic front, he had to handle the ongoing "stagflation," a combination of high inflation, high unemployment, and slow growth. The bank prime rate soared to 21%. I felt very nervous, especially with the high bank interest rate and the dwindling profit margins in all commodities. But our overhead remained high and we didn't know where to cut.

Despite the deteriorating business climate, our export continued its strong growth. Our excellent performance was finally recognized by the State of Oregon. In 1981, Governor Victor Atiyeh awarded K-C International the Best International Marketing Firm of the Year Award in the intermediary division. Subsequently, the Ministry of the Industry of the Republic of Korea awarded us a citation for the contribution our company had made toward the Korean Paper Industry in 1982.

President Ronald Reagan was now at the helm, but the stagnation affecting the entire nation finally caught up with our company, too. For the first time since the inception of our company in 1976, we started losing money like crazy every month. Running a legitimate business was not like turning a water faucet on and off. I valued all my employees and delayed downsizing as long as possible. I reached a crossroads where I decided not to chase too many rabbits at the same time. Except for the export of secondary fiber, I eliminated all the export items that required sales engineers with higher expertise. Thanks to the proper downsizing of our staff and the slowly improving market condition, we started recovering from the recession and our bottom line clearly indicated we were out of the danger zone. Letting go of some of our valuable employees during this recession period was an excruciatingly painful experience and a lesson I would never forget.

CHAPTER 30

BALANCING ACT

Time flew by. Almost eight years had passed since K-C International Ltd. was launched. We were still a small company, but we were well recognized and respected in our industry and not considered a small potato anymore. We had a stream of customers and sales agents from overseas visiting our company all the time. I rarely had a chance to take a real vacation with my family.

Myungki was never a nagging wife, but she started complaining about my absence and urged me to take some time off work to spend with our three daughters before they were grown up and off to college. I knew Myungki was right. This was a precious time in our girls' lives. Unfortunately, our company needed more time to recover from the long recession we had suffered. Now that we had begun to rebuild, we would have to hire more people. Until then, I couldn't get away from the office more than two or three days at a time. We didn't yet have the luxury of mobile phones or the Internet to conduct business while on vacation.

Thanks to their supermom, both Jenny and Christy were doing great at school. Little Didi was almost ready for pre-school. We discovered that Jennifer's musical talent was for the violin and Christine's for the piano. Myungki found the best teachers in Portland to give our daughters private lessons. The sound of the girls practicing their instruments filled our house all the time. It made me happy that they were so dedicated, though I sometimes found it annoying to hear sections of music being played over and over again; they rarely played full pieces.

Now in my early forties, I had succeeded in developing my business and giving my family a comfortable life, but I suddenly realized that I had not taken time to think seriously about my exit plan. There was a flaw in my management. I had heard that small entrepreneurs could face trouble by not preparing their retirement plan early enough; those who waited too long often ended up selling their companies at a bargain price. I was determined to be more deliberate and decided to start planning my retirement.

As it happened, I learned that my old friend Will Bone, who had helped me get a job with Connolly International Sales when I first came to Portland, had started exporting secondary fiber to Korea. He hired a young, intelligent guy named Bill Brooks, who had a keen interest in the recycling industry. They were not much of a competitor for me yet, but I soon recognized that Bill was doing a good job for Will's company. Less than a year after he had joined Bone and Company, I learned that he had left the company to start his own brokerage firm specializing in secondary fiber export. Bill and I saw each other at the recycling conferences, and we had played golf together a few times. Not only was Bill a good golfer, but he was also a straightforward and honest person with high integrity. He was the type of guy that I liked to work with, and given time, I thought maybe I could make him my business partner in the future.

Eventually, Bill did become my partner in 1985. I proposed to merge our two companies and he agreed to become a minority shareholder of K-C International Ltd. The synergy we created was phenomenal. He was strong in supplier development and had many large and reliable suppliers already lined up, especially on the Eastern seaboard. I was strong on the West Coast and had many loyal customers in Korea and Taiwan. Our sales grew and so did the profits and the credit lines from the bank. Bill was twelve years younger than I, and like me, he had three daughters. More than ever, I was convinced that my decision to bring him on board as my partner was the right one.

❦

In 1985, soon after Bill became my partner, I was invited to serve as president of the Korean Society of Oregon (KSO), founded in 1967. I hesitated, knowing the demands it would place on me at a time when things were at an even keel in my business and my personal life. There were approximately 20,000 Korean Americans, including students, living in Portland, Eugene, Corvallis, and Salem and the small cities and towns. The Oregon Korean community was small compared to cities like New York and Los Angeles, but it was a tight-knit community. Like most Oregonians, everybody was friendly and willing to extend a helping hand. But KSO had its growing pains like every other non-profit organization. Its mission was "to represent and secure the rights of Korean Americans in Oregon, and to preserve and promote our history, cultural heritage and values." It also had a subsidiary organization, the Korean Language School, where Myungki was serving as the principal of the school.

My friends overruled my objections and persuaded me that I was the man for the job. The committee elected me because the people in our community thought of me as one of the most successful businessmen, and they felt I could serve without using the position for personal gain. Ironically, however, my company and I were not doing well financially. We were still coming out of the dreadful economic recession that started during the Carter administration. We had to pay 23% interest (prime rate plus two points) for every dollar we borrowed from the bank. There was no way we could make any profit at that rate. Our company was heavily hemorrhaging every month, and there was no end in sight.

After much praying and pondering, and many days of discussion with Myungki, I decided to accept the nomination as the president of the Korean Society of Oregon, even though I was also involved in church matters. For the past seven years, I had been serving as an elder of the Portland Youngnak Presbyterian Church, and at the same time, I was heading the building committee, which required my time and energy in the never-ending fund-raising campaign.

Obviously, working for others and serving our community must have been in our blood for both Myungki and me. We couldn't resist doing things for the greater good and were able to forgo any selfish motivation. Perhaps we were naïve, but we couldn't help but serve others.

—ɯ—

CHAPTER 31

REUNION

One morning at the office, my mother called to invite me over for dinner that night. My mother was sixty-six years old and still in fairly good health. She lived alone in a small two-bedroom condo with a garage attached, only five minutes away from our house in Hartung Farms. She enjoyed her independence and had learned to drive a car soon after arriving in Portland. When she retired from Tektronix the year before, at her request, I had bought her a small tobacco shop in an office building in downtown Portland. She was not making much money, but she was happy to have something to do every day. It also gave her the freedom to buy gifts for her grandchildren without having to ask for handouts from my sisters and me.

When I got to her place that evening, my mother and I exchanged our usual greetings and she invited me to sit down. I suspected there was something important she wanted to discuss with me privately, as it was rare to have dinner alone with her. Usually the grandkids or my other siblings would be sharing a meal with us. I was curious to find out what it was.

"Abeom, remember your brother Sonsik whom you met in Seoul twenty years ago? You were in college, maybe a sophomore or junior."

She looked at me, waiting for my answer.

Indeed, I clearly remembered that occasion. My half-brother

Sonsik, who was six years older than me, had visited us at our rented room in Anguk-dong without announcement. There was no telephone in those days, and my mother was very surprised to see him. Naturally, I was stunned, too. My mother was still recovering from her cancer and hernia operations, and she was barely back to work at her job at the American Embassy.

"Of course, I remember him, Mother. What about him?" I asked.

"Your brother, his wife and their three sons are in financial trouble. They need our help." She added that Sonsik was in business by himself and was now on the verge of bankruptcy. My mother was wondering if she could invite Sonsik and his entire family to Portland and help them start a new life in this country. Obviously, she was at a loss and didn't know what to do except to discuss this matter with me.

I reflected on the day when Sonsik had visited us in Seoul. My mother went to the kitchen and quickly prepared lunch for my brother and me. I don't know how she managed it, but I saw kimchi and two bowls of beef radish soup with white rice on the small table. Before we started eating, I noticed Sonsik picking out the pieces of beef with fat on them. Like me, he didn't like fat. I saw that my mother had also caught what he was doing, and I read the subtle expression of disapproval on her face. She always reprimanded us if we complained about the meal. We had to finish whatever food was in our bowl or on our plates.

I was bothered by his arrogant demeanor and his attitude toward my mother. I instinctively realized that taking out the pieces with a little bit of fat was an act of silent protest against his mother. Without saying anything, I quickly put all the fatty chunks of beef my brother had pulled out of his bowl into my mouth before my mother could say anything about it. I couldn't bear to see my half-brother dare disappoint my mother with a small act like that. Beef was a precious delicacy in those days, and you didn't discard meat because it had fat on it. To this day, I don't like fatty meat.

I believe that is because of the time I had to swallow those fatty beef chunks for the sake of my half-brother, so my mother would not feel hurt by it.

"Kookjoo, what do you think? Will you do this for your brother and his family?"

I had to admit I felt a lingering resentment toward Sonsik. But strangely, I felt an indescribable affinity for my half-brother. His early life under the care of his stepmother after his father died could not have been easy. My sisters and I had gone through a lot too during the war, but we were blessed with our own mother's love.

"Why not, mother. It's a great idea. Let me find a lawyer who specializes in immigration matters and find out if he could help us."

Maybe Sonsik could help us out if he immigrates here, I speculated. Having helped my mother through multiple health issues and working day and night at my business had pushed me to the limit. Physically and mentally, I was exhausted. My mother needed to have someone else she could rely on.

Of course, my mother had no idea what kind of financial predicament my company was in at that time or the pressure I was under. All I could think was, here is a once-in-a-lifetime opportunity for my mother to repay whatever karmic debt she thought she owed to Sonsik and Woonsik by refusing the offer to live with her ex-husband and his girlfriend in Beijing. I couldn't ignore the fact that she must have been carrying a heavy burden of guilt deep in her heart all these years. I vaguely remembered my mother saying that my half-brother Sonsik had complained to her about abandoning her own children. Knowing my mother's character, I knew for certain that she was not thinking of her own interests when she made that agonizing decision, but about the wellbeing of her two babies. My heart instantly filled with sorrow and sympathy for her. I decided I had no time to weigh the pros and cons. I had to follow whatever God inside of me dictated.

"Mother, don't worry about anything. I will make sure they can come to this country as soon as possible."

I rarely called my mother "Mom"—not from a lack of love for her, but rather because she was both a father and mother figure to me. She deserved all the respect I could give her.

The next day, I found a top-notch immigration lawyer by the name of Bob Donaldson, who was serving as an Honorary Consulate General of the Republic of Korea. Bob said it was possible for my mother to invite her son and his family, except that someone had to guarantee their financial wellbeing while they lived in the United States. In other words, I had to submit my affidavit of support for the entire family of five. I agreed without hesitation.

Within a matter of six months or so, my half-brother and his wife and their three sons arrived in Portland. Even before they had completely settled into the apartment, my mother told me that her daughter Woonsik and her husband and daughter also wanted to come to Oregon. Apparently, the restaurant they owned in Seoul was not doing very well and they wanted to start a new life in America. Bob Donaldson said there shouldn't be a problem with their immigration as long as I submitted my affidavit of support for them. I agreed. Six months later, my half-sister Woonsik and her family were in Portland.

Financially, Woonsik and her husband were a lot better off than Sonsik. As soon as they arrived, they bought a small grocery store in Southeast Portland and would successfully manage it until their retirement. My half-brother Sonsik found a job at Nike and would work there until his retirement. My three nephews and niece would all graduate from college and go on to become successful managers and entrepreneurs.

Sadly, my mother's happy reunion with her son and daughter when they came to Portland seems to have lasted for only a brief moment. Both Sonsik and Woonsik were constantly bickering with each other for reasons I didn't fully understand and it pained me to see anyone give heartache to my dear mother.

Although my mother never complained about it, or shared her frustrations with me concerning Sonsik and Woonsik, I noticed the hidden tension and soreness between them. My half-brother and half-sister apparently didn't realize what my mother had gone through after her divorce or how she had struggled to survive the devastating war. Maybe I was mistaken, but it seemed to me that they never showed love, respect, and compassion for their own mother. Nor did I see any attempts on Sonsik's and Woonsik's part to genuinely understand and appreciate the sacrifice their mother had made for the sake of their wellbeing. For my part, I knew I would do everything humanly possible to accommodate the wishes of my mother and my half-brother and half-sister and their families to help them realize the American dream. But the greatest challenge I would have to face in the years ahead was helping my mother enjoy the remaining days of her life without undue anxiety and pain.

CHAPTER 32

TURN OF EVENTS

Stepping into my role as President of the Korean Society of Oregon (KSO) in 1985, I felt optimistic. My previous experience serving KSO in the capacity of secretary general and chairman of the Commerce Committee had given me an understanding of how things worked. However, that didn't mean our organization was a well-greased machine with proper personnel in place, except that I was fortunate to have our secretary general Dave Kim as my assistant. Dave and I worked very well as a team, but shortly after the inauguration of our one-year term, we were slowly sucked into a vortex of internal bickering between the old-timers and the newcomers.

Our KSO office space in a seven-story building in downtown Portland had been generously donated by Shin Jungdoo, who owned the building, out of which he operated Camera World (known nationwide). One day, we had an unexpected visitor to our office. It was John Lim, who would later become a multiple-term Oregon state senator and ran for governor as a Republican.

As soon as Dave and I exchanged greetings with John, he started tearing down the framed photos of the past presidents of the KSO hanging on the wall and throwing them, crashing to the floor. Dave and I were totally flabbergasted by John's sudden outburst. Not knowing why John was so upset, I had no choice but to wait until he had calmed down. He finally sat down on the sofa, still yelling cuss words at the pile of shattered glass and trashed photos. Dave seemed to understand why John had reacted so violently, but I had no clue. I had never been involved in any of the petty internal politics of our small community in Portland.

I hadn't realized that there were people like John in our community who were harboring ill feelings toward the so-called old-timers, who they imagined had control over most of the community affairs. I never realized that such tension existed. In fact, I thought John and I were friends, since we never had any bones to pick between us. But obviously, he considered me as one of the old-timers, too, even though he was seven years my senior. He wanted to show me where he stood by expressing his obvious displeasure about the way we were operating the Korean Society of Oregon.

This incident marked the beginning of the long and complex process during the transitional period of the Korean Society of Oregon in the late 1980s. At the end of that year, I wasn't surprised when John Lim was elected as the next president. I still wonder to this day why a gentleman of John's background and caliber would demonstrate such irrational behavior.

There was a tremendous amount of work to do for our growing community in Oregon. Dave and I had many good ideas, but we couldn't implement them because we were constantly called upon to attend meetings involving the issues of the by-laws and the different official functions, such as ceremonies commemorating the March 1st Independence Movement, and August 15th Independence Day, among others. Dave and I had made the decision to stay absolutely in the middle and never side with either the old-timers or the newcomers. Somehow, we successfully completed our terms, and were glad to turn our attention to our business.

❦

The economy was slowly reviving. With Bill joining me as my partner, K-C International started growing rapidly again, and we built some strong years together until late 1989. But I had learned from past experience that there was no such thing as an economy that would remain stable forever. In fact, the U.S. economy entered another recession in 1990 that lasted until 1992. During that time one of our largest buyers of specialty papers, the Poong Won Paper Mill in Korea, declared bankruptcy. They owed us a huge amount of money, close to a million dollars.

Bill and his beautiful wife Sarah were vacationing in Kauai, Hawaii, with their family at that time. I waited for him to return from his vacation to break the news. When I told him about the bankruptcy of the Korean buyer his face literally turned white. He asked me if the bankruptcy meant we would lose everything they owed us. I told him I wasn't sure, but that I would visit the buyer and my agent in Korea right away.

As it turned out, when I met with the owner of the mill in Korea two days later, I learned that their financial base was not as weak as we had imagined. He claimed that his hasty acquisition of a cement manufacturing plant, a totally different line of business from paper manufacturing, had caused a temporary cash-flow shortage and forced him to declare bankruptcy. I wasn't sure whether to believe the owner of the mill at the time, but he promised to complete the payment within one year, providing we would give him an additional 30% discount. We agreed to the terms.

When I returned home to Portland, Bill was happy with my report, but he didn't believe that we would indeed be paid as promised. Another six months passed. The Poong Won Paper company started remitting the payment little by little, and we became more optimistic about collecting the receivables. Eventually, they would pay the entire invoice amount less the discount we agreed to give. For both Bill and me, it came as a huge relief that Poong Won Paper was good for their word. I admitted to Bill that I had been nervous as hell, too. This kind of repayment settlement was not likely to happen in the United States. Once a company went into Chapter 11, it was well known that they paid out next to nothing.

We were extremely lucky that this Korean company eventually came through and honored their obligation to us, with the help of the discount we had to give. I learned a valuable lesson from this experience. In business, you need to be patient and assess the situation from all angles rather than making a rash decision, such as suing the company, which in this case would only have made the circumstances worse.

Hyunjoo, Myungjoo, Yoo Taejung, and Kookjoo. Portland, Oregon, 1992. This photo was specially taken to send to my half-brothers in North Korea.

PART THREE

JOURNEY
TO THE FATHERLAND

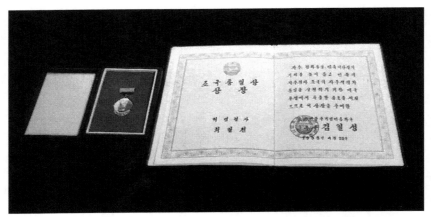

Kim Il Sung awarded the "National Unification Award" medal to Choi Il-chon. Vice Premier Pak Song Chol presented the medal to Yoo Taejung. The award ceremony was held at Mansudae Assembly Hall, Pyongyang, North Korea, in 1993.

Yoo Taejung in front of enlarged photo of a page from my father Choi Hyungwoo's book, *A Short History of the Overseas Korean Revolutionary Movement* (1945). Korean Revolution Museum, Pyongyang, North Korea, 1993.

CHAPTER 33

INVITATION TO PYONGYANG

In January 1993, my mother received a letter from the Overseas Korean Support Committee of Pyongyang, North Korea. It was an official invitation, dated January 18, requesting that my mother and her family visit Pyongyang during April or May that year. Several months earlier, we had learned that my half-brothers Dongjoo and Chuljoo were still alive and living in North Korea when we received handwritten letters from them. They informed us that they were the only family members who had survived from the Korean War. The rest of the family, including my father, were either killed or went missing. It was especially devastating for my mother to receive this news, because she was sure that my father was still alive in North Korea.

My half-brothers wrote several more letters to us. Their letters were always full of flattering remarks about their wonderful lives in the North Korean "paradise" under the care of the Great Leader Kim Il Sung. Meanwhile, they kept urging my mother and her family to visit them as soon as possible.

The official invitation letter from North Korea didn't entirely surprise my mother or me, because she had expressed her strong desire to visit her family in her correspondence with her two step-sons. Frankly, I was somewhat apprehensive about it, but the rest of the family was excited and happy to receive the invitation.

"Didn't I tell you guys, out of six family members, your father, my stepdaughter and her husband and three stepsons, who disappeared during the Korean War, at least one or two if not more could still be alive and living in North Korea?" my mother said.

For days, she kept going over possible scenarios, hoping to prove that my father was still alive. We didn't know how to respond to her questions.

"Your brothers told us in their letters that your father was killed during the war. But I can't believe it, do you?"

"Kim Il Sung could not have ordered to kill your father, could he?"

"They fought together against the Japanese in Manchuria. Your father was seven years older than Kim Il Sung who respected your father as a teacher."

My mother's monologues continued. Everyone listened to her, but we kept quiet. I couldn't give an opinion one way or the other. She continued talking to herself, visibly upset, as she struggled against the fear of a huge letdown.

"If he was not in North Korea, could he still be alive somewhere in South Korea? If he was, why didn't he seek out his own family a long time ago?"

"How could a man disappear from a tiny country like Korea without a trace?" she wondered.

She didn't want to believe what my half-brothers had said about my father in their letters—that he was probably dead. Understandably, she was in self-denial. But now I couldn't help wondering about the truth of this myself. The North Korean government was notorious for lying to its people, and what had happened to my father after he disappeared was still a mystery.

How sad that we children couldn't have sympathized with our mother's tormented mind while we were growing up with her, had we only known. My sisters and I had assumed that our father was killed during the war. I had never seriously put myself in my mother's shoes and wondered how she dealt with the loneliness without her spouse, and the unimaginable poverty and feelings of hopelessness.

While the speculations about my half-brothers and our lively family discussions continued, I was worried about the potentially huge expense we were about to incur for the prospective trip. I had heard from a friend of mine, Dr. Wang, who had recently visited his families in North Korea, how much money he had spent on his families and relatives. He was a very generous man, and he said it had cost him a fortune.

When I considered the high cost of airfare, the vast quantity of gifts we would have to buy for our poor relatives, and, of course, the cash expenditures permitted by law, it all seemed quite overwhelming. The poverty level and the living conditions in North Korea were beyond the scope of my imagination, Dr. Wang warned me. When he was ready to return to the States, he said he couldn't help but offer his brothers even the clothes he was wearing. It was disheartening and sad, and I could hardly believe what he was saying.

I knew that I could handle the expenses, and I felt embarrassed that I had been worrying about it. My mother and I now had the incredible opportunity to see my half-brothers and their families for the first time since the Korean War ended in 1953. I assumed that our visit would be a simple reunion with our families and relatives, nothing more. Maybe some sightseeing would be arranged by the North Korean government organization that had invited us. No one had any idea who my mother and I would be introduced to in Pyongyang.

My mother vividly recalled the day of September 21, 1950, when my father went out to secure more food for our family and never returned home. She had kept his memory alive all these years. But to receive an invitation letter to visit North Korea at this late stage of her life seemed almost meaningless if her husband was no longer alive. Yet she had many fond memories of taking care of her two stepsons for almost ten years until the Korean

War broke out. Dongjoo and Chuljoo were the tender ages of five and seven when she married my father in Beijing.

Until my mother received this invitation, my sisters and I hadn't realized that she had been secretly yearning for my father, hoping he was still alive in North Korea. Without such hope and faith in God, perhaps she could not have endured her many hardships. She had dedicated her entire life to raising us children and helping us to become successful adults. She knew how hard her husband had fought against the Japanese, that he had dedicated his entire life to the cause of the independence of Korea. For her, the only way to prove her love and pay tribute to my father was to present his fully grown and successful children to him. She would not disappoint him at any cost.

"Kookjoo, let's go and visit them in Pyongyang in April," my mother said matter of factly. "Ideally, your sisters should come along too, but I am not sure about that." Her voice trailed off. She knew it would be too much of a financial burden for her son.

"You can take some time off from business and accompany me there, can't you?" she asked.

I could see the resolve in her eyes. She was going to find out whether her husband was still alive in North Korea or not, once and for all. Suddenly, like my mother, I had the same realization about the significance of this trip. It didn't matter as much to me whether my father had passed away or not. But I needed to hear and verify the truth directly from my two half-brothers.

"Of course, Mother. I will come along with you. Don't you worry about anything. I will start processing the necessary paperwork right away."

—∭—

CHAPTER 34

LONGING FOR FATHER

My recollection of my father and my two half-brothers, Dongjoo and Chuljoo, from the first eight years of my life is hazy. When I was born in Beijing in 1942, Dongjoo was six and Chuljoo was eight years old. My father left his job in Beijing and moved our family to Seoul in 1944 to work for the Eastern Culture Publishing Company. Soon, he started writing his book on the history of the Korean independence movement that would be published in 1945 and 1946. Perhaps my brother Dongjoo took after my father, as I remember that he was very bright. His nickname at home was "Walking Dictionary."

Like most older siblings, my brothers were preoccupied with their own friends and rarely paid attention to me. And my father was busy with his writing, while also preparing to run for a seat in the National Assembly election on May 30, 1950. Naturally, he left all household matters, including the childrearing, to my mother. My mother always spoke highly of him and his dedication to Korea's freedom. While he might have appeared to be neglecting the household matters, he was fully occupied writing his books and newspaper articles. My mother said that he dearly loved her and all of his seven children, but that his passion was for the independence of Korea.

With his important work and all the important people coming and going at our house, my father must have seemed a romantic figure to me as a child. But I never experienced my father's love or bonded with him as father and son. At least, I don't recall ever being held in his arms and hugged. When my father and my two brothers suddenly disappeared from our life at the outbreak of the Korean War in 1950, it was a terrible shock to my mother and my two sisters and me. The question of what had happened to them would continue to haunt us. Thinking about them filled me with fear and pain; there was a blank space in my memory and a void in my heart that could not be filled.

I felt somewhat embarrassed at not feeling the kind of emotions I perhaps should have felt as his son when I learned that my mother and I would be going to North Korea. My excitement about visiting this country was clearly not as great as my mother's. All the same, I was excited about seeing my half brothers again, and grateful they were still alive. The idea that my father, too, might still be alive in North Korea felt strange, almost calming.

My father would be close to eighty-eight if he were alive. My mother was seventy-five. Many unsettling questions arose in my mind. Would he be in good health? If he were disabled or sick, would he be able to recognize us? I had to remind myself that in all likelihood my father had been killed during the Korean War. Perhaps I was only dreaming, but I felt my heart warming up at the prospect of seeing my father again for the first time in forty-three years. Perhaps I could have turned out differently, I mused, had I enjoyed the privilege of receiving my father's love and wisdom when I was growing up.

Beyond all doubts, my heart reached out to him—Father, I miss you very much!

—◆—

CHAPTER 35

PREPARATIONS

With the Poong Won Paper bankruptcy settled, I felt more re-laxed about taking the time away from business to make the trip to Pyongyang, North Korea, with my mother. Preparations for our trip were going well. The departure date was set for April 6, 1993.

When I contacted the North Korean government representa-tive in New York, he already knew about the trip that my mother and I were planning to take to Pyongyang. It was a big deal for anyone to receive a special invitation to North Korea at the re-quest of the government.

"We're glad to hear that you and your mother have decid-ed to visit the fatherland," he said. It was weird to hear the word "fatherland" in reference to North Korea, because I considered my homeland to be South Korea. North Korea was the father-land, the birthplace of my father. In essence, both motherland and fatherland in Korean have the same meaning as homeland. The representative instructed me to contact the North Korean Embassy in Beijing and apply for the visas for North Korea when we got there.

Meanwhile, my mother was very excited about our trip and busy buying gifts for everyone. Her primary concern was for the wellbeing of her stepsons Dongjoo and Chuljoo and their fami-lies. Strangely, my mother had not mentioned anything about my father since the weeks after she received the invitation letter from North Korea. She acted as though she had come to accept the reality that her husband was deceased.

My mother made many trips to Costco and started accumulating a mountain of gifts. She had bought heavy winter clothes, all kinds of vitamins, over the counter medicines, beef jerky, sausages, chocolates, and even some Korean ramen noodles. Three super-large suitcases were already stuffed with gifts for her stepsons and their families. The mere sight of it gave me vertigo.

"How in the world are we going to bring all these gifts to Pyongyang?" I protested.

"Don't worry, it is not you but the airplanes that will carry these for us," she replied.

I smiled indulgently at her little joke, but she must have thought I needed convincing.

"Can't you imagine how much they will appreciate these?" she said with a heavy heart. "I heard they are so dirt poor."

"Mother, North Korea claims their country is the paradise on earth. I don't think they would need anything from corrupt capitalists like us," I joked sarcastically with her. But I knew I couldn't stop her from buying as many gifts as she wanted to. I gladly agreed and assured her not to worry about the expense for the gifts or anything else.

Looking at her small frail body, wrinkled with age, I wondered how it had been possible for this petite woman to take care of her husband and seven children in China and Korea until the Korean War broke out, and then single-handedly raised me and my sisters through one of the most devastating wars in history. For a moment, I couldn't control my emotions, thinking of the hardships she'd had to endure. Many sad memories about my mother are buried deep in my heart. She was a wonder woman with her big heart and spirit, but she was not strong physically. The hardship and suffering she had endured had taken a toll on her health.

The day before our departure to North Korea, Bill came into my office and dropped a bombshell. He told me that he wanted to resign immediately and asked me to buy out his shares in the business. I was not prepared for this at all, because he had shown no sign whatsoever that he wanted to leave the company until that day. He could have picked a better day or at least have waited until my return from the trip to North Korea. He said his portion of guaranteeing the bank for our credit line was too much to bear and he had been losing sleep over it for some time. My gut feeling had told me that he might want to get out at the first sign of the market turning sour, but how could he desert our seven-year partnership just like that? I was really disappointed in his shortsightedness and felt betrayed. Emotionally overwhelmed by his decision, I foolishly told him I would buy him out as soon as I returned from the trip to North Korea.

The next morning at San Francisco International Airport, I called our fantastic duo salesmen Frank Crowley and Phil Epstein in our Newark, New Jersey, office. On our three-way telephone conversation, I told them about Bill's decision to leave the company. I asked them point blank if they also wanted to leave or stay with me at K-C International. They didn't hesitate but said they would stay and wished me to have a safe trip to North Korea. It really made me feel better and I decided not to regret the decision I made about buying Bill out immediately instead of giving him a long, drawn-out contract.

Bill's premonition about the market correction was right on the money. The U.S. economy continued its downslide for another six months or so. Whether Bill had any other reasons for leaving the company, I had no idea. But our company had become quite resilient and was not affected by the recession that much this time around.

Looking back, it was interesting to see that Bill Wiprud, my former boss, and my junior partner Bill Brooks and I had something in common. We were exactly twelve years apart in age, and we were all born in the year of the Horse. Both Bills were extremely smart and wonderful family men. They were fiercely competitive and did everything to protect their own interests in business and in their personal lives. For them, the loyalty in a business relationship could not be upheld if it meant sacrificing their own personal interests or if it was detrimental to their personal integrity. It took many years for me to understand this perspective and reconcile our cultural differences in order to let go of my ill feelings toward my former boss and my younger partner.

During the 1960s, '70s, and '80s, the mentality of Korean business in general, whether at a big or small company, was for employees to put the interests of the corporation above their own interests. Work hard and dedicate yourself to the betterment of the corporation and sacrifice your personal life and individual interests. In return, the corporation would take care of their employees as well as their families and assure them perpetual employment unless the employee made a huge blunder. Because of this extraordinary mindset in Korea and because of the enormous sacrifices made by this generation, South Korea was able to create the economic "Miracle on the Han River," rapidly transforming from a developing to a developed country, parallel to the "Miracle of the Rhine" of West Germany during the 1950s, with the rapid reconstruction and development of its economy.

CHAPTER 36

WELCOME ABOARD!

Naturally, I was happy to be taking my dear mother to North Korea and honor her wishes. But I was quite concerned, when we boarded the plane on the 6th of April, whether she would be strong enough to make the long journey to Beijing, Pyongyang, and return safely to Portland. Since my mother's hysterectomy, the cancer had never returned. However, she had experienced multiple problems with recurring hernias and had to be hospitalized to treat them. I had spent so much time in the hospital over the years that it began to feel like my second home. While I had the utmost respect for the doctors and nurses, I was sick and tired of the smell of sterilization and the foul hospital odors.

My mother had also been suffering from chronic bronchitis for many years. She was a heavy smoker and wouldn't quit despite the doctor's constant admonitions. She often said, "Cigarettes are only hobby and companion for me. Don't try to stop me." Her lung condition was so bad that once she started coughing, it was practically unstoppable. It was gut-wrenching to witness her coughing spells. Doctors had prescribed all kinds of medication for her coughing, but without success. She also suffered from insomnia, high blood pressure, and leg cramps—but strangely, no diabetes, thank God. Despite her pressing health issues, my mother, Yoo Taejung, was determined to take the long journey "home" to Korea.

We arrived in Beijing on the evening of April 7th. I had made a reservation for us at the Hotel New Otani Chang Fu Gong in downtown Beijing. It was a first-class hotel and my mother was pleased with our comfortable, spacious accommodations. I knew how she appreciated good taste. Although rare, she told me that my father used to treat her to dinners at the best restaurants in Beijing whenever the two of them had an opportunity to get away from us children.

The next day, on the 8th, I went to the Embassy of DPRK to apply for our visas. The visas were issued the following afternoon. The Embassy also confirmed our flight reservations with the Koryo Airline, scheduled to depart on April 10th. I was pleased that all the paper work was taken care of without a hitch.

Over the next two days, I took my mother for some sightseeing. I didn't imagine it would ever be possible to make another trip to Korea with her, and on behalf of my father. I wanted to make sure she had the best time of her life. Amazingly, she still remembered certain parts of the city, even though Beijing had been completely rebuilt with new high rises and massive commercial buildings.

On the first day of our tour, we visited the Forbidden City, the Chinese imperial palace complex from the time of the Ming dynasty to the end of Qing dynasty. For almost five hundred years, it had served as the home of emperors and their households and was the ceremonial and political center of the Chinese government. It now housed a Palace museum. We also visited the Great Wall of China. Unfortunately, we had to cut our sightseeing plans short that day, as my mother's bronchitis had flared up again.

My mother's coughing persisted all through the night. The medication she had brought from home did not help much. She blamed her cough on the poor air quality in Beijing. She was right. Every day, the city was polluted, windy, and dusty. The next morning, we went to see a Chinese doctor recommended by the hotel. The woman doctor prescribed a cough suppressant, and

I kept my fingers crossed that the medication would work for the duration of our trip.

After a restless night's sleep, we had a good breakfast at the hotel, checked out, and proceeded to the airport by taxi. We managed to check in all of our luggage at the gate without much hassle. Of course, I had to pay large tips to the porters handling our luggage at the airport. Money rules everywhere.

Our flight boarding was announced. We were about to leave for the country that we had heard so many unpleasant stories about, a country completely isolated from the rest of the world. The name DPRK alone stirred up anxiety in me. Horror stories such as North Korean agents killing and kidnapping innocent people abounded. No matter how big of a monster it might be, it was still my country, the home of my relatives—my own people. I had no choice but to accept them as they were. A feeling of compassion swept over me and restored my inner tranquility. All my fear vanished.

"Welcome aboard!" said a tall, beautiful stewardess in Korean as we entered the cabin. She spoke with a unique North Korean accent that was both sweet and pleasant. She spoke the same language as me. I already felt at home.

We were led to our seats in the airplane. My mother and I looked at each other and let out a big sigh of relief, though still feeling reservations. We had traveled a long way from our home in Portland, Oregon. The airplane we were on was an Old Russian Ilushin jet. The cabin decor was not fancy but plain, with an aura of austerity and discipline.

Maybe it was my imagination, but all the passengers seemed to have a grim, tense look on their faces. There were only a few Caucasian passengers on board. My mother and I tried to relax a little, but we simply couldn't do it. We were too excited at the prospect of meeting my two half-brothers Chuljoo and Dongjoo at the airport. How would they look? I wondered. Would we be able to recognize one another? I noticed that my mother had drifted off to sleep. She hadn't slept much the previous night due to her nagging cough. Maybe she was dreaming of reuniting with her long-lost husband. I reflected on all the terrible suffering she had endured in Korea, and the unimaginable hardships she had overcome. She certainly deserved a special gift from God on this trip. "Almighty God, please help us!" I prayed silently, and then dozed off.

We were awakened by the announcement of the stewardess. The airplane was now approaching Pyongyang's Sunan International Airport of DPRK. Looking out the window, I could see the airport terminal buildings below. The surrounding mountains and hills were barren, with hardly any trees to be seen. A few farmers were toiling in the fields. Surprisingly, only a few small airplanes were parked at the terminal and on the airfield. Two or three large jet airplanes with unrecognizable emblems were parked on the runways.

The flight from Beijing to Pyongyang took approximately two hours. When the airplane came to a complete stop, we were asked to deplane. A large passenger bus was waiting for us on the tarmac. I couldn't possibly describe the feeling when I first stepped on the North Korean soil! Briefly, I thought about the hundreds and thousands of people in South Korea who still had families in North Korea but couldn't even dream of going there to visit them. I am sure my mother was having similar thoughts.

At last we had arrived at the heart of the fatherland, Pyongyang, DPRK. I had never been to North Korea before this visit. And yet, this was my country and the place where my father was born. He had spent his entire life fighting against the Japanese for the sole purpose of recovering the Korean motherland in one piece, not divided as it is even today. He had foresight and yearned for Korean democracy. For that reason, he had chosen to move from Beijing to Seoul in 1944 before the official independence was declared on August 15, 1945.

I was filled with anguish over the inability of a small country like Korea to have found political solutions long ago to unify the divided country and reunite their people. What justification was there to artificially divide our country in half, forcefully separating millions of families against their wishes, and then controlling innocent citizens according to borrowed and half-baked ideologies? My heart was filled with anger toward the politicians ruling the governments of South and North Korea. What if my father, along with enlightened politicians such as Kim Gu, Kyu-sik, Lyuh Woon-hyung, and Cho Bong-am, had succeeded in their efforts to stop the division of the country during the transitional period before the Korean War?

Seoul and Pyongyang are in such close proximity, only 121 miles apart, and yet they are a vast distance apart in their political systems and ways of life. With the armistice in 1953, South Korea adopted a democracy with a free market economy and successfully industrialized their country to become one of the largest economic powerhouses in the world. North Korea, meanwhile, chose a different path. Old Stalinist communism was adopted in the beginning, and it slowly morphed into the pseudo-socialistic kingdom of Kim Il Sung and his family. In the name of self-reliance, they focused on indoctrinating their people to believe that Kim Il Sung was a Godhead. Now they boasted having a stockpile of H-bombs, A-bombs, ICBM and other formidable arsenals to vie for world power. What good were all these weapons when the civilians were dying from starvation and living in constant fear? Besides which, North Korea had not yet given up the ambition to conquer the South and put its fifty million people under the same yoke and shackles they had put on twenty-five million of their own people in North Korea. They claimed they must emancipate their brothers and sisters in the South from the monster of American imperialism.

Did this mean that all the politicians and generals in North Korea were lunatics? Were they really oblivious to the fast advancing industrial and technological revolutions around the world? They continuously blamed everything on the political,

Dongjoo (left) and Chuljoo (far right) with Yoo Taejung and Kookjoo meeting for the first time in forty-three years. Pyongyang Sunan International Airport, North Korea, 1993.

economic, and diplomatic sanctions imposed by the United States and its allies. Clearly, they were overlooking the fact that China and Vietnam, both communist countries, had adopted the free market economy and their countries were now thriving beyond their wildest dreams.

I believe the North Koreans knew very well that something was terribly wrong with their own political system. Their government seemed to care more about the people's loyalty to the Communist party system than the realities of their everyday lives—the logic of a cult system. The tragedy was that the North Korean populace had (and continues to have) absolutely no voice in deciding what type of government they have. They were locked inside the iron trap of their dictator's invention and desperately needed help from outside their borders. I felt as if I could hear the muffled screams of the North Korean people. My heart ached and bled for them.

—ɷ—

CHAPTER 37

VIPs

Two middle-aged, slender men with dark complexions, look-ing older than their age, were waiting for us in a large waiting room inside the terminal of Pyongyang Sunan International Airport. Instantly, I recognized them—they were my half-broth-ers, Dongjoo and Chuljoo. I was not surprised that my father was not standing beside them. I glanced at my mother and we nodded to each other, acknowledging our mutual disappointment. Our long-shot hope of reuniting with my father had been crushed, but we did our best to control our sadness.

My half-brothers knelt on the carpet and bowed to my moth-er. Then we hugged each other and cried. No words were neces-sary. Briefly, I wondered whether my two half-brothers had been forcibly taken to North Korea after the war or had gone there voluntarily. I assumed that they had been given a choice. Did they desert my mother and their young half-brother and sisters because she was not their biological mother? Maybe they thought they would be better off living with their father and had expect-ed to meet him in North Korea. These questions lingered in my mind for the duration of our stay in North Korea. I was hoping that Dongjoo and Chuljoo would voluntarily open up and share their own experiences with us—the predicaments and hardships they had inevitably gone through. They never did. Perhaps that was because there were eyes and ears everywhere watching every move our family made day and night.

Two gentlemen walked over to join us and Dongjoo introduced them: Mr. Lee, from the Overseas Korean Support Committee, and Mr. Yoon, from the History Research Institute of the DPRK. The government agents were very kind to my mother and me the whole time we stayed in North Korea. I didn't realize when we first met them that they, and especially Mr. Yoon would be accompanying us like shadows wherever we went, like personal bodyguards.

A green-colored, old but clean Mercedes Benz was waiting for us outside the arrival gate of the airport. A good-looking young man greeted us and said, "Welcome to our fatherland." He would be our private chauffeur until the end of our stay. My two brothers sat with my mother in the back seat. I sat in the front seat with the driver.

Traffic on the streets was very light. It was the spring season in Pyongyang. The weather was crisp, and the air quality was pure, without any pollution—unlike Beijing. Briefly, I noted the irony of the benefits of clean air and an unpolluted environment due to the slow industrialization process of this country. The streets were fully decorated with beautiful flowers and hanging plants. The driver informed us that the great leader Kim Il Sung's birthday was around the corner on Saturday, April 15th.

We had expected our hosts to put us up at one of the local hotels in downtown Pyongyang. Contrary to our expectations, our green Mercedes arrived at a gated compound. At least fifty beautiful and spacious villas were scattered around inside the walls. These guesthouses especially catered to people invited from overseas, I later learned. Soon our car stopped at a nice two-story villa painted light pink. A middle-aged, kind-looking woman and a young maid came out and greeted us. They would take care of our meals and the house cleaning during our stay, we were told. This extraordinary hospitality was totally unexpected, and my

Villa in Pyongyang where Kookjoo and his mother stayed during their two-week visit. Back row: Dongjoo (far left), Chuljoo (center), and Mr. Yoon (right); front row: Mr. Lee (left), Yoo Taejung, and Kookjoo. Pyongyang, North Korea, 1993.

mother and I were quite surprised. We felt like we were being treated like VIPs.

My two half-brothers helped unload our heavy luggage and carried it up to the villa. After we were all settled in our rooms, the government agents departed and left our family alone. I sensed that my brothers were relieved, as they immediately relaxed. Dongjoo and Chuljoo helped my mother to get comfortably seated on a sofa, and then kneeled and gave deep bows to her again. I also got on my knees and bowed to my two half-brothers. Forty-three years had passed since the war. My half-brothers were fourteen and sixteen when the war broke out in 1950. They were quickly conscripted by the People's Army and forcibly put into the war. They must have gone through hell during the war. Their worn, wrinkled faces told the story without their saying anything. My mother embraced her stepsons. No one spoke a word. Everyone's eyes overflowed with tears, expressing our long pent-up emotions.

❦

Over the next few days, Mr. Yoon and Mr. Lee gave us an escorted tour of all the typical places first-time visitors must visit, such as the humble house where Kim Il Sung was born. Then they drove us around the city, showing off their many wonderful buildings and monuments. They were proud how fast they had rebuilt the city from ashes after the war. The city buses were filled with passengers and there were long waiting lines everywhere. In North Korea, most of the people rely on public transportation. Their subway system, built underneath the ground at least one hundred meters deep, was clean and beautiful. I was told it was also designed to serve as an escape shelter in the event of "imperialist" American bombings and invasion.

❦

On April 14th, Mr. Yoon brought us an invitation card to attend a government-sponsored general meeting to celebrate Kim Il Sung's birthday the following day. My mother and I still couldn't figure out why they were giving us VIP treatment. No one, including my two stepbrothers, had ever hinted at the significance of this invitation to such an important government function.

On the evening of April 15th, we attended Kim Il Sung's eighty-first birthday dinner party at Kumsusan Palace. It was held in a huge auditorium with at least five hundred people in attendance. Norodom Sihanouk, the King of Cambodia, was attending the party. I noticed many foreign dignitaries in attendance, mostly from socialist countries, I assumed. My mother and I were seated at one of the many tables reserved for VIPs.

Kim Il Sung appeared with an entourage of women in black and white modern-style Korean dresses. They were all young, in their twenties, and beautiful. He smiled broadly and waved his hands to all the guests in attendance. He looked very healthy without a hint of the scary dictator. Rather, I felt as if I was looking at my father's old friend. Indeed, he was my father's friend, wasn't he? That was a question I could not yet answer.

While the formal toasts were being exchanged between King Norodom Sihanouk and Kim Il Sung, our table of ten or twelve guests just followed the formalities without exchanging any conversation whatsoever. I saw no openness in the faces of the guests, and there was a peculiar feeling of uneasiness at our table throughout the evening.

Six days had passed since our arrival to Pyongyang, and my mother and I had visited many different places, but we had spent little time with my brothers, and we hadn't yet met their families. The day after the dinner party, my mother complained to Mr. Yoon that we were in Korea to visit with our families, not for sightseeing. She demanded to meet her stepsons' families immediately.

We learned from my brothers that they were not living in Pyongyang but in remote cities, and it would take time to bring their family here. Later, I would understand this logistical problem. I knew that people who were not living within the city limits of Pyongyang were considered second-class citizens, and they led a miserable life. My suspicion that the North Korean government had executed my father during the war now grew stronger. Perhaps that was why my two half-brothers and their families were not considered part of the elite class and were not allowed to live in Pyongyang. But then, why were the North Koreans giving my mother and me this extraordinary hospitality and VIP treatment?

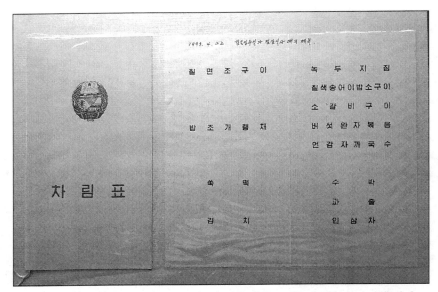

Menu from luncheon with the great leader Kim Il Sung. Broiled turkey, chilled clam salad, mugwort cake, and many other delicacies. Jusukgoong Palace, Pyongyang, North Korea, 1993.

—m—

CHAPTER 38

LUNCH WITH GOD

On April 21st, my mother and I were relaxing at our villa. We still hadn't met my brothers' families. That afternoon, Chuljoo and Dongjoo, along with the two agents, surprised us by walking into the room. Shortly, thereafter, a woman formally dressed in a black skirt and white Jeogori visited us. Her name was Kim Jong Nim. My brothers, along with Mr. Lee and Mr. Yoon, sprang up from their chairs and stood stiffly.

Kim Jong Nim explained to us that she was from the History Research Institute of the DPRK. She withdrew a letter from a formal envelope and began reading out loud:

"Dear Mrs. Yoo Taejung, Our Great Leader Kim Il Sung would like to extend a cordial invitation for you and your family to attend a luncheon specially prepared for you at the Jusuk Goong (the Kumsusan Palace) on April 22nd."

The great leader Kim Il Sung was going to personally meet us. We were shocked. Until that moment, no one had given us the least hint that a meeting was scheduled with Kim Il Sung. This was destined to be a truly historical moment for our family. From what I had heard, Kim Il Sung rarely allowed people from foreign countries to meet him personally, unless they were important heads of the government or ultra-rich people who would donate millions of dollars to the DPRK.

Now it dawned on me why they might have waited to extend this invitation until now. They had been closely observing my mother and me, often recording our words in a notebook—perhaps especially whenever we spoke about my father. It occurred to me that they may have cross-referenced the information with their own records. Everything must have matched; my mother was confirmed to be the genuine wife of Choi Hyungwoo (Ilchon), the patriot, comrade of Kim Il Sung, and a hero of Korea. My mother was very happy about the invitation, as she hoped to learn more about her husband's whereabouts.

My brothers were excited that they had been invited, too. My second brother, Dongjoo, was especially happy and couldn't hide his joy. He said he was now ready to invite us to his new apartment in downtown Pyongyang and meet his family. Apparently, his move to this new apartment had occurred within the past few days. My mother and I couldn't be happier, but we were puzzled why my first brother, Chuljoo, was being treated differently and was still living in the northern province of Pyonganbuk-do. It was absurd that people in North Korea had absolutely no freedom to move around and live wherever they chose, and it angered me. But for now, I knew it would be wise to keep my mouth shut and continue following the carefully orchestrated plan for our visit.

The apartment building looked reasonably new, judging by its cleanliness and the condition of the paint. However, the elevator didn't work due to lack of electricity. We had to walk up to the fifth floor. I was nervous about my mother's bronchitis and her weak physical condition; holding her arm, we slowly and carefully ascended the flights of stairs. At last, we reached the door to Dongjoo's apartment. The family was gathered there at the door to greet us. We met Dongjoo's wife, their daughter Eunjung and son Taehyun, and the grandchildren. The other two children were away. Dongjoo bragged about how wonderful his family's life was under the care of the great leader Kim Il Sung.

He said he was thankful for his job as a civil engineer. There were many structures and monuments in downtown Pyongyang that he had designed or helped to build. The DPRK was "a true paradise," he said. The government provided everything for everybody. My belief in his remarks was quickly shattered a few minutes later when I used their bathroom. There was no running water to flush the toilet. Instead, I had to use the bucketful of water standing beside the toilet to flush it. I wondered how the people who lived on even higher floors managed their daily life with a restricted supply of electricity and water. It was not difficult to imagine how miserable the life of the people living outside of Pyongyang must be. The most basic necessities would be lacking or in short supply. Daily survival would be the prime objective of their lives.

❦

At a luncheon specially prepared for my mother in memory of my father, in Jusuk Goong, Kumsusan Palace, the great leader Kim Il Sung himself attended and personally greeted my mother, my two half-brothers, and me with a warm, grandfatherly smile. He didn't come across as the ruthless dictator he was known to be. I was surprised how healthy he looked at age eighty-one. Other than a huge lump on the right side of his neck (from a calcium tumor, I later learned), there were no signs of any physical debility.

Before Kim Il Sung led us to his office to reminisce and tell his stories about my father, he suggested that we have a photo taken in front of a huge oil painting of beautiful mountains and waterfalls. I assumed it was either the famous Kumgangsan or Myohyangsan. After the photo session, we all sat together around a large semicircular table. My mother and I and my two brothers were seated across from Kim Il Sung. There, he told us stories about several patriots, including my father, who had helped him and his cause during the early resistance movement days in Manchuria. He also confirmed that it was my father and his father-in-law, Mr. Byun Daewoo, who had suggested he change his name to Kim Il Sung (Sun of a Nation) from Kim Song Ju, another nickname Kim Il Sung (One Star) was given earlier by my father's best friend Kim Hyuk.

I knew many people who were confused about Kim Il Sung's name change. His confirmation of my father's account in his book helped to clear up that confusion in my own mind. I had heard rumors that the leader's authenticity was also questioned; some claimed that he might not be the same man who had fought valiantly against the Japanese. However, the way Kim told the story and reminisced about his days with my father and other fellow compatriots in Manchuria seemed natural and plausible, without any hint of fabrication or deception. This was the real Kim Il Sung. I had no further doubts or suspicion about it.

My mother did not want to miss this opportunity to ask Kim Il Sung if he knew of my father's whereabouts. Without missing a beat, he said matter-of-factly that South Korean reactionary agents had killed my father in South Korea during the war on November 5, 1950. His answer came out so quickly that my mother and I were a little taken aback—we knew this was not the case. It was North Korean agents that had captured my father and taken him to Namsan Mountain for execution on the eve of September 27, 1950, the day before the recapture of Seoul by the Allied Forces. When the search party for my father had returned empty handed the next day, we had all assumed that he was taken to North Korea as a prisoner. But obviously, my mother and I would not dare to voice our objection and confront Kim Il Sung with the truth. We just absorbed what he said with pain in our hearts.

Kim Il Sung had a very charismatic personality, with the aura of a great man. Mr. Kang Suk Soong, the director of the History Research Institute, and Kim Jong Nim, deputy director, were also seated at the table. The dining room was not large but compact, with an upper level concealed behind long dark-mirrored window panels. I assumed the great leader's loyal security guards with their formidable weapons were watching every move of the invited guests in that room. I tried to maintain my composure, but I couldn't shake the eerie sensations I felt on my back throughout the whole luncheon.

The lunch menu was fabulous. The waiters served many North Korean specialties: frozen potato sesame noodles, fried mushroom balls, scallop salad, grilled rainbow trout, smoked turkey, grilled short ribs, and mung bean pancakes, followed by fresh fruit and ginseng tea. Kim Il Sung mentioned that he had ordered the kitchen to serve the frozen potato sesame noodles for us because he and my father used to eat that same dish during their desperate days in Manchuria. My mother and I told Kim Il Sung that everything was delicious, and we thanked him profusely for this unexpected hospitality.

My half-brothers were absolutely frozen stiff under the immense pressure of sitting with God, the great leader Kim Il Sung himself. This was truly a life-changing moment for them. They would cherish this experience for the rest of their lives. Attending a meeting with the great leader face-to-face, let alone sitting down at the same table to dine with him, was totally unimaginable for ordinary citizens in North Korea. My brothers' social status would be dramatically enhanced and solidified, and their lifestyle would be forever changed from this day forward, I assumed.

Kim Il Sung talked most of the time to all of us. He reminisced about his meetings with my father and his father-in-law, Mr. Byun Daewoo, in Ogaja. He said they were the leaders of a small community in Manchuria who had helped young Korean independence movement fighters like Kim Il Sung. He had stayed at Mr. Byun's house every time he visited there.

At a sign from Mr. Kang, the head of the History Research Institute, my brother Dongjoo surprised me by bringing out photocopied pages from my father's book, *A Short History of the Overseas Korean Revolutionary Movement Vol. 2.* He then read a few paragraphs about Kim Il Sung and his brilliant success against the Japanese. My brother handed me the papers and asked me to read a paragraph as well. As I was sitting right next to Kim Il Sung, I felt nervous, but I read the unrehearsed paragraph loud and clear. The great leader complimented my reading.

At the end of the luncheon, Kim Il Sung asked my mother whether she would be interested in moving back to North Korea. He said he would make sure that she was well taken care of, with a house, a car, or whatever she needed. He said he knew that life in the United States must be very difficult for her, with the racism, high cost of living, language problems, and adapting to the customs of the American culture. He said he was well aware of the racial violence triggered by the police beating of Rodney King in 1991. My mother just listened politely and thanked him for his generosity and consideration.

Kim Il Sung was like God in North Korea. He was feared and revered by everyone. Desecrating newspapers or posters with his picture was considered a capital crime and the offender would be sent to a concentration camp automatically without trial. After the luncheon meeting with Kim Il Sung, everything seemed to have changed, including the attitude of everybody who was helping us. I had no more doubts about our VIP status in North Korea.

Interestingly, the great leader Kim Il Sung was not at all pretentious. Nor did he give any indication that he was fabricating the stories he told. He was simply remembering the past and the people who had helped him during the days of the independence movement, stories that were told in his memoir, *With the Century,* published the previous year.

It was not too difficult to imagine Mr. Kang and his staff at the History Research Institute hard at work helping Kim Il Sung with his reminiscences, crosschecking the historical facts relating to my father and Kim Il Sung in my father's two-volume book, published in 1945 and 1946. I was proud to see copies of several book pages enlarged, framed, and beautifully displayed at the

Korean Revolution Museum in Pyongyang.

Sitting next to the Great Leader at the luncheon that day, I couldn't help but speculate that perhaps my father's account of the movement had information that might contradict certain claims in Kim Il Sung's "reminiscences." The timing of our official invitation to Pyongyang, just months after the publication of Kim Il Sung's memoir in 1992, was too perfectly coordinated to overlook this possibility. (The first volume was published in April 1992; the next seven volumes were published from 1995-1998).

First, I speculated, they would have found my brothers Chuljoo and Dongjoo living in the northern provinces of Hamgyongbuk-do and Pyonganbuk-do. My brothers would have been informed where my mother and I were living in the United States and asked to write to us, after which the government sent us the formal invitation. I felt as if my convoluted brain had finally started untangling, and the thick smoke screen was clearing away. My father, who was now being honored for his patriotism through this invitation to our family, was more than likely a victim of the North Korean slaughter of political leaders in South Korea who threatened their shaky and corrupt regime.

In this light, the lavish luncheon Kim Il Sung provided for our family at his palace seemed a cruel irony—were it not for my father's unfortunate demise, we would not be in the presence of the great leader. I hadn't realized the full implications until that moment. And yet, I was not sure that I could blame Kim Il Sung personally for my father's death. It was the hunters, the Korean Communist Party's hired assassins, that would have committed the execution.

The author and Yoo Taejung paying tribute to father and husband Choi Il-chon (Hyungwoo) at Patriotic Martyr's Cemetery, Pyongyang, North Korea, 1993. The floral sprays were sent by Kim Il Sung and the North Korean government.

CHAPTER 39

DEATH OF A PATRIOT

On April 20th, we were notified that the North Korean government would be sponsoring an official funeral service for my father the next day on April 21st. He would be posthumously entombed at the famous "Patriotic Martyrs' Cemetery" located in Sinmi-dong in Pyongyang.

It was a crisp morning under blue skies when my mother and my brothers and I drove out to the cemetery with Mr. Yoon. The North Korean government had erected a headstone at my father's gravesite that was inscribed with the date of his birth and alleged death: October 11, 1905–November 5, 1950. Two enormous standing sprays of flowers sent by Kim Il Sung were placed on either side. There was a red carpet leading to the memorial shrine under the headstone as a sign of honor.

Alas, there was no corpse of my father to be buried at the gravesite. Instead, a small black-and-white photo of him had been put inside a small box to be buried in his place. Solemnly, we gathered around the site and watched as the miniature casket was lowered into the ground. Quite a few government dignitaries had come out to the ceremony to pay their respects to my father. I had no idea who they were. We bowed to one another.

After the dignified burial service, we were escorted to a different location inside a huge auditorium where the government of North Korea awarded my mother a medal of honor on behalf of

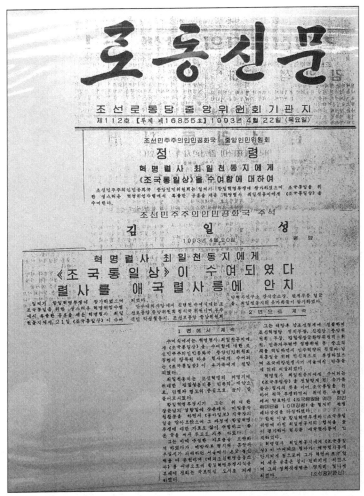

Article published in the newspaper *Rodong Sinmun* describing the burial of Choi Il-chon (Hyungwoo) at Patriotic Martyr's Cemetery, and the National Unification Award presented to Yoo Taejung on behalf of her husband. Pyongyang, North Korea, 1993.

my father, the "National Unification Award." We were not especially happy about this honorary distinction, but politely followed along with the formalities as instructed. My mother and I shook hands with the group of dignitaries.

Rodong Sinmun, the official North Korean daily newspaper, featured a picture of my mother, my half-brothers, Chuljoo and Dongjoo, and myself on the front page the next day. A long and elaborate article about my father and his contribution to the independence movement during the Japanese occupation was published in the newspaper with the photo.

Our family had become celebrities overnight in North Korea. But it was little consolation for the loss of my father from our lives, and my mother's long years of torment, wondering whether he had been killed or was alive somewhere in North Korea. I believe this memorial helped to give my mother closure and peace. I too was grateful to honor his memory. But I was not convinced that we had heard the whole story. For me, there was still some unfinished business and I secretly resolved to find out the truth.

Chuljoo's family in Taechon. Back row: Chuljoo standing beside Kookjoo with his wife and three sons. Front row: Three daughters-in-law and five grandchildren. Taechon, Pyonganbuk-do, North Korea, 1993. My family was poor, but healthy and happy.

House of Chuljoo in Taechon, North Korea, taken by the author on visit in 1993. When I noticed that the fence was freshly painted, I felt something was not right, but held my tongue in the presence of the agent.

—⚏—

CHAPTER 40

LIFE IN PARADISE

Twelve days had passed since our arrival in Pyongyang. Tentatively, we set our new departure date for April 26th. I asked Mr. Yoon to make the return flight reservations for us. I explained to him that I had a family and a company to take care of back in Portland, Oregon.

The previous day my mother had quietly asked me if we could return home sooner. Her chronic bronchitis had flared up again, and she was coughing constantly. She was exhausted from all the planning, travel, and all the activities involving her husband. And the constant surveillance was tiring.

"I see people here have no freedom whatsoever," she complained in a hushed voice. "You noticed your brother Dongjoo constantly putting his index finger on his mouth whenever I try to say something about your father, didn't you? Don't you think this is absolutely absurd? I can't put up with this nonsense anymore. The Great Leader promised me a good life if I decided to move here. Honestly, I don't care. I could never live in this country."

She continued complaining about the government. To her mind, this was not the way people should be treated and live their lives. She was a strong-willed person, but she knew she was helpless and there was nothing she could do about it.

My brothers had warned us that our rooms were heavily wired, and my mother and I knew that we needed to be extremely careful not to say anything derogatory about North Korea. I had known about this before we came, but I was getting very tired and didn't think I could put up with the suffocating situation any longer either.

How on earth can people carry out their daily lives without freedom of any kind? Do people back home and in other countries in the free world appreciate having a government that supports democracy? A government that allows the freedom of speech, religion, and basic human rights? There is no such thing as a perfect political system, but I was deeply thankful for my life in the United States and South Korea. Briefly, I thought about the South Korean leftists who still yearned for the political system of North Korea, and I wondered if they truly understood what it meant to live under that kind of dictatorship.

It wasn't easy for me to keep holding back my emotions, which were all mixed with unanswered questions, mysteries, and puzzles surrounding my father's books, his death, and just how closely connected he was to Kim Il Sung. For the time being, I had to let it all go, although, deep down, I felt that my father would never rest in peace until I knew the truth about what had happened to him.

"By the way, when can I visit your family, Chuljoo?" my mother asked her stepson, while also looking at the agents, Mr. Lee and Mr. Yoon.

"How many times did I ask you guys about this? Is there something wrong? You know I can ask the Great Leader Kim Il Sung to make the arrangement for me and Kookjoo, don't you?" she demanded in loud voice.

The two agents jumped from their chairs when they heard my mother mention the name of the Great Leader.

"Please don't worry, Mrs. Yoo," said Mr. Lee. "It will be arranged within the next few days." He hesitated a moment and then added, "They live far in the northern part of the province and it is not easy to get around that part of the country."

Actually, my brother's house was located only eighty miles north of Pyongyang in Taechon (Pyonganbuk-do). They were sweating about their answer for some unknown reason.

The next day, my brother Chuljoo and his wife came to our villa. We were surprised to see my brother's wife for the first time. She had a dark complexion and looked very tired from the long train ride she had made overnight. Mr. Yoon said they had decided to bring my brother's wife to Pyongyang rather than ask my mother to make the long trip to visit them. Immediately, my mother walked over to my brother's wife and gave her a long and warm embrace. No words were exchanged.

Mr. Yoon announced that they would take me to visit my brother's family at their house the next day. My mother insisted she wanted to come along, too, but I persuaded her not to, using her weak physical condition as an excuse. But I was also concerned about what we might find there.

⟨

The road to Taechon was unpaved and very rough. The trip took almost three hours. When we pulled up to the house, my brother Chuljoo and his wife and their whole family of three sons, with their wives and the five grandchildren, came out and met us in the green Mercedes. The house had a typical red-tiled roof and there was a high white wooden fence in front and a pigpen in the yard.

It seemed that my brother and his family would be happy living in such a house. However, I couldn't get over the strange sensation that something wasn't quite right. The house looked rather big, and the fence was newly painted. Also, I got the impression that the pig wasn't being raised by my brother. He was too frail and weak to care for farm animals. Could this be someone else's house? I wondered. Did the party people just move my brother and his family into this house to impress me and show how well ordinary citizens like my brother lived in the DPRK? Chuljoo had been forced to retire early due to his back injuries. He and his family were totally dependent on government subsidies.

A few neighbors came out and looked at our Mercedes with curiosity and envy. My brother and his family seemed proud that he had just met the Great Leader Kim Il Sung and had lunch with him. The neighbors must have heard about it or read the news in the *Rodong Sinmun*, a North Korean daily newspaper. I couldn't tell how far the effect of my brother's meeting with the Great Leader would go. Maybe it had already changed the status of his life.

The dining table was covered with many delicacies, including dog meat, which was beyond my expectation. Dog meat in North Korea was very popular but very expensive. I knew I would go all the way to entertain my brother if he visited my home in Portland, but this meal was clearly well over his budget. I complained to my brother for spending so much money for my visit. I told him I had just wanted to see how he and his family lived and enjoy a simple ordinary dinner with him. To my surprise, he said the party secretary, who was in charge of this particular town, had provided the dinner for us. The dinner was prearranged by the higher ups in the party. Was it a sign of my brother's change of status? Didn't the party people have higher priority work than tending to small family affairs like ours?

After dinner, I suggested to my brother that we take a walk in the neighborhood. Mr. Yoon was reluctant, but he agreed to accompany us. It was a quiet neighborhood. I saw hardly anyone outside on the street. I thought maybe it was because everybody was having dinner. It gave me the impression of any small town you'd see in the countryside of South Korea.

Once again, I realized how little time I'd had for a heart to heart conversation with my brothers since my arrival in North

Korea. Dongjoo was somewhat aloof and spared his words. He rarely asked me any questions or volunteered to speak his mind. He seemed to be on constant alert and watched that my mother and I did not go overboard when discussing anything related to my father. To me, he was a typical communist, and I felt sorry for him.

My brother Chuljoo was very reticent too, but he was warm-hearted. When Mr. Yoon left for the day and no one was around except us, he opened up and said how sorry he was that he had decided to go to North Korea instead of staying in the South and taking care of my mother, my two sisters, and me. I knew he meant it. After all, he was only nineteen years old when he had to make that decision during the repatriation.

At the outset of the Korean War, Chuljoo was one of the first to be captured and conscripted by the People's Army before our family had the opportunity to escape Seoul. He said he had fought in many battles. Then he was captured by the South Korean soldiers and sent to Geoje Prison Camp, a prisoner of war camp located on Geoje Island at the southernmost part of Geyongsangnam-do, South Korea. Geoje Camp was built to hold North Korean and Chinese prisoners shortly after the outbreak of the Korean War.

On July 27, 1953, the Armistice Agreement was signed between the United Nations Command, supported by the United States, the North Korean People's Army, and the Chinese People's Volunteers. Unfortunately, South Korea was not among the signees, although the Armistice called upon the governments of South Korea, North Korea, China, and the United States to continue peace talks.

Inside the Geoje-do prison camp, there were many uprisings by North Korean prisoners. One time, they forcibly captured the camp commander, General Francis Dodd, and his aide, Lt. Col. Wilbur Raven. Lt. Col. Raven narrowly escaped before he was taken into custody. However, General Dodd was held in the center of the prison for seventy-eight hours before he was released through the negotiation of General Charles F. Colson who was rushed to the island to take command. Many embarrassing concessions had to be made to secure General Dodd's release, which subsequently led to General Dodd's demotion to colonel and his early retirement the following year.

After the long, drawn-out armistice negotiations, they agreed to repatriate approximately 75,000 North Korean and Chinese POWs in December 1953. My brother Chuljoo was one of them. He explained that he was torn as to whether he should stay in South Korea or go to North Korea, where he thought his father and his two brothers and his sister and her husband might be. He chose to go to the North. His eyes were filled with tears as he said this. After many years, he found Dongjoo, who had also chosen to go to North Korea. But they never found my father or their elder brother and sister. I wondered whether he now regretted choosing to desert his stepmother and his young half-brother and sisters. Perhaps he later realized what a terrible mistake it had been to go to North Korea and suffer all these years. I could read on his face that he did not want to elaborate any further. I had no way of knowing the truth. I wondered, not for the first time, whether my mother could have had an easier life if she'd had the help of her step-son after the war.

It was getting late at night. We laid down side by side on the futon. The room had a warm floor, and it reminded me of the old rented room in Seoul that I had shared with my mother and sisters. The size was almost identical. It was an incredible feeling to be lying beside my dear half-brother for the first time in forty-three years. We couldn't have been any closer to each other. And yet it felt as if the distance of an ocean existed between us.

In the darkness of the night, I whispered a question to him.

"Dear brother, can you tell me more about your experience in Geoje Prison Camp?"

Silently, he put his right index finger over his mouth and

winked at me a couple of times. Then he pointed to several places in the walls and ceiling. I got the message—hidden microphones. My saddened heart sank still deeper. It was a terrible feeling to know we were being spied on. We couldn't even have a private conversation between two brothers in our own house. I felt like I couldn't breathe. This was not a paradise. This was a living hell.

The reason North Koreans have been able to survive since the Armistice of the Korean War in 1953, despite the unbelievably long economic sanctions and other political restrictions imposed by the Western countries, is due to their survival instinct and the resiliency of the human spirit. This was similarly demonstrated by the Germans and Japanese when they were defeated in the Second World War.

It was insane that the North Korean government allowed two to three million people to perish during The March of Suffering, 1994-1998. This number far exceeded that of the war casualties resulting from the Korean War. The world community should feel ashamed to have let this tragedy run its full course and leave an indelible stain in human history.

Material depravity is one thing. But the worst enemy of being poor in North Korea was the perpetual fear and stress; the fear of not being able to feed your own family and the inability to move elsewhere in the country to find better opportunity. In truth, these people were living in hell. I thought about the deprivation of millions of North Korean souls from the lack of civil liberty for the past seventy years. And what about the psychological impact on people who are constantly under government threat and surveillance? We had heard that even the ruling family members did not trust each other and had to be extremely careful not to speak their mind.

My brother had fallen asleep and started snoring. Would he and his family be all right? I wondered. Would the government start to take better care of them in the future? Was it fair for them to be treated as specially classified citizens and receive extra food and rations? Many questions like these haunted me throughout the night.

In my dream that night, I donated a large instant ramen noodle manufacturing plant to the North Korean government. My mother gave me a big hug and said, "I am proud of you. Your father would be happy in heaven."

CHAPTER 41

FINAL TRIBUTE

We had about four days left in North Korea until our scheduled departure date on April 26th. My mother and I felt we had accomplished our goal by meeting her two stepsons and their families. Certainly, meeting the Great Leader Kim Il Sung was the highlight of our visit, although we didn't feel there was anything especially "great" about him, once we spent some time in his company. And we were hardly impressed with North Korea's political system. We were worried about how we could stand to live through several more days with no freedom of any kind. And yet, I was surprised to find myself slowly getting used to their system. I had become less sensitive to the tension-filled atmosphere and class-oriented behavior. Given enough time, maybe I, too, would become immune to this horrible political system of fear and oppression, just like the citizens of North Korea.

Our guides kept us busy for the rest of the week. We visited the beautiful Mt. Myohyang, a Buddhist Temple, Pyongyang Maternity Hospital, Mansudae Art Studio, the National Museum, and Kim Il Sung University. They even took us to the DMZ and showed us the wall crossing east and west, allegedly built by the South Korean government.

We went back to my father's burial site at the Patriot's Cemetery on April 25th and bid him our final farewell. After dedicating some fruits and alcoholic beverages on the tombstone, we bowed our heads and prayed again. All the while, I was making a silent vow that I would ultimately find out what really happened to my father.

All told, the visit to North Korea was a life-changing experience for my mother and me. And it was incredible how much money, time, and energy was spent on our behalf by the North Korean government. Everything was free, and our hosts did not demand any money or other form of remuneration.

🍃

My mother and I left Pyongyang on April 26th and arrived in Beijing the same day. Compared to North Korea, China was a wide-open free country on the surface. My mother and I did not exchange much conversation until we checked into our hotel. We both felt sad and depressed. What impacted us the most was the level of poverty we had witnessed. Everywhere we went, we observed a lack of confidence in people, much as they all valiantly defended their system and their great leader Kim Il Sung. They did their best to hide the truth from us. Even the civilians we saw in the subways and buses looked at us with eyes full of suspicion. Rarely did we see smiling faces. The complexion of most of these people was dark, and their face muscles and bodies looked tense. And those were the people living in Pyongyang, who were supposed to be the elite class.

It was getting late in the afternoon, but we weren't yet hungry enough for dinner. My mother and I were completely exhausted, physically and mentally. We decided to take a nap. I woke up around seven o'clock. I noticed that my mother was already awake and was looking out the window viewing the city she had once known rather well. All of the offices and commercial buildings were brightly lit, and the streets were filled with cars. There was not a trace of resemblance to the old Beijing.

Quietly, my mother prayed to God and thanked Him for the opportunity to meet her stepsons and their families in Pyongyang. She was grateful that the Great Leader Kim Il Sung had given a government sponsored funeral service for her late husband and let him be buried at the Patriot's Cemetery.

I was deeply moved by her prayer. Despite her old age and failing health, she had come all the way from Portland to visit her family in Pyongyang. This was possible only because she was a truly compassionate human being. At the same time, she did it for the sake of her deceased husband, who she knew was looking down from heaven.

My mother slowly turned around and saw me watching her. She said, "I am so happy and glad that we came. I have no more wishes in this life."

"Of course, Mother, I am happy for you, too."

"You helped me to invite my son Sonsik and daughter Woonsik, your half-brother and half-sister, and their families to Portland ten years ago. You've done so much for me. You gladly signed all the paperwork including the Affidavit of Support for everybody. You also helped me invite my sister and her families to Oregon. You did so much for so many people, but you never frowned or complained. Nor did you turn down any of my requests and wishes all these years. Without your financial support and unselfish heart, this trip could never have happened. You are a wonderful son, Kookjoo. Thank you."

"Mother, you don't have to thank me. I simply followed my heart as God in heaven guided me."

After all, how could I not want to help her? She had done everything humanly possible for her husband and all the children God assigned to her custody in this world. Her life was an ultimate act of self-sacrifice and self-denial. She gave everything back to God. I was overwhelmed by the aura of this great human being who was my mother.

Yoo Taejung with stepsons in the garden at the villa in Pyongyang, April 25, 1993, the day before our departure. My mother and her stepsons show their genuine love and happiness. They were singing old songs together.

PART FOUR

COMING HOME

Christmas party at author's home in Hartung Farms, Portland, Oregon, early 1990s. Front row: Hong Sonsik's wife and sister-in-law, Myungki, and Kookjoo with Coco. Second row (left to right): Yuni (sister), Hong Woonsik (half-sister), Hong Sonsik (half-brother), and Kim Sangman (Woonsik's husband). Back row (left to right): Benjamin Lim (nephew), Hyunjoo (sister), Amanda (niece), Gregory Charr (nephew). Although my half-brothers and half-sisters were not yet fully settled in the land of opportunity, they were grateful and happy.

CHAPTER 42

FRIENDSHIP

It was the end of April 1993 when my mother and I returned safely to Portland from North Korea. We were grateful for our trip together, but also very relieved to be back in the land of the free. Although tired and depressed from the long trip, I was pleasantly surprised to learn when I called the office the next day that our business had started picking up at a much faster pace than anticipated. Frank and Phil were doing a phenomenal job coordinating all the sales and procurement of secondary fibers on the East Coast. The international market was back to normal, our order files were full, and our office was running smoothly and with excitement.

Ever since I first started my company, the ultimate goal in my long-term business plan was to go public and list our company in NASDAQ at some point in future. My banker friend told me that to qualify for a listing in the NASDAQ, our company would need to have a manufacturing plant of our own to prove we were a full-fledged producer and marketing company. We couldn't just rely on other suppliers to meet the demand from our overseas customers.

With enough cash built up in our retained earnings, and solid credit lines secured from the bank, we started looking in the New Jersey and New York area for a potential secondary fiber-producing plant to acquire. We located a possible candidate in New

Jersey, but the company's balance sheet looked weak and the management was somewhat shaky. We decided to wait and watch.

About a year after my return from North Korea, two FBI agents visited me in my Portland office, unannounced. They politely gave me their cards and wanted to ask me some questions about my visit to North Korea the previous year. I was not surprised by their sudden visit because I had already advised American Ambassador Stephen Bosworth in Seoul about my visit to Pyongyang on my way back from North Korea in April, 1993.

The FBI agents said they were primarily interested in learning about North Korean terrorist activity and wanted to know whether I had been asked to participate in any covert scheme. I told them that no one had approached me about a scheme, and explained that the reason for my visit was that my father was being honored as a patriot and posthumously entombed in the Patriotic Martyrs' Cemetery in Pyongyang, North Korea. Although their visit was cordial and low key, I will never forget how eerie it felt when I realized that my mother and I had been watched by Big Brothers—not only North Korean but U.S. agents as well.

The following July, I scheduled a trip to Los Angeles to visit a few of our secondary fiber suppliers in Southern California. Upon arriving in LA that evening, I was planning to meet one of my best friends, Paul Kim, for dinner. Paul's brother-in-law Ko Byungok owned the Korea Plywood Manufacturing Company where I had worked before coming to the United States in 1969. Paul was the owner and president of Sunrise Enterprise Inc. in Pomona, California. The recycling industry was booming in the United States at that time, and his company was highly successful and expanding rapidly. His main business was the marketing of recycled waste paper, aluminum, metals, plastics, and other materials.

Paul had been living in the Los Angeles area for more than fifteen years after moving there from South Korea. Like me and many of our fellow compatriots, he was still struggling to adapt to the American way of life despite his considerable success. And like me, his English was average at best. He admitted that he was still uncomfortable attending meetings or parties conducted in English. But in each other's company we felt at ease, like brothers. Paul dearly missed his relatives and friends in Korea, and often said that he wanted to be buried in Korean soil. He and his wife must have listened to their inner voices or perhaps they were simply following their natural homing instinct, because years later, he sold his business and they moved back to Korea permanently. He was such a humble, honest, open-minded gentleman and friend. I dearly miss him.

Paul and I cherished our close friendship because we shared similar values and beliefs in life. We often discussed the role and mission of the Korean church in the United States. Paul thought it was God's mission for him to help his fellow Koreans, especially the newcomers to the United States. He tithed gladly and gave happily to his church. He often said he felt blessed in so many ways and giving back was his way of thanking God. I agreed with him wholeheartedly. I gave generously to my church in Portland as well, with a willing heart, gratitude, and a deep sense of community service.

The Korean churches provided a perfect venue for newcomers to gather, share ethnic food, sing, and speak Korean with each other. They gathered to pray, repent for their sins, and give glory to God. They asked for blessings from God and released pent-up frustration that inevitably arose from living in the newly adopted dreamland where opportunities appeared to be far from their grasp.

Paul was an elder at a large Korean Presbyterian church in LA. He and his family attended one of the over three hundred Korean churches in the area. The services were generally conducted in Korean, although most churches provided English-speaking pastors at a specially allocated time and place. Paul and his wife were involved in church business meetings, overseas evangelical mission work, revival meetings, choir, holiday services, special fund-raising events, and prayer meetings for cities or countries stricken by natural disaster. As one of the respected elders in the church, he was also expected to attend weddings and funerals. It was a non-paying full-time job for both of them. The church was the most important part of their lives, their purpose for living. I often wondered how they had any time left for their own family and running the business. And yet, Paul's business was thriving, thanks to the support of his brother-in-law, who owned and operated one of the largest newsprint manufacturing plants in South Korea.

While I was more progressive than Paul when it came to discussions about our Christian faith, we just tried to be good, honest, unbiased listeners. Bertrand Russell once said, "The whole problem with the world is that fools and fanatics are always so certain of themselves, but wise people are full of doubts." Paul and I didn't want to be on either side of this argument. We knew that the time was approaching when the people of the world would start looking beyond religions, ideologies, races, and borders and become united as One in the name of God.

Paul had in-depth knowledge of the bible, especially the Old Testament, and used to teach adult classes in his church. One time, to poke fun at him, I said, "You know so much about the history of Israel and the bible, but do you know the names of the three most important Korean sacred books?" He couldn't answer. They are *Chon Bu Gyong, Sam Il Shingo,* and *Cham Jon Gye Gyong.* The reason I posed this question to Paul was that many Korean Christians tend to have blind faith in the bible and ignore the Korean sacred texts that contain as much profound wisdom and truth as the bible.

Like the majority of the world's fundamentalist and monotheistic religions, Christianity maintains its beliefs with self-righteous conviction. Many practitioners forget the fact that all human beings are the children of God, whether they know Jesus Christ and have faith in a particular religion or not. God is the spirit that resides within all of us. Realizing this truth will bring us salvation and happiness. Jesus Christ was an enlightened man full of love, compassion, and humility. He taught human beings to reflect on themselves rather than looking at his name or image for deliverance from suffering. I believe in one living God within myself and others. As far as I am concerned, as long as you have faith in God, the diverse ways of reaching Him shouldn't matter. My hope is that all the religions of the world will become more tolerant of other denominations and begin engaging in interfaith dialogue and move beyond our differences.

—ɱ—

CHAPTER 43

THE GREAT LEADER

After my plane landed in LA, I took a taxi to Korea Town to meet Paul for dinner. In Korea Town, it's easy for native-born Koreans to feel at home. Most of the signs are in Korean, once you step into certain areas and streets. Living in Portland, I sometimes missed the authentic Korean dishes available in Los Angeles, which has the largest Korean community in the U.S. Paul took me to a me-dium-sized Korean restaurant in Orange County. The restaurant was already filled when we walked in, obviously a popular spot. It wasn't a fancy place, but it was clean, with good ambience. The hostess recognized Paul immediately and greeted us with a broad smile. She led us to a cozy corner table that Paul had reserved for us, away from the crowd, with a view of bamboo plants encased in glass and perfectly lit.

The sweet smoky aroma of bulgogi and galbi cooking on the grill filled the air. It touched off my nostalgia for Korea and made me feel happy and even hungrier. Rather than order my usual drink, Johnny Walker Black Label, Paul and I chose the tradi-tional inexpensive soju (Korean vodka with a low alcohol con-tent of 18-21%) as the ideal companion for dinner that evening. I couldn't wait to take my first sip of Soju filled to the brim. Soju is the commoner's drink and is rarely served by waitresses or wait-ers. Friends pour drinks for each other, which creates a more in-timate feeling.

While settling down in our chairs, I noticed a couple of medium-sized, Korean-made Samsung televisions hung on the walls of the dining room. A Korean musical entertainment program was playing. Suddenly, a male news anchor appeared with a grim look on his face and interrupted the program. There was breaking news:

"North Korean Leader Kim Il Sung has died at the age of eighty-two. The exact cause of his death is unknown but is suspected to have been caused by a stroke. His death occurred in the late morning on July 8th 1994."

The news anchor continued reading the script with a hint of excitement, expressing his concern about the future of South and North Korea. It did not strike me as odd that the announcement of Kim Il Sung's death had been withheld from the public for thirty-six hours. We all knew that the North Korean government was secretive about its affairs.

Although most South Koreans abhorred the communist dictator Kim Il Sung for his invasion of the South on June 25, 1950, everybody knew he was a legend and had fought valiantly as an independence movement fighter against the Japanese. He looked healthy in the recent photos of him that flashed across the TV screen and he still had such amazing charisma. The great leader had ruthlessly ruled the northern half of the peninsula for almost fifty years.

Paul and I, along with the rest of the customers in the restaurant, were shocked by the news. There was dead silence for a few seconds. Then, quite spontaneously, everyone stood up, raised their hands, and yelled out "Man Sei!" (Hurray!) We all shook hands, as if the reunification of the two Koreas were now imminent.

Overwhelmed by the news, I felt the urge to cancel all of my appointments with the suppliers and return home immediately. Instead, I decided to cut my schedule in half and cancel the rest of the appointments. Although Kim Il Sung's death would not affect my business one iota for now, I had to admit that the news of his death was particularly troubling. Personal ill feelings toward Kim Il Sung and his regime aside, I had seen the potential for doing business with North Korea. With Kim Il Sung's help, we could have avoided a lot of the red tape.

The next day, I made the round of visits to our suppliers and managed to board an Alaska Airlines flight back to Portland that afternoon. While snuggly nestled in my window seat, I closed my eyes and reflected on the trip to Pyongyang with my mother. It was amazing to think that, only a year ago, we had met the great leader himself.

Kim Il Sung and his people from the Party History Research Institute were exceptionally kind and extended such hospitality to my mother and me. And yet, I felt like the whole country and its people were heavily weighed down with the Juche (self-reliance) ideology, and had no flexibility or room whatsoever for the different views of the Western world. My family members were no exception. My half-brothers Chuljoo and Dongjoo never opened—or perhaps could not open, their hearts to me. Nothing meaningful was ever discussed. It felt as if my mother and I were facing huge concrete walls. We had no choice but to turn away from our dear family feeling absolutely helpless, desperate at not being able to help them in any way.

I thought about my dear die-hard fundamentalistic Christian friends who stubbornly refused to discuss the views of other faiths or religions of the world, not to mention our beautiful Korean sacred texts. They were trapped behind their own walls like the North Koreans in terms of their rigid doctrines and their illusion about the infallibility of their beliefs.

"Would you care for a drink?" I was startled by a tall, smiling stewardess.

After ordering a glass of orange juice, I thought about how fortunate and blessed my life was in the United States of America. Myungki was fifty and I was fifty-two; we were still in our prime, with two daughters in college and one in junior high school. The business I had started eighteen years ago was on solid ground and prospering. Like my friend Paul, I felt that God had blessed me in so many ways. But there is an old Korean saying, "Too many blessings often bring about misfortune." I was totally unprepared for the terrible trial that lay just ahead.

—ᗰ—

CHAPTER 44

NIGHTMARE

When I returned from Los Angeles that afternoon, my head was still reeling from the shock of Kim Il Sung's death. The Great Leader had looked healthy when my mother and I met him at his palace, Ju Suk Goong, the previous year. I even felt a little sympathy for the aging dictator, who had been gracious to my mother and me on behalf of my father. In the back of my mind, I was still considering doing business with North Korea. Supplying the raw secondary fiber material to the North Korean paper mills seemed like a fantastic idea, as I had noticed they had virtually no forestry resources, and not enough waste paper was being recycled domestically. Besides, the great leader Kim Il Sung himself had told us he would gladly help my mother with whatever she asked for.

Myungki was out when I got home, but Jenny, our eldest daughter, was in the living room watching TV. After exchanging hugs and brief pleasantries with Jenny, I went upstairs to wash up and change into comfortable clothes. Then I poured myself a drink, my favorite Johnny Walker Black on the rocks, and sat down next to Jenny on the sofa.

Around eight o'clock, Myungki returned, surprised to see that I was already home.

"Hi Hon, when did you arrive? I thought you would arrive late this evening. Did you have dinner yet?" she asked.

"No, not yet, but I am not hungry," I said.

"Would you like some doenjang jjigae (fermented soy bean soup)? I can make it in no time for you."

"Of course, honey, you read my mind."

She knew that doenjang jjigae was one of my favorite soups and I wouldn't complain. Without listening to my answer, or even changing her clothes, she immediately pulled out some ingredients from the fridge and started chopping potatoes, green onions, and tofu, then put them in the pot to cook.

While watching her cook, I asked her how things were going at her job. She had recently joined a new real estate firm as a sales associate. After teaching music in elementary school, and then serving as a teacher of Korean Language at Portland State University, she said she was tired of working for such low wages. There were times when she had said she felt jealous that I was making so much money. "It is not fair that men get paid more than women," she used to complain. She said she wanted to venture into the real business world to make lots of money.

Whether she was joking or serious, I was not sure. As the wife of a CEO and owner of a successful company, she knew it wasn't necessary for her to earn more income for our family. Nonetheless, she decided to go into the real estate business. Her first step was to take the exam for the brokerage license. She toiled through many textbooks for quite some time, and then easily passed the exam. Now she was a licensed real estate agent and was proud of her accomplishment.

Against my wishes, and even before I had finished my dinner, she said she needed to return to her office to take care of some unfinished paperwork. I was annoyed.

"Are you sure you really have to go back to your office at this late hour?" I angrily protested. "Can't you see that I have just returned from a long trip? We need to spend some time together and talk about how things are at home and about our children."

I blurted all that out, hoping to prevent her from going out, while knowing full well that I was guilty of not spending enough time with her and our children.

Myunkgi didn't respond to my question. When I looked up, she had quietly slipped away from the table. I thought she had gone to the bathroom; then I heard the sound of the car engine starting. I rushed out the door to prevent her from leaving, but she had already backed out of the garage. She saw me standing in the garage in the headlights and stopped the car in the middle of the driveway. I couldn't see her face in the dark, but she gave me a hand sign saying she would be back home soon. Helpless and tired, I gave up and went back inside to finish my drink.

I realized how important this job must be to Myungki. Only four years after she started teaching, she had become pregnant with Jenny, soon followed by her pregnancy with Christine. She stayed home raising our daughters, but as soon as the girls started school, Myungki became restless. She accepted an appointment as the principal of the Korean Language School and started teaching Korean Language classes at Portland State University. Then our daughter DeAnna was born. Yet she still managed to keep up with our daughters' school activities and private music lessons.

She was so incredibly busy all the time that my mother and I advised her to slow down and at least cut back on volunteer work. Myungki was a deacon of the Portland Young-Nak Presbyterian Church. She said she did it for the pure joy of helping others. She was eager to help newcomers from Korea, sort of like an on-call emergency doctor.

Myungki was a super mom as well as an angel in many people's lives. She was proud of our daughter's progress in school and their success in music. Jennifer and Christine won the Oregon State Championships for violin and piano and had both been accepted to prestigious universities. Their younger sister Didi was destined to shine with her musical talent, too.

Myungki encouraged them every step of the way and did everything possible to assure their success. She would never listen to my advice about slowing down. No sooner had two of our girls gone off to college than she went into high gear with the new real estate job.

I waited for Myungki for a couple of hours before going to bed. I wondered what was so important about the unfinished paperwork. Soon, the effects of the alcohol and the tiring trip to LA overtook me. Feeling immensely tired, I went to bed around eleven o'clock, and fell asleep.

From far away in the distance, the telephone rang. It rang a second time. Half awake, I grabbed the receiver while looking at the alarm clock. It was 1:25 AM. Strangely, Myungki was not in bed. Feeling dazed and nervous, I cautiously answered the phone.

"Hello, is this Myungki Choi's residence?" A man with a grim sounding voice on the other side asked.

"Yes, it is, I am her husband. Who is this calling?" I asked bluntly.

"Mrs. Choi was in a car accident, and she is in critical condition. I am a nurse at the Emmanuel Hospital on the east side of Portland. Could you tell me your name and address, please?"

I hesitated a moment. I felt as if I had been struck by a lightning bolt. Why me? I thought, and then, Why *not* me? I struggled to grasp the meaning of "critical," desperately wanting to believe Myungki was in a better condition than the nurse had indicated.

I awakened my daughter Jenny, who was home from Oberlin College for the summer. Together, we rushed to the hospital. Myungki was already in the intensive care unit. Her face was full of scrapes and cuts, with a tracheotomy tube attached to her throat. Her left arm was heavily wrapped with bandages. Her left eye was tightly closed, but her right eye was open wide; it was dilated and fixed. She looked like Mrs. Frankenstein. She was intubated with all kinds of medical devices measuring her vital signs attached to her body. My heart sank to my stomach. I froze and couldn't say a word. My mind went totally blank, shell shocked. The attending head nurse told us Myungki had sustained a traumatic brain injury and was unconscious and in critical condition. Now, I fully realized what "critical condition" meant. It meant Myungki could die at any moment. She was dangerously close to death.

There was nothing Jenny and I could do to help in the intensive care unit. The nurse advised us to go sit outside in the visitors' waiting area. It was still early in the morning and there was hardly anybody in the room. The gravity of the situation started creeping up inside me. Jenny and I sat down on a long bench-like sofa and remained silent for quite some time.

What now, I wondered. What was going to happen to my family? To Jenny and Christine and Didi? What about my company and my thirty employees?

Slowly, I managed to climb out of the darkness, and asked Jenny how she was doing.

"I am all right, Dad, how about you?"

"I am fine, too. Thanks, Jen," I answered, holding back my tears and emotion.

I leaned against Jenny and embraced her, saying, "I love you very much, Jen. Don't worry, Jen. Mom will recover quickly and will come home very soon, before we know it. You know how strong a person she is, don't you?"

She was quiet and speechless. I knew my consoling words must have sounded hollow. She was just as devastated as I was—perhaps more. I couldn't yet fathom her mind. She was very close to her mom. Myungki was exceptionally caring for her first daughter and cherished her musical talent. In a way, Jenny was fulfilling Myungki's own childhood dream of becoming a famous musician. At twenty, Jenny was now a grown-up daughter. Be strong baby, be strong! I wanted to say to her. But the message got stuck in my heart and the words wouldn't come out. I felt like my soul had left me. Indeed, it had. My soul was following after my wife, who was wandering in purgatory.

The full police report explained what had happened at the scene of the accident. It was almost midnight by the time Myungki was on the way home from her office, only fifteen minutes away on Northwest Cornell Road. She was driving her small 1986 white Mercedes 190E north of Bethany Blvd heading to Hartung Farms where we lived. She stopped at the traffic lights at the intersection of Bethany Blvd and the Hwy 26 access road, which ran parallel to Sunset Freeway on her right side. The speed limit was 45 mph. There was another car stopped at the red light waiting to turn. When the light turned green, Myungki proceeded. From the road to her right, a 1980 black Ford Bronco driven by a sixteen-year-old boy with his friend was driving west to access Hwy 26 straight towards her car. They saw the light turn yellow but decided to beat it. Another car filled with their friends was following right behind them. The boy floored the pedal. By the time he reached the traffic light it was already red. He saw Myungki's car in the middle of the intersection, but he couldn't stop. Myungki's small Mercedes was smashed on the right front side. He was driving at least sixty miles an hour, or perhaps faster, according to the witness at the scene who happened to have had twelve years of experience as a paramedic.

Incredulously, Myungki had no seat belt on, according to the police report. She was flung into the passenger seat and hit her head on the metal frame of the window, knocking her unconscious. The witness jumped out of his car and quickly adjusted her head to establish the airway, and then called 911. Amazingly, the ambulance arrived in less than seven minutes. The first paramedic who treated her looked into her eyes and said that they were fixed and dilated. He shook his head and said to the first officer that had arrived, "I don't know. She is in bad shape." They saw her body begin to convulse with labored breathing.

The ambulance had taken her to the Emmanuel Hospital and Health Center, on the Northeast side of Portland, designated as one of the main hospitals equipped to treat trauma patients like Myungki.

At the emergency room, Myungki's diagnosis looked grim; the Glasgow Coma scale, measuring the condition of the victim, registered at 4 when she was admitted at the hospital. Earlier at the accident scene, she was at 3, the lowest, meaning she was totally unresponsive and unconscious. She was virtually dead.

Notwithstanding the incomprehensible medical terminology and its implications, I was happy to learn that none of the doctors predicted that Myungki was going to die soon. I was sure that her condition had now changed from critical to serious. I was learning quickly. Still unconscious, Myungki was now officially in a comatose state. However, her Glasgow Coma Scale had improved from 4 to 9, and she was easily aroused by sternal rubbing, which caused involuntary movement in her body. My hopes rose a bit.

While Jenny stayed at the hospital with her mother, I drove out to pick up Didi at the Delphian School in Sheridan, Oregon, about fifty miles southwest of Portland. I was wondering how to explain her mother's accident and her condition to Didi. She was thirteen years old, going through the most tender and vulnerable period of adolescence. Besides, I knew she did not have a good relationship with her mother at this time. Didi was happy to see me at the school. I explained Myungki's situation to the school administrator and requested Didi's immediate withdrawal from school. On our way to the hospital, I told Didi about her mother's accident in more detail, though I didn't tell her how bad the prognosis was or what kind of shape her mother was in.

Once at the hospital, Didi and I went directly to see Myungki. As soon as Didi saw her mother lying in bed with all the medical devices attached to her body, with her left eye shut and her right eye fixed and dilated, she froze and couldn't move. She didn't say a word or start to cry. She just stood there. It was painful for me to watch her react that way. I told her not to worry about anything and assured her that her mother would recover and come home soon. It seemed odd that she didn't show any emotion toward her mother. She acted as if she were a total stranger. But Didi was in shock. How could she not be?

Not knowing what was going through my baby daughter's mind, my heart was torn with anguish. Being the youngest daughter, Didi had always received the most attention and love from me. Her older sisters also loved her very much. Myungki and I had provided everything possible for our daughters. No money was spared to give them the best possible education and the comforts of life. I never wanted our daughters to have to experience the kind of hardships that I had experienced growing up in Korea. But there was no way for me to spare them the terrible hardship we were faced with now as a family.

The doctors were unable to give us a prognosis as to when Myungki might come out of coma. In fact, no one could predict whether she would come out of the coma at all. "Only God knows," we were told repeatedly.

—ɯ—

CHAPTER 45

IN GOD'S HANDS

Myungki would spend two weeks in the emergency room of Emmanuel Hospital before she was moved to a skilled nursing home. It felt like my life and my business career had been turned completely upside down. I couldn't even begin to fathom how my life would evolve from that point forward.

All of the major projects on the table, including the possible acquisition of a recycling plant in New Jersey, had to be put on hold indefinitely. I called both Frank and Phil, who were now minority shareholders in the company, and asked them to take full charge of all matters pertaining to our sales. Sue Litton, our CFO and General Manager of our Portland Office for seventeen years, was also instructed to tighten our operation and make sure to stay on top of all the accounts receivables and payables. Actually, Sue was such a thorough and tough supervisor that it wasn't even necessary for me to say anything. Besides, she was Myungki's eldest sister, and she knew what I was up against with my family situation.

On July 27th, fifteen days after the accident, and while Myungki was still in the ICU, we received the following Neurosurgical Consultation report from Dr. Martin Johnson: "Multiple injuries with severe closed head injury." The earlier diagnosis by Dr. Reuben Morris was similar: "Diffuse axonal injury with a severe closed head injury."

Dr. Johnson added the following comment and prognosis: "Neurologically, she will not recover to her pre-injury state. In all likelihood, in twelve or eighteen months, she may be ambulatory with a cane or walker, with secondary left hemiparesis and ataxia athetosis. She undoubtedly will be dysarthric secondary to the basal ganglion brain stem portions of her injury. I think she will probably remain homebound with the need for help with her daily living. I will discuss this with her husband."

Simply put, the doctors were saying that Myungki would survive, but with severe disabilities, possibly reducing her body to worm-like movement, especially on the left side of her body. She would also experience a speech disorder, with difficulty of articulation and stammering caused by nerve damage. Their prognosis was all predicated on whether Myungki could come out of coma in the near future.

Yes, gratefully she was alive, but the prospect of Myungki not coming out of the coma became more real every day. The social worker from Kaiser Permanente had forewarned me that if Myungki didn't come out of the coma, she would no longer be able to stay at Emmanuel Hospital. She would be discharged to the Friendship Skilled Nursing Home in Portland. Sadly, my hope that she would beat the coma before the discharge date was now dashed.

My wife and I had been long-time members of Kaiser Permanente in Clackamas, Oregon. Because we were relatively young and in excellent health, we had neglected to designate primary care physicians for ourselves. We simply didn't visit the clinics very often, and even skipped our annual physicals many times. In hindsight, we realized how important it is to have a primary care doctor on your side who can advise, counsel, and guide you when your dear loved one suffers multiple injuries from a car accident like Myungki's. It was a nightmare not knowing what was happening or what course of treatments were being planned and executed for my wife. However, under the kind guidance and direction of the social worker Meg Munger at Kaiser Permanente, Myungki was finally discharged to the Friendship Skilled Nursing Facility on the Southeast side of Portland on August 2nd. The Kaiser medical insurance would allow Myungki to stay for three months in this facility. Within that period, she was supposed to come out of her coma, and then she would begin receiving a prescribed amount of physical, occupational, and speech therapy. That all depended upon the results of the final evaluation by the Kaiser social worker. Myungki would have to demonstrate self-motivation and the will power to withstand the many therapies given by the facility; only then would she be eligible to become a candidate for further rehabilitation at the Rehabilitation Institute of Oregon (RIO), the nation's top institution for rehab patients like Myungki, to this day.

If she didn't come out of the coma or failed the test, we would have no choice but to bring her home or send her to a special nursing home that exclusively housed comatose patients.

With the clock already ticking, we were racing against time. No one in my family wished Myungki to go to a special care nursing home. I couldn't imagine how devastating it would be for our daughters and the rest of the family.

During this time, I often had a dream in which Myungki was lying in bed with other comatose patients in a special nursing home. I would wake up in the middle of the night, struggling to come out of this nightmare, and find myself drenched in sweat. The other side of the bed, where Myungki should be sleeping, was empty. I could never go back to sleep. Before I knew it, the day was dawning.

Daily prayers and meditations became routine. There was nothing else I could do for Myungki. Our pastor and many friends from the Portland Youngnak Presbyterian church visited my wife at the hospital and prayed for us. I attended Sunday services religiously, as if my belated diligence might somehow appease God and spare my family further suffering.

One day, I suddenly recalled my response when I received the phone call from the emergency room nurse at Emmanuel Hospital. My first thought was, Why me? and then I thought, Why *not* me? After all, what makes me so special not to have any bad luck? I was no different than other people. I had been graced with a long and blessed path from the day I arrived in Portland from Korea in 1969 until the day of Myungki's accident twenty-five years later. When I arrived in America, I only had two-hundred-and-fifty dollars in my pocket and a passport stamped with a three-month business visa. Come on, I said to myself, look at you and your flourishing family now. This could happen to anyone. Stop whining and bravely face the challenge. My inner voice took over and commanded me: *You can handle this situation.* I knew that I must handle it!

All of a sudden, the terrible situation I was dealing with no longer seemed that improbable. It was part of life. We all go through ups and downs, and all of us, without exception, must face many trials in life. I knew God would continue watching over me and help me to handle things. I decided not to worry anymore about how soon Myungki would come out of her coma. It was in His hands, not mine. Let Him do His job. Whatever was within the realm of human capacity, I would give my best effort to do. I felt like a renewed man. Momentarily, I was under the illusion that I could easily handle all of the challenges and difficult tasks that lay ahead of me. Only later did I realize that a dreadful depression was slowly encroaching on my being, threatening to destroy me.

CHAPTER 46

OLD WIFE, NEW WIFE

Even though I continued to see a positive outcome for Myungki, in reality, her condition did not look promising at all. We received three different consultation reports from her neurologists before she was discharged from the hospital to a nursing home.

One neurologist, while sitting in front of Jennifer and me, said to us: "At best, Myungki will be like a vegetable or a worm." We had already received a similar prognosis from Dr. Morris, though not in those words, so I was not surprised to hear it. We knew that most doctors were direct and not very diplomatic. But we thought this doctor was rather cruel. I felt miserable inside. I was wondering how I could alleviate the psychological pain Jennifer had just suffered.

We stepped out of the doctor's office at Emmanuel Hospital, located on the east side of the Willamette River. We walked quietly along the sidewalk outside the hospital, still trying to digest the awful words the doctor had just uttered. Ironically, the morning sky was cloudless and sunny, as if trying to give us the message, "Everything will be alright." It was late July. I had forgotten how beautiful the summer weather was in Portland.

The best prognosis came from another neurologist: "She could become ambulatory with a walker, but she will have the mentality of seven-year-old girl." All three doctors positively agreed on one thing. That I was not going to have my old wife back. She would be a different person, as her personality would change, too.

The news from the consultations did not affect me very much. I was just happy that none of the doctors had said that Myungki's death was imminent. She was going to live. I was now totally convinced of that. But no doctors or nurses had said that Myungki was likely to come out of her coma in the near future.

I had the full support of my three beautiful daughters. I also had my great mother's love and prayers. My mother-in-law was busy tending her own husband, as my father-in-law was sick with stomach cancer in the hospital. My two sisters, Hyunjoo and Yuni, helped me every step of the way. I was not afraid anymore. My energy level seemed to have improved, too.

Our neighbors in Hartung Farms were wonderful during that trying time as well, especially right after Myungki's accident. Those of us who had chosen to raise our families in this neighborhood were more or less in the same age group. All of our kids felt close to each other, as they had grown up together. Our neighbors poured out their love, prayers, and care, and brought over meals for me and my daughters.

Even with all the support, I sometimes got overwhelmed with Myungki's care. After listening to my numerous pleas and protests about the difficulties of managing my wife's care, Kaiser finally appointed a primary care physician, Dr. Harold Nevis, on August 9th. I felt good about this because I could now go to Dr. Nevis with questions pertaining to future treatment and other medical concerns. The important lesson I learned during this critical period of caring for my wife was that you and your family members must stay on top of everything. Naturally, the doctors and nurses would all do their best within their professional capacity. But that additional attention to detail in the care of a patient could make a critical difference between life and death—especially in the case of a coma patient who has no control or the power to make decisions and is completely at the mercy of the medical professionals.

On the morning of August 17th, thirty-six days after the

accident, I received a phone call from my brother-in-law Sungki, Myungki's older brother. He said that my father-in-law had passed away early that morning. Saddened by the news and with a heavy heart, I went to see Myungki at the nursing home. I sat next to her hospital bed, held her right hand, and started praying. At the end of my prayer, I told Myungki about her father's passing.

I had been talking to her constantly over the weeks and playing sacred music on the radio and CD player all the time in the hope that she would hear it and come out of the coma. That day, I decided to try something new. I asked her to squeeze my hand once if she understood what I had said. Immediately, I felt a sensation in my hand. I asked her again to squeeze my hand. She responded with a slight squeeze. I was totally ecstatic. I thanked God and my father-in-law for saving Myungki's spirit and soul. It was the most beautiful moment of my life. I had found my true wife again. God had returned her spirit and soul to me. Yes, her consciousness was back, I was sure of it.

Filled with joy and excitement, I ran to the nursing station and asked to see the doctor on duty. I explained to the doctor what had just happened with my wife and her response to my command. The doctor was a bit skeptical, but he followed me to Myungki's room to examine her. He held her hand and commanded a few words. No response. He tried again. But still, no response. A few more tries still produced no results. My heart sank and my enthusiasm quickly evaporated.

The doctor tried to console me by explaining that Myungki's response was a typical involuntary reaction that commonly occurs with coma patients. It didn't mean that she was actually coming out of coma. He encouraged me to continue my conversations with her and play music as much as possible. He also reminded me that I should be looking for another nursing home, one that exclusively cares for comatose patients.

At the kind advice of the Kaiser social worker, I did my due diligence and had already visited one such facility. They showed me a room with five coma patients with feeding tubes attached to them. The oldest coma patient had been there for five years; the others, from one to three years. They looked like aliens to me. They were alive and sleeping, but it seemed as if they were devoid of soul and spirit, like zombies. *NO, NO, NO!* My inner voice loudly screamed. I couldn't stand the idea of Myungki lying in the same room with these zombies. My mind was set now. If she didn't wake up in time, I was going to bring her home. There was no way I would choose to put her in such a facility.

The weeks flew by quickly, without any sign or positive response from Myungki. Her mandatory discharge date was fast approaching, only about a month away. The possibility of her not coming out of coma became more and more real. Starting physical therapy for her was out of question, since that could only begin once she was out of a coma and lucid enough to follow instructions from therapists.

It was now almost two months since the accident. I was distraught and nervous, and the distress was taking a toll on my body. Signs of physical deterioration started appearing. Constipation was routine. I couldn't digest food very well. Acid reflux developed. My physician referred me to a gastroenterologist. A stomach ulcer was detected from the upper GI endoscopies and many polyps were removed by laser during a colonoscopy. The doctor ordered me to immediately stop drinking alcohol or eating spicy foods, and to avoid stress. He warned me that any remaining polyps in my body could potentially turn into cancer. Nexium, the anti-acid medication, was prescribed. The doctor said I would need to take it for a long time. Avoiding spicy food and alcohol I could do easily. But how was I going to avoid the stress from dealing with the responsibilities of work, family, and Myungki's recovery?

CHAPTER 47

THE AWAKENING

On that day you will realize that I am in my Father,
and you are in me, and I am in you.

(John 14: 20)

The fall season was fast approaching. It became chilly in the early mornings and evenings. I stopped by my office in Cedar Hills to read fax messages from overseas agents and customers and sign a few checks. I discussed the overall condition of our company with my general manager and CFO, Sue Litton. I talked on the phone with my East coast managers Frank and Phil in the Newark office in New Jersey. I dearly missed Bill Brooks, my long-time junior partner of seven years in the Portland office, who had resigned the previous year. He was such an honest and reliable businessman.

While driving down Canyon Road on my way to the Friendship Skilled Nursing Home, I suddenly realized what had happened at the accident scene on July 11th. The off-duty EMT (Emergency Medical Technician) had saved Myungki's life. Without his prompt response, adjusting Myungki's head to protect her airway and spine, she could have died at the scene. He did not lose any time calling 911, and the EMS (Emergency Medical

Service) vehicle arrived within seven minutes, according to the police reports. Another angel in my life.

Perhaps Myungki was not meant to die yet, I thought. If God had enabled her to survive such a terrible crash, then wouldn't it be logical for God to bring her out of the coma? I knew it was not very rational thinking, but it made me feel better. She was supposed to have been dead by now, according to the statistics, and yet she was not. The fact that she was still alive after three months gave me a renewed sense of hope.

"Good Morning, Yeobo (Honey), I just got here," I said to Myungki. "How are you feeling today?"

As usual, I greeted her in Korean, just as if she was a normal person. The doctors and nurses told me that she could be hearing and understanding everything we said to her, even though she was still unable to express a response to it. All of my daughters as well as our relatives and friends had been told about this, and so everybody talked to her as if she was awake and well whenever they visited Myungki.

I turned off the radio and sat down beside her bed. Then I held her right hand and started praying as usual. At the end of the prayer, without much hope or expectation, I asked her to squeeze my right index finger—once, if she did not understand what I was saying; twice, if she understood. I reversed the order of the command to make sure I would not be mistaken if she did respond to me.

"Can you hear me and understand what I say? Squeeze twice, OKAY?"

She feebly squeezed twice. Startled and with a pounding heart, I cautiously asked the same question again. She definitely responded, squeezing my finger two times.

Next, I asked, "Are you hungry now?" She squeezed once, which meant No.

I repeated the questioning a few more times, but with different questions. For example, I asked her to confirm our daughters' names. She answered correctly. I noticed that she was looking at me with her right eye as if she knew who I was. The right eye had been wide open from the beginning, but we couldn't tell whether she was able to see anything or not. For the first time, she opened her left eye, which had been shut since the accident.

"Do you know who I am?" Again, she squeezed twice. She even smiled at me. She definitely knew who I was.

Oh my God! I thought. She is back! God has returned her soul and spirit to my family and me. I hugged her and cried, and cried, and cried with happiness.

I had found a new wife. Oldwife was the one with all sorts of physical handicaps with broken bones and scars all over her face and body. Oldwife was the one who was stubborn and had many shortcomings. She looked ugly physically. It didn't matter. To me, she was the most beautiful wife in the whole wide world. Knowing that her God-given pure soul and spirit was back in her body, her outer appearance and old mind was not going to matter anymore.

Why didn't I see this truth about who my real wife was before? I asked myself. Was I such a perfect husband myself? Don't I have as many shortcomings of my own, if not more? After all, don't I have the same soul and spirit inside of me as my wife? Is there a color and gender in spirit? Of course not. Doesn't that mean we are one in spirit? And didn't Jesus Christ spend his entire life trying to teach others and convince his disciples of this truth? We are all one in God.

God gave my wife back to me. At the same time, I had just received the biggest gift of my life from Him. I felt as if the thick scales were lifted from my eyes. All my bottled-up questions and doubts about Christianity and other religions had been cleared away. This was a true awakening moment for me. This experience was something I would never be able to forget, even if I tried. Like swimming or riding a bike, once you learn how to do it, you may stumble once in a while, but you will never forget. I felt like I was a free man again. God's spirit resided in me now.

There was nothing I needed to fear or worry about. Whatever I did for Myungki and my family, I also did for myself and for God. Whatever I did for our parents, our children, our family members and others I was also doing for myself and for God.

Myungki, recently discharged from Friendship Skilled
Nursing Home, with daughters Jennifer, DeAnna and
Christine, 1994. My family was happy to have her home
for the first time since the car accident five months earlier.

—ɯ—

CHAPTER 48

OUR THREE DAUGHTERS

Weeks later, I still could not forget the squeezing sensation I had felt on my finger on that awakening day. The sensation was real and the conviction that God had saved Myungki's life was embedded deeply in my heart and soul. When the doctors and nurses officially confirmed that Myungki was out of the coma, it felt like a miracle. But it was not as if she was totally healed of her injuries and back to normal by any means.

Myungki had been off the tube feeding for some time, and she had started eating porridge and soft food. But she couldn't talk or do anything else. She could barely follow verbal instructions. Besides which, she started having emotional outbursts. In the presence of anyone that she didn't like, she would lose control of herself. She would scream, kick her feet, and swing her arms wildly. It was very frustrating for all the family members present. It was very painful for me to watch her going through these emotional outbursts. Thankfully, they usually didn't last too long, and she would calm down and act as if nothing had happened.

Meanwhile, Jenny, who had been helping me to care for her mother all these months, returned to college for the fall semester. She had expressed the desire to skip the next semester to take care of her mother and me. Being the eldest daughter, she was always very caring and considerate, especially for her mother and younger sisters. But I encouraged her to continue her college education without any interruptions. She was studying to become a classical violinist, and I did not want her musical career to be affected by her mother's accident. Myungki would have insisted on it as well if she were able to understand the situation. This I knew for sure.

Jenny's musical talent was exceptional. She had her first solo violin debut with the Portland Youth Philharmonic in Portland at sixteen. She was also invited to perform with the major symphony orchestras in Oregon—the Oregon Symphony, the Vancouver Symphony, and the Olympia Symphony in the Pacific Northwest. Musically, Jenny was exceptionally gifted, though she was not a prodigy. She had that rare quality of staying power and the spirit of never giving up. She started playing the violin when she was six years old, but only seriously at age ten. In the world of violin virtuosos, that was old. Instantly, she was hooked on the instrument and she never gave up on it. She took lessons from many famous teachers in the United States, and would breeze through the top schools she attended, Oberlin College and then the Juilliard School, while winning many awards in various competitions.

Our second daughter, Christine, who was about to start the second semester of her sophomore year at Northwestern University in Evanston, Illinois, called and offered to come home to help me and her mother. This was quite unexpected on my part, but all the family members convinced me that I needed her help and should not try to do everything by myself. Besides, I knew it could be a life-changing experience for Christine to take some time off from school and help her mother and father through the most difficult circumstances of our lives.

In no time, Christine arrived home. When I saw Christine walk into the hospital one afternoon, I felt as if a strong army had come to my rescue. I always felt she was like a son to me. She was always dependable, and with her quick mind and keen intelligence, I never had to worry about anything for her. She cheered everybody up with her positive attitude, especially her younger sister DeAnna, who was going through her adolescent years.

Christy was already an accomplished classical pianist. Like her older sister Jenny, she had won both the Oregon Music Teacher Association's Award and the coveted Oregon State championship trophy. Before leaving for Northwestern that fall, she had played her first solo piano concerto, Beethoven's Piano Concerto #2, with the Rogue Valley Symphony in Oregon. Myungki and I had the pleasure of attending this performance.

From an infant until she went off to college, Christy was such an easy child, with an outgoing personality like her mother. Christy was also very athletic like her mother. She was a varsity volleyball player in high school and loved all kinds of sports. I don't recall that she ever complained about anything. As a father, however, I sometimes worried that she was holding back her inner feelings instead of sharing with her sisters or me. How on earth could anyone be free of anguish or anxiety?

DeAnna was perhaps the smartest of our three daughters. She was different from her two sisters. While Jenny and Christy were easily persuaded by their mother's admonitions, Didi was headstrong and not easily bent. Nonetheless, she was my favorite daughter and I tried to make up for some of the fatherly duties I had neglected with her two older sisters. Myungki had a tough time guiding her, except when it came to music and singing. It was a passion they shared.

Didi didn't always get along with her mother, but she had great affection for her Grandma Choi. Even at a young age, she showed unusual concern and love for her grandma. She tended to her grandma's illnesses or wounds more than anyone else in the family. One summer when Didi was three years old, we had a family vacation at Seaside, Oregon. While cooking lunch, Grandma Choi spilled hot water and scalded her hand. It didn't look too bad, but she decided to stay inside and not join the party outside. Everybody was enjoying themselves on the sunny beach when we suddenly realized that Didi was missing. I ran back to the hotel room and found Didi sitting next to her grandma.

My mother scolded me not showing more concern for her wounded hand. "What kind of a son are you?" Then she embraced her granddaughter and said, "Oh my precious one, you are the only one in this family who loves and cares about me. I love you very much, Didi."

Didi didn't express her thoughts. But I knew that her caring personality would never change because it was a blessing from God. Like her two older sisters, Didi had the spirit of never giving up that always brings rewards in the end. She would attend Oberlin College for a year, and then graduated summa cum laude from the Berklee College of Music in Boston.

During these trying years, I regretted that I couldn't be more helpful and pay more attention to our daughters. I wished to have had more heart-to-heart conversations with them regarding their traumatic emotional experiences during Myungki's recovery. I knew my tendency to have tunnel vision. While focusing on Myungki's recovery, I often neglected to be a more caring and loving father to our daughters. I kept telling myself to take action and narrow the emotional gap I had created between my daughters and me. Alas! Our beautiful birds would soon be leaving the nest.

CHAPTER 49

MENDING WINGS

Although Myungki was out of the coma, she was still far from being normal by any means. Whenever she felt uncomfortable, she kicked her feet and swung her right arm wildly, sometimes pulling out the J-tube (Jejunostomy tube; a soft plastic feeding tube). When the tube was pulled out, she had to be transported to the emergency room at Kaiser hospital and the doctors had to put it back in place. This was always a traumatic experience for me and my family, as we were concerned about possible infection and other complications from the surgical procedure. To prevent this from happening, the nurses had to bind her arms to the bedrail except when I was present.

Contrary to my initial expectations that Myungki would recover quickly once she was out of her coma, the speed of her recovery was ever so painfully slow. She recognized all of her family members, but she was not able to express herself, other than to respond to our questions with a simple yes or no answer by gesturing with her right hand. Her emotional outbursts and screaming appeared out of nowhere, especially when I gave her showers with help from the nurses and family members. Some coma patients come out of a coma as if they were waking up from a long refreshing sleep, and immediately communicate with doctors and family members. We had seen this in the movies and knew it happened to people in real life. But that rosy picture was totally misleading in our case. Myungki's slow recovery was due to the severe impact of her head injuries, which had shearing effects inside her brain. After all, one doctor had forewarned us that, at best, Myungki would be like a worm or vegetable. The only consolation I had at this time was that she was far better looking than a worm or vegetable!

One day in late September, Dr. Nevis, the Kaiser Permanente primary care physician, finally ordered to remove the J-tube and Myungki started eating soft food. She consumed the porridge specially prepared by my mother without any problem. This was a very encouraging sign, and we noticed that Myungki was gaining strength.

Subsequently, the physical and the occupational therapies started. Myungki did not have enough physical strength or willpower to follow the instructions of the therapists, and we only had about a month before Myungki would be discharged and go home. She had to demonstrate that she was physically and mentally strong enough to be accepted as a patient at the Rehabilitation Institute of Oregon. I felt that Myungki would recover faster once she had begun the excellent therapy at RIO. It was Meg Munger, the social worker at Kaiser Permanente, who would make the final determination whether or not Myungki would qualify to be admitted to RIO.

In early October, with Christine and Didi at home helping me care for their mother, I was happy we had successfully cleared the first major hurdle of bringing Myungki out of coma. Now we were all concentrating on her physical recovery. However, I noticed that my own health was deteriorating fast, with constant fatigue and acid reflux. I already knew about my physical condition from medical checkups I had a while ago. But this time, something inside of me was waving a red flag. I knew I had to be careful and pay more attention to our daughters' health and wellbeing as well. I suggested to Christine and Didi that we join Lee's Black Belt Academy in our neighborhood and take Taekwondo training. They liked my idea and we went over to the Academy together the next day.

My daughters lasted a few months and got their yellow belts. I kept up with the training until I received the first-degree black belt. The benefits from the Taekwondo training and workouts were huge for me. Not only did I get rid of my acid reflux and other minor health problems, but the training also ended my frequent attacks of depression.

Because of the all-out effort poured into Myungki's diet, the various therapies, and the caring support by both Myungki's family and mine, Myungki demonstrated that she had built enough strength and had the willpower to begin therapy at RIO. I'll never forget the nerve-wracking meeting with Meg Munger while she evaluated Myungki's progress one last time. She gave her passing grades instead of a negative report. I knew that Myungki was close to failing. Myungki's discharge date from the nursing home was set for November 9th; she would be admitted to RIO on November 20th. It was another victory for Myungki and the happiest moment of my family's life.

On November 9th, Christine, Didi, and I went to the nursing home to discharge Myungki and bring her back home for the first time since the accident on July 11, 1994—almost exactly four months earlier. To me it had seemed like four years. I wasn't sure how much Myungki was aware of the whole situation, but she gave us a broad, bright smile when she saw Christine, Didi, and me at the nursing home. All my pent-up emotions of sadness, happiness, and gratitude poured out, and I simply couldn't hold back my tears; they streamed down on my cheeks. Christine and Didi were standing beside me wiping their tears, too—tears of joy and happiness. We embraced each other and thanked God for what He had done for Myungki and our family.

Having Myungki back home was a huge morale booster for everyone. I felt like one of my broken wings had been mended and put back again. I didn't have to sputter on the ground any more.

Myungki, in RIO graduation hat, with Kookjoo, after being discharged from Legacy Brain Rehabilitation Institute of Oregon; Portland, December 1994. Although she was still in a wheelchair, I felt confident that my wife would fully recover and be independent in no time.

I couldn't fly yet, but I knew I would be able to fly again soon. Seeing Myungki lying next to me in our bed made me feel like I had become a whole person once again. I realized that part of my soul had been lost for the past four months, and now it returned to where it belonged.

Eleven days later, Myungki was admitted to RIO in downtown Portland. She would stay there and receive intensive physical, occupational, and speech therapy under the care of the nationally known physiatrist, Dr. Danielle Erb. The RIO was drastically different from the Friendship Skilled Nursing Home. RIO offered patients and their families a complete approach: round-the-clock medical and rehabilitation services in a caring environment, as well as therapy and counseling, all in one location. The therapists who helped Myungki were excellent. Dr. Erb was very thorough, and great at communicating with my family and me.

Myungki stayed at RIO for forty days and was discharged in a wheelchair on December 30, 1994. She was finally coming home permanently, five months and nineteen days after the day of the accident. Despite the all-out efforts of the doctors, nurses, and the therapists, Myungki was still far from walking independently. Since she demonstrated that she had enough strength, my family and I didn't doubt that she would be able to walk within a few months. Our entire family celebrated Myungki's discharge from RIO. She had received the best possible care available from the many great doctors, nurses, and therapists. There were no more treatments they could provide for Myungki at this time. The question of whether she would become independent or permanently dependent on caregivers now relied on Myungki's own willpower and determination.

CHAPTER 50

NO MERCY

In the home setting, Myungki needed full assistance from me to go to the bathroom, take a shower, or sit at the dining table or on the sofa to watch TV. During the night, she would attempt to get out of the bed and crawl to the bathroom on her own, but I would have to get up and help her get safely to the bathroom and back into bed.

Doing these routines twenty-four-seven was quite overwhelming. I was constantly sleep deprived and on the verge of a nervous breakdown from the constant fear of her falling and hurting herself. I couldn't imagine what kind of setbacks we would encounter if Myungki fell and broke her hip or injured herself in some other way. I soon realized it was time for me to get some professional help. I hired a full-time caregiver during the daytime without further hesitation. It gave me a reprieve, but the evening duties were still mine. Unfortunately, the first caregiver I hired didn't work out well and I had to let her go.

While I was looking for another caregiver for Myungki, my younger sister Hyunjoo, who owned and operated a small dental lab, called and volunteered to become the full-time caregiver for Myungki during the day. My sister and Myungki were good friends, and I had no doubt that Hyunjoo would do a good job, even though she lacked professional skills as a caregiver. I knew she would be terrific support as well when it came to household matters. She turned out to be a God-sent angel. Not only was she fantastic at taking care of Myungki, but she also took care of everything from cleaning the house to cooking for Didi and me. I didn't have to worry about anything during the daytime.

My focus now was to make Myungki walk independently without any assistance as soon as possible. Myungki was religiously taken to the outpatient physical, occupational, and speech therapy sessions without fail. I also sought the advice and opinions of local physical therapy experts to learn how fast Myungki might be able to walk without any help. Since Myungki had a problem with severe double vision, we had special consultations with Dr. Brad Coffey, an optometrist at the Pacific University. Myungki was also tested by the neurologist Dr. Owen Black to see how her problem of balance, a vestibular disorder, could be improved. These nationally known doctors gave us much valuable advice.

We tried to assist her walking with various types of canes, but without success. However, everyone was still very hopeful that Myungki would be able to walk independently. Dr. Erb, her physiatrist, recommended to use a walker as a last resort. She warned us that once Myungki started using the walker, she would be hooked on it and would never want to let go of it. She had already fallen a few times at home, though without serious injuries, thank God. We decided to wait as long as possible before we introduced a walker for Myungki.

The next challenge for me was to reorient Myungki to our home environment and help her to become a normal mother for our daughters and wife for me. Before the accident, she was one of the most active women in our community. However, she showed no desire or interest in going out to meet her parents, siblings, and friends. Basically, she had lost the executive function of her brain due to the injury. My only hope was to wait until the healthy and undamaged part of her brain took over for the damaged cells, and then help her to relearn everything all over again.

First things first. I began by taking her out of the house to visit all the family members who had extended their love and care to support us over the past several months. I asked our daughters to come home from college to visit their mother as often as possible. Although Myungki was still very weakened by her physical handicaps, I took her everywhere I could to make our lives worthwhile. She was fragile, so I had to stay on top of her every move.

We did not hesitate to make the long trip to Louisiana State University in Baton Rouge, where Jennifer was performing at a concert. Traveling with Myungki in the airplane and pushing the wheelchair everywhere required great energy and mental sharpness on my part. But it didn't matter. Sitting beside Myungki in the front row of the LSU music hall and proudly listening to our daughter Jennifer's violin performance was a gift sent by God for Myungki and me.

In June 1995, when our daughters were on their summer break, I took the whole family to Kona, Hawaii, for a one-week vacation. Our daughters were ecstatic and so was Myungki. Quietly, I was soaking in all the joy and happiness internally, reminding myself who I am as a spiritual being in this universe. The innocent laughs and smiles of my family humbled me. I thought about how my mind and body had been tainted by pursuing material happiness most of my life. For the first time, I was able to see that I had learned something far more precious and meaningful. The price I had paid for this gift was incredible—beyond comprehension. But I doubted that such a profound realization about who I am would have come about in my mind by chance. The business setbacks and material loss sustained in the process didn't seem important any more. I was simply happy to know that my relationship with Myungki was now on a different path and my love and devotion was unshakable. Our beautiful daughters also came around for their mom and me. Our family bond continued to grow stronger day by day.

Two years flew by quickly. At a medical consultation session, Dr. Jean Wiles, the physiatrist at Kaiser Permanente, bluntly told me that Myungki had recovered physically as much as she could. The doctor added that her mental capacity would continue improving, but there was no way she could become the normal person we had known before the accident. I clearly recalled the other doctors warning me about this prognosis in the past. Obviously, I had been in self-denial, and did not want to believe what the doctors were saying. Giving up the hope of Myungki's full recovery had never entered into my mind.

In the summer of 1996, I took the family to Banff National Park in Alberta, Canada. It was a long 700-mile drive from Portland, but Myungki never got tired and was happy that our daughters were with us. On our way up to Banff, we stopped at a hotel with hot springs facilities. We thought it would be a good idea for Myungki to soak in hot mineral water and heal her damaged body. When Myungki and the girls came out of the warm mineral bath, our youngest daughter DeAnna told me that her mom had found a lump in the left side of her breast. Apparently, she found it accidentally, and we all gathered around her and discussed what we should do. As our suite in the Fairmont Banff Springs Hotel had been reserved and was already paid for, we decided to proceed with our planned vacation. We all had a great time, though my concern about the lump in Myungki's breast stayed with me until we returned to Portland the following week.

As soon as we returned to Portland, I took Myungki to Kaiser Permanente. The oncologist who examined Myungki came out and told me the biopsy revealed cancer in the breast on her left side. The size of the lump was quite large, and it would require either a lumpectomy or a mastectomy. The oncologist recommended the latter without hesitation, due to the seriousness of her condition and her age, and asked the nurse to admit her immediately. The surgery was successfully completed the same day. Her doctor prescribed eight weeks of Chemotherapy and prescribed Tamoxifen for the next five years.

One blessing was that Myungki seemed to have been oblivious

about what was happening to her body until the day she was discharged from the hospital. She weighed only about eighty pounds. All of us had been so focused on her physical rehabilitation from the accident that it never occurred to anyone that cancer cells were quietly consuming her body.

Myungki's cancer surgery was a huge setback for my family and me. I felt totally defeated after all the effort we had poured into Myungki's physical recovery over the past two years. Although the mastectomy was a success, the doctors were guarded about their prognosis for her. Any cancer cells not removed by the surgery could potentially spread to other parts of her body. My priority for Myungki now shifted from physical therapy to cancer survival mode. I was convinced that she was now sentenced to death and would die within a matter of a year or two—that is, if she was lucky. Honestly, I did not believe that her weakened body from the car accident could withstand the attack of cancer. After all, it was third-stage cancer and the chance of cancer cells metastasizing was greater than fifty percent, according to her oncologist. Once again, I would have to trust in God, who had been generous to my family so far, to show mercy on Myungki and save her from this devastating disease.

—⚭—

CHAPTER 51

NEW PRIORITIES

Weeks after Myunkgi's surgery, as if coming out of a dream, I woke up and realized that I still had a company to run. Ever since Myungki's car accident, I had not been able to function properly as the CEO of the company I had started eighteen years before. To be honest, I had lost interest in running the business. I knew I was not thinking rationally, but I couldn't help it. Fortunately, the world economy was recovering fast and our business was thriving without my day-to-day involvement. My partners and the employees were all fully supportive of me and allowed me to focus on Myungki's recovery. By this time, I had built a respectable export brokerage house specializing in marketing recycled fiber products and other commodities. We exported to over a dozen different countries, mostly in Asia. We had offices in Newark, New Jersey, Los Angeles, Sao Paulo, and many agents in Asia. To build this business, I had worked very hard, traveling overseas two to three months of the year.

Looking back, I realize how hard it must have been for Myungki to take care of our three daughters while also taking care of our huge house in Hartung Farms by herself all those years. I was grateful that I had been able to delegate most of my daily duties and responsibilities to my partners and employees during that critical period of our lives. My devotion to Myungki and our daughters had brought us closer together and helped to heal our family. And thankfully, my business hadn't suffered from my absence.

Early in April 1997, Phil Epstein, my junior partner in the New Jersey office, called me bright and early one morning.

"Hey, Ken, there is a company that's interested in buying our company. Are you interested in selling?"

Up until this time, we were still looking for a company to buy, and then determine if we could become a public company by ourselves. I learned that a very large and well-integrated waste management company called KTI Industries located in New Jersey had expressed interest in purchasing our company. They were already registered in the NASDAQ and its shares were publicly traded. The only thing this company appeared to be lacking was the competent marketing of their own products. What caught my attention was the huge volume of recycled fibers KTI was producing every month—well over 150,000 tons of various grades of secondary fibers. By this time, my company was exporting an average of 30,000 tons monthly, about fifteen-hundred 40-foot containers, and we were hungry for more suppliers that could back us up. All of a sudden, my heart start pounding rapidly. It was my dream that K-C International would become the number one secondary fiber exporter in the United States. There was no question in my mind that I could handle the marketing of the entire tonnage being generated by KTI, and then we would soon become the leader in the industry. At this point, I had no idea how much KTI would offer to purchase our company, nor did I know the appropriate price to ask if I decided to sell.

Dr. Ross Pirasteh, the Chairman of the KTI, came out to visit me and our company in July 1997. I noticed that he was quite impressed to witness first-hand that our company was already fully automated, with an up-to-date computer system that controlled our inventory and logistics as well as our documentations. Until now, only a handful of the companies in our industry had adopted a computerized system to manage their marketing. Our staff was well trained, and we could handle substantially more business with the same number of employees. Prior to coming out to meet me in Portland, Dr. Pirasteh had examined our audited financial statements for the past five years and he was satisfied. He admitted that although his company was much larger, their computer system was not as sophisticated as ours, and most of their products were sold to domestic mills only.

Dr. Pirasteh and I sat down to talk in a quiet Italian restaurant in downtown Portland. I learned that he had once served as Finance Minister in Iran; after the fall of the Shah regime, he exiled to the United States. He expressed tremendous compassion regarding the political dilemma faced by the divided Korean peninsula, especially when he heard the story about my father and my visit to North Korea. I also mentioned that there was a remote possibility of investing in North Korea by introducing a newsprint manufacturing plant for which we would supply all the raw material they would require. The combined tonnage that KTI and K-C International could generate would easily support a mill or two in North Korea. The reason I even mentioned this idea to Dr. Pirasteh was because I was cautiously optimistic about the possible breakthrough in political, diplomatic, and economic relations between North and South Korea and the United States at that time.

In October 1994, the United States and North Korea had signed an agreement, the Agreed Framework, calling upon Pyongyang, suspected of being part of a covert nuclear weapons program, to freeze operation and construction of nuclear reactors in exchange for two proliferation resistant nuclear power reactors. The agreement also called upon the United States to supply North Korea with fuel oil pending construction of the reactors. An international consortium called the Korean Peninsula Energy Development Organization (KEDO) was formed to implement the agreement. The terms of the Agreed Framework also revealed the commitment of the United States and North Korea to move forward in normalizing economic and political relations by reducing barriers to investment, opening liaison offices, and ultimately exchanging ambassadors. The prospect of normalizing the relations between the United States and North Korea looked better than ever.

After signing the Memorandum of Understanding between KTI and K-C, the due diligence of reviewing our accounting records followed at a rapid pace. It indicated that KTI was seriously committed to buying our company. I was very excited by the prospect of having a tremendous amount of secondary fiber available for marketing internationally. I also welcomed the opportunity to fulfill my dream of becoming part of a public company registered in the NASDAQ. I made up my mind to go ahead and proceed with the sale of the company. I resumed negotiations with KTI and eventually agreed to sell the company. Per Dr. Pirasteh's request, I agreed to serve as one of the board members of KTI and remain as chairman of K-C International for the next five years.

It was September 1997. I had started the company with practically nothing in 1976, just six years after coming to the United States. I felt like I had finally realized my American dream. The sales price offered for my company was not great, but I did not want to delay the process, simply because I was fully charged up with the prospect of marketing the huge recycled fiber volume KTI plants were generating. At the same time, I knew full well I was not going to become super rich like some dotcom company owner who becomes a multimillionaire overnight. However, with the substantial personal savings I had already built before the sale of my company, I knew that Myungki and I could continue making a comfortable living if we were careful and maintained our humble way of life.

In November 1997—a mere two months after my company was sold, the Asian Financial Crisis shocked the world economy. The crisis started in Thailand, known in Thailand as the Tom

Yum Goong crisis. Indonesia, Thailand, and South Korea were the countries most affected by the meltdown. Impact from this financial debacle dealt a severe blow to most of our customers in these countries. The price of raw materials dropped sharply, and order volume decreased drastically. However, due to the sale of my company to KTI, K-C International was not affected that much by this particular Asian crisis, and we were able to maintain the sales volume since we had already diversified our marketing to other countries like India, Brazil, and China.

One sunny afternoon in the late spring, I took Myungki out to the deck behind our house where I had put in a new koi pond, along with a beautiful custom-designed gazebo with a built-in shower. I had stocked a dozen koi fish in the pond for Myungki's enjoyment. We had a half-acre lot where I had planted many trees and flowers in our back yard. The brilliant yellow forsythias were gone, but pink azaleas were in full bloom. Their sweet spring scent was still in the air and I felt immense peace inside of me. Dressed in warm clothes and wrapped in a blanket, Myungki also looked happy and content. Her outgoing personality and beautiful smile had not been lost while battling with rehabilitation and cancer treatments. She had regained most of her weight and she looked like a normal person for the first time in a long while.

It was hard to believe that five years had gone by since the car accident. As we sat there, I wondered, as I often had, whether Myungki could remember anything about the accident. I knew that most people with serious head injuries did not remember anything about their accident. But I decided to ask a few questions anyway. As expected, she could recall neither the accident nor the mastectomy. Her short-term memory was severely impaired and maybe would never come back. Surprisingly, she had retained most of her old memories, and had no trouble remembering the

Myungki with family while undergoing chemotherapy treatments. Portland, Oregon, 1997. She had withstood all the
odds and was recovering beautifully. My daughters and I
were happy and full of hope for Myungki to beat the cancer.

birthdays of her family members and the names of her high school
classmates.

As her physiatrist Dr. Erb had warned me, due to the injury
to her frontal lobe, Myungki would not be able to take her own
initiative about anything in daily life except for very basic physical
needs, such as going to the bathroom. She couldn't even express
that she was hungry or complain of pain or discomfort in her
body. To make sure she didn't lose touch with her nervous system
controlling her sensations, I pinched her occasionally to test her
reaction. I pinched her arm lightly and she flinched. Quietly, I let
out a sigh of relief.

While looking at Myungki sitting in a comfortable chair on
the deck, I was slowly awakening to the reality that my wife was
physically alive and well, but her mind was partially gone, and
perhaps she would never become a whole person again. Her soul
or spirit was within her, but not her mind in the normal sense. She
responded to stimulation and simple questions properly, but she
never asked a question or initiated anything on her own. I knew
she cared about our daughters, but she never seemed to worry or

think much about them. She was living in the present, without the capacity to think about the past or future.

One by one, Myungki's friends stopped calling. Even her own siblings and family members seemed to have given up any hope of her full recovery and showed less interest in Myungki and me. We were basically on our own. I had no choice but to adapt to the challenging new life ahead of us. From now on, I would have to think and act on her behalf. Even though she was not fully present, her soul and spirit were right here with me. We are all one in that sense. And it was comforting to know that we had nothing to worry about financially. With the sale of my business, our future was secure. I had realized my American dream in business.

CHAPTER 52

GIVING, SHARING, CARING

Share even a piece of bean with your neighbor.
—Old Korean saying

In 2002, I officially retired from K-C International Ltd. The buyer of my company, KTI Inc., based in New Jersey, decided to keep our employees in the Portland, Los Angeles, and Newark offices. I was also happy that KTI would retain the name K-C International Ltd. and continue marketing their products under this name. My business was given a new life.

Coming to the United States in 1969 with no money, I essentially created something very valuable out of thin air. Within a matter of years, after gaining invaluable experience in the international trading business, I founded my own company. K-C International Ltd. offered job opportunities to many hundreds of employees in America and overseas. Looking back, this success was possible, not because I had a college degree, or because somebody gave me a how-to book on how to run a company. What I had going for me was my youth, good health, a sound mind, and a few good teachers along the way.

My management style was to trust and empower all the employees 100%. Our managers and top executives were given absolute freedom and allowed to exercise their discretion and judgment in all business dealings. At the same time, as the CEO, I tried my best to stay on top of everything going on in the company's sales, accounting, and marketing departments with utmost transparency, honesty, and integrity. Due to my weakness in the accounting area, I made sure we had top-notch accountants with CPA certificates to oversee our financial dealings with the banks, the customers, and the suppliers. I also hired only the best-qualified people, those who had graduated from the top universities, for our managerial positions. I firmly believe your company is only as good as the people managing and running the company. All of our employees were compensated properly according to their level of skill and experience. I simply paid top salaries commensurate with the experience and demonstration of productivity. I did not hesitate to share the company's profits with a few key employees—Sue Litton, Frank Crowley, and Phil Epstein, and eventually made Frank and Phil my junior partners.

One of the most important lessons I learned over the years was that you get rewarded a hundredfold when you practice giving and sharing with others. The same principle applies to our personal lives too, of course.

One rainy day after the Thanksgiving holiday in 2003, Mr. Peter Chun, my dear friend of many years and the owner of Thermo Industries in Clackamas, Oregon, invited me out for lunch in downtown Portland. Peter was serving as the chairman of the Oregon Korea Foundation (OKF), a non-profit organization serving the Korean community in Oregon. Peter and I had jointly served as director and president of the Korean Society of Oregon (KSO), another non-profit organization, for many years. His contribution to the Korean community was well known and everybody loved and respected him.

As soon as we sat down for lunch and before the meals were served, he asked, "What is your perception of the Oregon Korea Foundation and its role for the Korean-American community?"

I was a little taken aback by his abrupt question, but I quickly realized that he had serious concerns about the future of OKF and the growth of its endowment program. Peter and a few other board members had joined in an effort to initiate a permanent endowment fund and had successfully raised $85,000 within a matter of two years. This was truly a remarkable accomplishment, and it was only made possible by the generous donation of $50,000 from Harry and Rockie Park, $20,000 from Chris and Stephanie Kang, along with $15,000 donations from fifty-four individual donors, including myself, who eagerly participated in establishing the "Harry and Rockie Park Endowment" at OKF in 2002. This was a historic event for the Korean American community in Oregon. As far as we knew, the OKF was the only Korean American organization in the United States with a permanent endowment program.

Initially, the primary purpose of the OKF was to manage the community building acquired in 1985 when I was serving as the president of the Korean Society of Oregon and Mr. Yoonshik Shin was chairman of the building committee. It was being used as the Korean Language School, where Myungki had taught for many years, and for various other community-related functions. Most of the directors were past and present presidents of the Korean Society of Oregon, but they did not show much interest or enthusiasm in its management.

The management of the community building soon became problematic. The leaders of the community expressed a strong desire to establish a separate entity specifically geared toward the care and management of the community building that undoubtedly would become a valuable asset and a legacy for our future generations. Ten years later, in 1995, the Oregon Korean Foundation was founded and incorporated for the purpose of maintaining and enhancing the Korean Community Building. By introducing the endowment concept to benefit the Korean community in 2002, OKF's mission and vision were more clearly defined and firmly established. Peter was serving as the third chairman of the board of OKF. He asked me if I would be interested in serving as the fourth chairman of OKF, for the 2004-2006 term, subject to the approval of the board.

I knew Peter was a very intelligent and thoughtful guy. I was sure he and his nominating committee members had carefully thought about whom they should nominate, because the new chairperson would have to be someone who could carry on the beautiful legacy without interruption. I felt honored by the invitation, but I also sensed the enormous amount of responsibility that would be involved. I told him I would have to think it over. Peter knew about Myungki's recovery from the car accident and her survival from breast cancer. He also knew that I had sold my company and officially retired in 2002.

Now that I was retired, I was looking forward to truly enjoying my retirement with Myungki by traveling and playing golf more often. However, I couldn't deny the fact that I had started to feel a certain emptiness and sensed in my heart that something was missing in my life, beyond the fact that I was no longer running a business. I thought maybe God was trying to give me a message.

This notion came into my mind a few days after Peter Chun offered me the position of chairman of the Oregon Korea Foundation. It was a big responsibility and it seemed unfair to Myungki for me to take on more public duties on top of the care-giving. Besides, a non-profit public organization like OKF would require a certain amount of expertise in fundraising and marketing. My only previous experience with a non-profit was serving as the president of the Korean Society of Oregon in 1985, and I didn't feel I had accomplished anything meaningful during my tenure. The Oregon Korean community was going through a lot of soul-searching during the 1980s, revealing many hidden conflicts between the so-called old-timers and the new immigrants. Not that there were many conflicts of interest commercially, but the newcomers felt that the old-timers were reluctant to let go of the control of the leadership of the community, such as the presidency of KSO and other similar posts.

As president, I absolutely refused to take sides and stayed neutral until the next election came around. One of the newcomers got elected and many of the old-timers, most of whom were my long-time friends, thought I had betrayed them and shunned me for a long time. We had elected the new president through the most democratic election process and the person who got the most votes won. Naturally, I was very disheartened by the narrow-mindedness displayed by some of my old friends, which reminded me of the deep-rooted and never-changing partisan politics in South Korea. I firmly believe that community leaders have to be selected by a democratic voting process, electing candidates who demonstrate passion and willingness to serve the community and its people.

Now faced with the question of whether I would serve as chairman of the Oregon Korea Foundation, I felt a certain urge in my belly and an idea popped into my mind. Perhaps God wanted to give me another opportunity to serve the community and vindicate myself for my mediocre performance during my tenure as president of KSO. When I was serving the Korean Society of Oregon, I had nothing to gain personally or business-wise. Most people knew that my motivation was unselfish and viewed me as an unbiased president who cared about KSO and its members. By now, most of the people in our community were aware that I was fully retired from business and had no commercial ties in our community.

I would soon turn sixty-two-years old. Although, I had begun to think about starting some type of new business, for some reason, it didn't strike me as a good idea. I kept praying and meditating, looking for clear guidance about what to do in the next chapter of my life. After a longer than usual meditation one evening, a blissful feeling arose from deep inside of my heart. I asked myself, when did I stop feeling stressed from taking care of Myungki and my other family members? When did I start feeling happiness from doing things for others? It was right after my awakening nine years earlier—the day in the hospital when I saw my wife as a spiritual being and realized that I, too, was a spiritual being, and we are all One in God.

After that experience, I no longer found the care-giving responsibility for Myungki challenging. Doing anything at all for her felt the same as if I were doing it for myself. I also noticed that I had no internal conflicts with anyone, including my own family and relatives. I truly felt as if I was a renewed person—not necessarily in Christian terms.

A Chinese philosopher once said, "Doing good deeds for others will bring ultimate happiness in life." I couldn't agree more. This was the answer. My next task in life was to find something that would bring happiness by serving others.

It was almost midnight by the time I had reached my decision. I had to hold back the urge to pick up the telephone and call Peter right away to let him know that I would gladly accept the nomination to become the next chairman of the Oregon Korea Foundation.

CHAPTER 53

OREGON KOREA FOUNDATION

The more he does for others, the happier he is.
The more he gives to others, the wealthier he is.

—Lao-tzu, *Tao Te Ching*

Peter and I met the next day at a Japanese restaurant called Shinju in the Pearl District in Portland. I told him that I would gladly accept the nomination and serve for a three-year term starting in 2004. It was rather a long time, I thought, but I calculated it would take at least a couple of years to bring in new board members and revamp the organization. Peter was happy and expressed his thanks for my accepting the nomination pending the final approval by the board members.

I called the first board of director's meeting on March 15, 2004. The first thing I proposed was to conduct all of our future board meetings in English. The reason was simple. Most of the board members, including myself, the so-called old timers, were accustomed to using our very comfortable mother tongue, Korean. This prohibited many young and old talents who could not speak Korean from joining the Oregon Korea Foundation even if they wanted to. Besides, the globalization of the world was in full swing and English was being taught even to Korean kindergarten students. I firmly believed that using English in our board meetings would improve communication between the members, especially with the younger generation, and expedite the transformation process, which was urgently needed in our community.

The second item I proposed was to set our endowment goal for $1,000,000 in the first year and $10,000,000 in ten years. All the board members gasped at this audacious goal. They looked at each other in total disbelief. Then, I proudly announced an additional endowment of $155,000 that I had quietly raised during the months of January and February after I was nominated as the chair. This was possible due to generous donations by my dear friends Chris and Stephanie Kang, Peter and Helen Chun, Drs. David and Candace Jun, and Seungri Kim.

We now had a total of $240,000, including the pledge amount from two families. I personally donated $50,000 in the name of my mother, Yoo Taejung, and requested the board to earmark the fund for the benefit of the possible refugees from North Korea and any expenses related to the reunification of the two Koreas. The board members were surprised and impressed with the size of the new endowment I was able to raise in a mere two months. With the support of many conscientious and passionate friends in our community, I did not anticipate a problem raising the rest within a year or so. Alas, I was wrong in my estimation and we miserably failed to reach that goal. Finding like-minded people was not as easy as I had imagined.

The third item on my agenda was to hire a professional Executive Director for OKF. Most of the board members had a full-time job and it was next to impossible to expect the board members to fulfill their duties satisfactorily. The professional ED would fill the void left by the board members and add his expertise to enhance and grow the foundation. My intention was to remake the OKF as a legitimate and professionally run organization. I succeeded in convincing the board to hire Bill Failing as our first Executive Director. He was an immensely qualified person with a profound knowledge and interest in the Korean community. Working closely together, he and I were able to raise the status of OKF to a higher level, making the people in our community feel proud to support and nurture the organization.

My last proposal was to adopt OKF's motto: *To Serve with Compassion.* In a nutshell, I truly wanted to reinvent OKF as the most beautiful non-profit foundation, serving not only the Korean community, but reaching out to other ethnic communities as well. The unspoken agenda behind all of this was to appeal to the Korean Americans in our community to practice caring, giving, and sharing, which would ultimately bring true happiness to everybody. By practicing giving and sharing in their daily life, people in our community would become happy and prosperous, and eventually become beautiful citizens of this great country.

The Oregon Korea Foundation is now very well established, with an endowment of over $500,000, along with hard assets including the buildings and land worth millions. Under the leadership of the current chairman, Mr. Yu Hyongjin, a dear friend of mine and a compassionate person, the OKF is flourishing with many young, dynamic board members as well as prominent advisory board members. Our mission statement reads:

> *The OKF's mission is to promote, preserve, and share Korean cultural heritage and to improve the quality of life for Korean-American communities in Oregon and Southwest Washington by raising, managing, and providing funds to such organizations.*

Some of the groups and institutions that OKF supports are: Korean Society of Oregon, Senior Citizens Welfare Fund, Korean Language School, Scholarship Fund, Korean Culture Fund, Future Leadership Training Fund, Public Defense Fund, Portland Art Museum, Portland State University.

I was truly honored that I had an opportunity to serve our community for three full years. It gave me pleasure and true happiness. It was hard work, but I didn't mind losing a little sleep at night, or making cold calls to potential donors, or encouraging reluctant board members to participate in a worthy cause like the Oregon Korea Foundation. And while I was devoting my time and energy to OFK for the benefit of the people in our community, God stepped in and took care of Myungki and my family without a hitch.

CHAPTER 54

CROSSROADS

I was happy when my three-year term as chairman of the Oregon Korea Foundation was winding down in March 2006. It was twelve years since Myungki's car accident. Christine was already happily married, and DeAnna and Scott were engaged. Jennifer, our eldest daughter, was planning to marry her fiancé Bruno del Ama in Spain later that year. It seemed like the right time for me to revisit the question of Myungki's and my life together. I wanted to carefully evaluate our current situation and plan for our future as best I could. Myungki hadn't experienced a recurrence of her breast cancer since the mastectomy ten years before. Despite the short-term memory loss and malfunctioning executive function of her brain, her overall physical condition was excellent, except that she had to rely on a walker to get around the house. Basically, she was homebound and still needed twenty-four-hour supervision.

I had arrived at a crossroads and needed to make some serious decisions about the future course of Myungki's rehabilitation and what kind of lifestyle we needed to create moving forward. Should I continue spending my time, money, and energy on Myungki's rehab, which seemed to have no end to it, and sacrifice my own interests and goals in life? Myungki's physiatrist Dr. Erb and Dr. Wyles at Kaiser had already told me that Myungki had recovered as much as she could physically. Any further improvement in the future would be insignificant. Dr. Erb suggested that Myungki and I just start living our life as normally as possible. She told me that it would be extremely difficult for Myungki to let go of her walker now that she was so accustomed to it. While continuing to push her to walk on her own, I realized it was time to start paying more attention to my own health. I decided to explore different possibilities for enriching our rather depressing pattern of living.

In April 2006, some close friends of ours in Oregon invited Myungki and me to visit them at their vacation homes in La Quinta, California. Both couples owned beautiful houses in the PGA West Golf Resorts. As soon as we arrived at the resort, I fell in love with the amenities and the six world-renowned golf courses. The weather was dry and very comfortable. Myungki and I decided to buy a vacation home there right away, although I knew the hot summer weather would be brutal. It didn't matter, because we did not plan to live down there during the summer months. The only disadvantage was that we would be far away from our family members who had been giving us their love and support all these years.

In June, we purchased a 3300-sq.-ft. home on Spanish Bay Street in the PGA West Resorts overlooking the 11th green of the Jack Nicklaus Tournament golf course. I wanted to make sure our vacation home was large enough to accommodate my three daughters and their husbands and future families. We sold our house in Hartung Farms in Portland and moved into a two-bedroom condominium not far from where my mother lived. It seemed that I had created the most ideal retirement lifestyle I could dream of.

In October 2006, our daughter Jennifer got married to Bruno del Ama in Madrid. They had met in New York, where Bruno was working as an executive at a reputable financial firm, and Jennifer was busy pursuing her dream of becoming a world-class violinist after graduating from the Juilliard School. It wasn't easy traveling to Madrid with my whole family—Myungki and our three daughters, my sisters Yuni and Hyunjoo, Myungki's sister Sue Litton and her husband, and her brother Chanki and his wife. But it was a fun and meaningful experience for all of us and well worth the long trip.

The wedding took place at the Grand Cathedral in Madrid. It was a traditional Spanish wedding with about three hundred people attending. Our beautiful daughter and her handsome husband looked like movie stars. Myungki and I were impressed to meet our in-laws, Dr. Carlos and Marisa del Ama and their families— all wonderful, inspiring, and warm-hearted people.

Returning home to Portland, Myungki and I began our annual ritual of making the 2200-mile roundtrip migration, spending winter months at our place in Southern California. The traveling was physically stressful for me, but Myungki seemed to enjoy the drive. We stopped at resting spots, tried out different restaurants, and sang duets to keep our spirits high as we drove along the freeway. While not neglecting Myungki's physical therapy in La Quinta, I played golf as much as I could. Our friends from Oregon provided us with much support, including frequent dinners with delicacies from their kitchens.

The following year, in October 2007, I decided to take Myungki and our baby daughter Didi to Seoul, Korea. I never dreamed the day would come when Myungki would be recovered enough physically to make the long trip to Korea. Many of her old high school friends and family members were anxious to see her face to face. They had kept in touch over the years. This was the first time she was returning to Korea since the accident.

For Didi, this was the first trip to see her parents' birthplace and get acquainted with the country she had never paid much attention to in the past. She was living and working in New York at the time and struggling to decide on her career. She couldn't quite make up her mind between an accounting career and pursuing her dream of becoming a singer and starring on Broadway.

—ᴍ—

CHAPTER 55

GONE TO THE DIFFERENT WORLD

The most desirable thing in this life is death. Your death will bring you to
Jesus Christ. Is it not difficult to be free from all the suffering on this earth?
By leaving this life on earth, we will be reunited with God. Let us separate
ourselves from this earth then walk together with God.
—Yoo Taejung (*from her journal, September 22, 1986*)

The years passed by. Myungki and I continued to spend winters
in La Quinta and summer and fall months in Portland. Didi had
been accepted to the Berklee School of Music in Boston to study
voice performance. Jennifer had become a prominent chamber
musician and was also performing contemporary music with different groups. After graduating from Northwestern University
with a Communications degree, Christine worked in the marketing department at CISCO systems for few years, then switched
to the real estate brokerage business. With her pleasant, outgoing
personality, she was blossoming in the real estate business. Our
daughters were living up to their promise.

Meanwhile, I couldn't help but notice that my mother had
aged over the past few years, and she didn't seem to be enjoying
life as much as she used to. The number of appointments with her
doctors increased, and my sisters and I had to make frequent trips
to the emergency room at the hospital to treat her extremely high

blood pressure and pneumonia-like symptoms. Her only activity was going to church with Myungki and me every Sunday, and occasionally dining out at different restaurants.

My mother was fading away. More and more, she spent her days in a waking dream. She shared stories with me about her strange encounters with the ghosts of her stepson and stepdaughter, Seokjoo and Youngjoo. She said she heard someone knocking at the door calling a name that sounded like "Mother." She was sure it was the voice of either Seokjoo or Youngjoo.

Not long after these episodes in the spirit world, she collapsed and had to be taken to the emergency room at St. Vincent Hospital. Initially, she was diagnosed with acute pneumonia, but further lab test results revealed that she had a far advanced case of liver cancer. Until then, even her doctor had not detected the rapidly advancing cancer. Rather abruptly, her health declined dramatically. Within a matter of about two weeks, her doctor ordered hospice service at home.

My mother started going in and out of consciousness and was suffering much discomfort and pain in her body from the dreadful liver cancer. We gave her morphine to ease the pain. A month later, the wonderful hospice nurse notified my family that my mother would have only about one week before she would die.

At my mother's sickbed, I pleaded with my half-sister Woonsik to please reconcile with her brother and sister-in-law before our mother passed away. Although my mother never complained or shared her frustration about Sonsik and Woonsik with me, I was aware of the never-ending tension between them. Deep down in their hearts, they probably still harbored ill feelings toward their mother, whom they thought had betrayed them. But Woonsik and her brother and his wife made no attempt to reconcile with her at the end. It reminded me of something my mother had said: "Children will never understand their mother's profound love and compassion for them until their mother has gone to the different world."

My mother passed away on January 9, 2009. When she died, I felt as if I no longer had my energy source; it felt like my spirit had left my body. I had lost the only support I'd had all those years. Despite her failing health, she had done everything possible to help Myungki and all of our family members during the last fifteen years of her life. It was painful to admit that I also felt huge relief from the heavy burden of taking care of my mother throughout my life. At the same time, I was happy that she no longer had to suffer from physical pain or the mental anguish caused by her own children.

After the mortuary services carried my mother's body away, I slept in her empty bedroom for three nights. None of my siblings volunteered to spend the nights with me. They said they were afraid. According to Korean customs, the formal funeral services are usually performed three to five days after the death of the family member. I wanted to hang onto my mother's spirit as long as I could. I wanted to console her soul and pay my final tribute to a great mother and a wonderful human being.

Yoo Taejung in formal dress. Vancouver, Washington, 1995.

CHAPTER 56

PROPHESY

During the months of mourning, the beautiful spring season came and went. The stress from taking care of my mother's funeral services and dealing with squabbling siblings, in addition to the care-giving responsibilities for Myungki, had worn me down. I was literally fed up with living in Portland. The cold dark winter months were especially hard on me. Besides which, I felt like I was about to fall into another depression. I consulted with my wonderful internist, Dr. Kilo. He perfectly understood my situation and was willing to prescribe the appropriate medications, but the possible side effects of antidepressants were not worth the risk. I knew it was time for Myungki and me to make a major change in our lives.

In June 2009, six months after my mother's passing, Myungki and I decided to move to La Quinta permanently. We were still reasonably young, at sixty-five and sixty-seven, but driving back and forth annually had become very challenging for me because of Myungki's need for constant care and supervision. I was fully aware of the intensely hot weather in the desert, but I wanted to test our patience and resiliency.

Three months after we permanently moved down to La Quinta from Portland, the heat was becoming unbearable for us. Despite our neighbor's assurance that our blood would become thinner in no time and we would have no problem withstanding the heat, I started having serious doubts about living there year-round. One night I heard a strange warning in a dream.

"Abeom! Abeom! Wake up, wake up! You can't live in this house any more. Move somewhere else as soon as possible."

It was my mother's voice. When I awoke from the dream, the alarm clock showed just past four o'clock am. I was sweating, and the room temperature felt like a hundred degrees, even though I had set the air conditioner at seventy-eight.

I thought Myungki and I could tough it out until November when the temperature would start falling quickly. It was only September now. My dream was real, and my mother's voice was so clear that I was wide-awake and had to sit straight up on the edge of the bed for a while.

"Did I make a mistake moving down here to La Quinta permanently?" I asked myself. "Was I too hasty?" I thought that maybe Mom didn't approve of my move and was upset with me in heaven because we had moved too far away from her grave.

Myungki was still deep in sleep but I decided to wake her up. She responded quickly and asked why I was up so early. I told her about my dream of my mother urging us to move right away. Without hesitation, she said she agreed with my mother and said we should move again. I couldn't believe how fast she reacted. She added that she had never liked the idea of moving there but went along with me because she knew how much I loved to play golf. I was flabbergasted. After all the work and hassles selling the house, buying the condominium in Portland, and buying the new one in La Quinta, and now she claims that she never liked the idea of our moving to the desert? I might have yelled at her if she was a normal person. But I knew she was innocent and was speaking her mind.

Another hot day, with temperature ranging from 100-115 degrees, was about to begin. About ten o'clock that morning, I called my seasoned realtor Sandi Phillips, who had helped me buy our house four years ago. She was surprised to learn that we wanted to sell the house so soon, but she understood our circumstances. I knew the real estate market had started nose-diving ever since we purchased our house in 2006. There were no signs of the market improving any time soon. I told her I was willing to entertain any offer as long as the potential buyer was serious about buying the property. I knew I had to sell and incur substantial losses. I didn't care.

Thankfully, as soon as I listed the house for sale, my mind settled down and I felt peace in my heart. While waiting to receive buyers' offers, I called our daughter Christine in Saratoga, who had become a very successful as a realtor over the past several years. She was surprised to hear about our decision and asked what I had in mind. She soon suggested that we should consider moving to San Jose and live close to her rather than moving back to Portland. I jumped on her suggestion and asked her to research the availability of a single-level condominium with two bedrooms and two baths.

After I hung up from my conversation with Christine, I sat on our back porch with a glass of Chardonnay. Our house was located overlooking the putting green of the 11th hole of the Jack Nicklaus Tournament Golf Course. Although it was still very warm, the summer breeze was quite pleasant and made the temperature bearable. The sun was slowly setting on top of the Santa Rosa Mountain ridge and the sight was absolutely gorgeous, out of this world.

Momentarily, I thought about the scary incident while driving on the I-60 Pomona Freeway the month before. Frank Crowley, my ex-partner at K-C International, called me one day and wanted to know if I could make myself available for lunch with him at a hotel in Huntington Beach. He was attending a business conference there for the next few days. I was really happy to hear from him and agreed to see him without hesitation.

The next morning, I left my house in La Quinta around ten o'clock. From my house to the hotel in Huntington Beach was approximately 120 miles and it would take roughly two hours. About halfway to Huntington Beach on the Pomona Freeway, I felt a dizzy sensation in my head. I wondered if I was dehydrated, so I started drinking water. The dizziness would not go away and my eyes were getting blurry. I couldn't detect any shortness of breath, but I wondered whether this was an early symptom of heart failure; I had never experienced these symptoms before. I panicked. Immediately, I pulled my car over at the next exit.

Fortunately, there was a Ramada Inn adjacent to the freeway. I parked my car in the parking lot and decided to take a little rest, hoping my dizziness would go away. Contrary to my expectations, my condition only got worse—now I felt short of breath. I knew I should call 911 immediately, but I didn't want to risk fainting while making the call and die in my car. I forced myself to walk to the hotel to ask one of the employees to make the emergency call for me. At least that way, someone might find me if I fainted in the parking lot on my way to the hotel. Fortunately, I was able to wobble to the hotel lobby and the front desk clerk called 911.

While waiting for the paramedics to arrive, I called Frank and told him I would not be able to see him that day. He was shocked and immediately offered to come out and take care of me, but I told him I'd already called 911 and he didn't need to worry. In no time, the fire engine and the paramedics arrived and took me to the Anaheim Regional Medical Center. They put me through all kinds of tests for the next couple of hours. The ECG (electrocardiogram) and all the lab tests results came back negative. I was immensely relieved with the reports, and by then, I felt good and back to normal.

It was already past midnight. I wanted to leave the hospital and go home right away. I realized I hadn't had a chance to call Myungki. My iPhone didn't show any calls from her either. By now, she would be in bed asleep. She would be incapable of thinking about the implications of her husband's absence. My heart ached intensely with deep empathy and love for her. I called her.

After prolonged ringing, she finally answered the phone. I was relieved to learn that she was safe in her bed.

"Where are you now? Why are you not coming home yet?"

She couldn't remember that I had left home that morning to have lunch with Frank in Huntington Beach. I told her briefly what had happened and assured her that I was fine and would be on my way home shortly. I told her to go back to sleep.

The on-call emergency room doctor wanted me to stay overnight for observation. But I had no such luxury to stay in the emergency room overnight while Myungki was one hundred miles away and home alone. She wouldn't remember my phone call due to her severely impaired short-term memory. Instead, I decided to call my best friend Paul Kim in Orange County. He arrived quickly and offered to drive me home to La Quinta the same evening. When he arrived, I asked him if there was a Korean restaurant nearby open twenty-four hours. I had not had lunch or dinner and I was extremely hungry. My intention was to carefully observe my physical condition while having dinner and ask Paul to drive me home only if I felt uncomfortable driving.

We soon found a restaurant, and I emptied a large bowl of galbitang (short-rib soup with rice) and many side dishes, including kimchi. I felt better and was ready to drive myself home.

The Pomona Freeway merges into the I-10 San Bernardino Freeway. There was hardly any traffic. My head was clear. I realized that La Quinta may be a heaven on earth for a lot of people, but not for us. Myungki and I needed to be closer to our family. A huge doubt was embedded in my mind about living in the desert without any family members nearby. When I arrived home that night, I knew my decision to sell our house was the right one.

Because of the depressed economy and the real estate market, there were hardly any offers to buy our house in La Quinta. One day in December, my realtor Sandi called and said we had a serious offer from a buyer in San Francisco. Since we had listed our property substantially lower than the market price, it didn't take long for the buyer and I to agree to a price and close the deal. The closing date was set for the end February. That meant we had to move all the furniture out of the house and turn over the keys to the new owners by the first of March. It took five months from the day our house was listed until it sold in March 2010.

Temporarily, we moved into our daughter Christine's house in Saratoga and started looking for our new home in San Jose. Being one of the most successful young realtors in the Bay area, it didn't take long for her to find a beautiful and cozy 1600-sq.-ft. two-bedroom condo in The Villages Golf and Country Club in southeast San Jose, a senior living community with an 18-hole golf course and many beautiful hiking trails in our back yard. Myungki and I couldn't have been happier.

𝄞

It was exactly six months since my mother had appeared in my dream urging me to move away from La Quinta. The temperature in San Jose was a welcome change from La Quinta's desert heat. Weather in San Jose is very gentle and comfortable throughout the year. It was October by the time our contractor had finished the extensive remodeling of our newly purchased condo, and we were able to move in. Compared to our house in La Quinta, the condo seemed very small, but it was comfortable. Gradually, we put all the household goods in order and quickly adjusted ourselves to the new environment. Myungki and I soon joined the Kaiser Permanente Health System and found wonderful primary care physicians for us. At her doctor's recommendation, Myungki started new weekly physical therapy. I also hired a physical trainer to come to our house once a week and work with Myungki on her balance and muscle strength. I joined the men's golf club and started playing golf more often. I also resumed my morning walk routine, a minimum of forty-five minutes a day.

One afternoon in August 2011, I felt a sharp pain in my back and the right side of my abdomen. I thought it may have been caused by moving some heavy boxes of books. I rested overnight and took some Advil, but the pain would not subside. Rather, it was getting worse and I could hardly move in the morning. I called my doctor and asked Myungki's caregiver Rita to take me to the Kaiser San Jose facility. He immediately ordered a CT scan, concerned that I might have appendicitis. The CT scan revealed no sign of appendicitis; however, they found a small but suspicious-looking enlarged lymph nodes deep in my abdomen. Dr. Abrams immediately referred me to an oncologist, Dr. Yavorkovsky, who recommended a biopsy.

A long huge needle was stuck into my back and a small tissue sample was taken from an enlarged node in my abdomen and sent to the lab. The sample was positive, and the radiologist diagnosed a possible lymphadenopathy, swollen lymph node, suspecting a low-grade Non-Hodgkins Lymphoma. Dr. Yavorkovsky, or Dr. Y (as he was called at his clinic), agreed with the radiologist's opinion. He said I had a low-grade indolent Non-Hodgkins Follicular Lymphoma, which is a form of blood cancer in the lymphatic system of the body. Unlike other forms of cancer, such as stomach, lung, and liver cancer, the problem with this type of cancer is that it is incurable. There is no way to destroy all the cancer cells in your blood stream, not even when treated with chemotherapy.

The news was devastating, to say the least. We had moved to San Jose from La Quinta barely ten months before and were about to start enjoying our new life. My God, what kind of a terrible deal was this, I wondered. I had done everything within my power to help others. I had taken care of my mother until her passing, been Myungki's caregiver for the past seventeen years, supported our three daughters and financed their college education and weddings—now this. Why? Besides which, I had volunteered and served the Korean community for three full years before retiring to San Jose. What had I done to deserve this dreadful cancer at this late stage of my life? It seemed totally unfair. For the first time in a long while, I couldn't hold back my tears and began to cry when Dr. Y briefly left the office. Christine, who had accompanied me that day, gave me a very warm and consoling embrace.

Not knowing the implications of this type of blood cancer, I feared that my days left in this world were numbered. Perhaps I would die within a matter of a few years. The only consolation from Dr. Y was that this type of cancer was very slow-growing. He said he could start treating me if the cancer cells became aggressive or I started showing symptoms such as enlarged glands, night sweats, itching, or drastic weight loss.

Hearing his prognosis eased my fear a bit; however, I couldn't help but feel I had been dealt with another blow from God. It shook me upside down and to the core. What do I do now? I wondered. Suddenly, I remembered my mother's warning in the dream urging me to move from the desert.

"Did I catch this terrible disease in the desert?" I asked Dr. Y. I speculated that maybe the cancer in my body would have been aggravated if I had stayed there and not moved.

Dr. Y said there was no way of knowing how I had contracted this disease. I asked the doctor if he had any recommendations to prevent the cancer cells from proliferating or to slow down their growth. He had none.

"You mean, there is nothing you can advise me to do?" I asked. I thought he might recommend a special diet or some form of exercise. He said there was no proof that this particular cancer had anything to do with food or exercise.

"Just try to live your life normally. Eat, drink, and exercise smartly and reduce stress as best you can."

That's all he said. "Let's wait and watch" was his prescription.

Kookjoo and Myungki at the Tom Weiskopf golf course in PGA West Resorts, La Quinta, California, 2007.
I never imagined that Myungki would be out on the golf course with me driving the cart, and yet here we were!

CHAPTER 57

SOUL MATES

Myungki's wellbeing was always foremost in my mind, but now it was compounded by my own health issues. I helped her to create a daily routine that would give both of us pleasure and health benefits. Starting in La Quinta, after physical therapy and exercise with her personal trainer, I would take Myungki out on the golf course with me as often as possible. Of course, she couldn't play golf, but she enjoyed accompanying me and often pointed out what I was doing wrong whenever I missed a shot. She used to be a pretty good golfer herself. I also let her drive the golf cart on the flat terrain when no other golfers were around. At first, she was afraid to drive the cart, but slowly began to enjoy it.

I bought her a resistance chair with a small stationary bike attached to it that allowed her to do a full-body workout from a safe and comfortable seated position. She used this equipment religiously at least thirty minutes every day. Another safe exercise program I introduced to her daily routine was a senior yoga program done in a chair. We simply put in the DVD and she followed the instructions given by the instructor.

When she finished these physical exercises, she often would play the piano. I was amazed when I discovered that she hadn't forgotten how to play the piano or lost her theoretical knowledge, though naturally she wasn't as proficient as she used to be. There was no way of knowing how much knowledge she had retained or lost, but it was a miracle for our family when she started playing the piano again. These days she enjoys playing the electronic organ rather than the grand piano, which we traded in when we moved to San Jose. We also started singing together, mostly from the hymn book. Her singing voice changed drastically after the accident, but she still has a wonderful alto voice. Since I am a tenor, we make a great duet whenever we sing together. Many times, she ends up crying when we hit some great notes in harmony. It is a beautiful experience and we usually end by thanking God for His grace and give blessings for our health, wonderful daughters, and caring families—especially my sister Hyunjoo and my dear mother in heaven.

For my own pleasure and sanity, and for the sake of Myungki's enjoyment, I started memorizing and singing many of the great classical songs, such as "Ave Maria," by Franz Schubert and Charles Gounod, "The Lord's Prayer" in English and Spanish, "Panis Angelicus," "Una furtiva lagrima," "Core 'ngrato," "Non ti Scordar di mi!", "Ich Liebe Dich," as well as some Korean songs. Without fail, she always yells, "Encore!" and "Bravo!" and claps her hands. Then I yell, "Pavarotti and Andrea Bocelli, eat your heart out!" Myungki is the greatest cheerleader for me and for our daughters when they perform for us.

Amazingly, not only has Myungki's overall health improved remarkably over the years, but her memory also seems to be a lot sharper than before. Although her lack of short-term memory continues to be problematic, she acts like a normal person and her pleasant personality always keeps my spirits up.

Because Myungki didn't have any hobbies of her own, I decided one day to teach her how to play Blackjack to stimulate her brainpower and memory. While we were living in the California desert in the winter, there weren't many things Myungki and I could do during the evenings except watch TV. The next best thing was to go to the casino to see shows or movies. Interestingly, I noticed that whenever we went to the casino, Myungki's whole demeanor changed, and she showed extraordinary enthusiasm when we crossed the casino floor. Her steps became more confident (with a walker, of course), and the long walk across the casino didn't seem to bother her at all. Walking anywhere else, such as on the street, she generally refused to walk for any distance. It was weird, and I couldn't explain it.

One day, I bought a book for Myungki called *How to Play Blackjack*. She started reading it, but I knew she would not be able to follow the instructions. Instead, I decided to teach her about this magical table game myself, as I knew how to play the game.

I was surprised how fast Myungki learned to play the game. After a few days of practicing at home, we decided to venture out to a casino and put her skills to the test. Even though I knew that the house always has the advantage, I was hoping for some beginner's luck for Myungki.

There was an empty seat available right in the middle of the blackjack table with a minimum bet of five dollars. I helped her to sit down and pulled out a hundred-dollar bill and bought twenty five-dollar chips for her. She bet five dollars each hand. I watched a few hands and let her decide whatever she wanted to do. She won couple hands and lost three or four times. She struggled a bit whenever she was dealt with 16 against the dealer's face card. I encouraged her to take the card according to the tips learned from the book. She also didn't know what to do when she had soft 12, 13, 14, 15, 16 cards in her hand while dealer's hand showed 4, 5, or 6. A soft hand is any hand of two cards that contains an ace card. I taught her to double down the bet. There were a few more basics she needed to learn, like when to split the same cards, or to double down whenever your hand shows 9, 10, and 11 against the dealer's face card showing 4, 5, 6 etc. She mastered the basics in no time. There are times when you need to press or reduce the bets and learn how to manage your winnings and so forth. Myungki showed no interest in learning those rules; she wanted to stick to her own game plan of making steady five-dollar bets each time. She didn't seem to show any emotion, even when she was on a losing streak and her original investment was down to a few chips. I noticed that the only time she increased her bet was when she saw the chips piled up in front her and knew that her winning had increased at least fifty per cent. She was a natural gambler.

Over the course of many years, her playing habits have not changed and she rarely loses her original investments. Of course, the reason for this success is that I always watched over her shoulder and pulled her away from the table whenever she was winning or before she lost her last five-dollar chip. Ironically, I was the one who occasionally donated big bucks to the casinos due to lack of emotional control and self-discipline. I have since graduated from serious gambling. It's a blessing that Myungki doesn't remember how much money she's made or lost once she leaves the casino. She is simply happy playing with me there beside her.

The purpose of teaching Myungki how to play blackjack was for brain exercise and to let her enjoy being out and about with me. I truly believe that making trips to interesting places, eating at different restaurants, and seeing shows and concerts has enhanced her overall health and wellbeing. I have no doubt that every dime I have spent for her was well worth it. Despite the mental and physical burden her dependency has placed on me, I came to realize that I was permanently, lovingly, glued to her—as if we were conjoined twins in life.

———∿∿∿———

CHAPTER 58

WINTER TREES

Sometimes our fate resembles a fruit tree in winter.
Who would think that those branches would turn green again and blossom,
but we hope it, we know it.

—Goethe

Seven years had passed since I received the cancer diagnosis. The follow-up PET scans showed nothing unusual, and the annual lab tests had been consistently normal. Now Dr. Y wanted to see me only once a year instead of twice a year. He thought I was doing really well, though he had not yet declared that I was cancer free. The only thing I added to my routine was a two-hour hike twice a week with my friends in the Villages; a six-mile round-trip course with steep and strenuous trails. Mild weather, a fair amount of exercise, and moderate eating and drinking seems to have been the best medicine for preventing cancer cells from turning aggressive. I was glad that I heeded my mother's warning in the dream and quickly escaped from the hot and harsh desert climate and moved to San Jose, with its comfortable, mild weather. Life in San Jose is enjoyable. Every time my regular Korean foursome gets together on the golf course, the first thing we say is how fortunate we are to have been endowed with good health and live in a place where we can play golf as much as we want.

Ever since Myungki and I had entered our sixties, we realized that we were driving downhill at sixty miles an hour. We were now seventy-five and seventy-seven and averaging seventy-six miles an hour; pretty soon it would be eighty. That's really fast and well over the speed limit of most freeways in the United States. Looking back, it was incredible how Myungki and I managed our lives and watched our three beautiful daughters grow up, now happily married and successful in their own ways and chosen fields. It sure has been a long and arduous journey for me and my family.

Perhaps the biggest letdown was my failure to make Myungki physically independent, without the help of a walker or a wheelchair. It was a decision I had to make twenty years ago, when I prematurely introduced a walker for Myungki, fully knowing the potential consequences that she could become permanently dependent on it. The option for me seemed clear at that time. Will you spend the years ahead repeatedly going back and forth to therapists and doctors' offices without any guarantee that Myungki will become independent? Or would you rather do something more enjoyable with your life now, despite the burden of constantly supervising Myungki's mobility? What prompted me to make my decision was that Myungki showed absolutely no will to become independent physically. I tried every possible trick and coercion and did everything in my power to get her to walk again.

The end result is that I have a happy wife who goes everywhere with me, sleeps with me in the same bed, and truly shares my life. Our daughters have more time with their mother and frequently communicate with her on FaceTime. Indeed, we have been living a very good life, simple and normal. I am fully aware that our daughters missed their mom's wisdom and guidance in the crucial years of their growing up and maturing. But, let's face it. Who said life was fair and perfect without trials? From the many ordeals we had to go through together as a family, I am sure our daughters learned many valuable lessons in life that cannot be learned in schools. At the same time, I am convinced that our three daughters are well prepared to face any adversities in life that may unexpectedly be presented to them in the future.

A friend of mine once asked me why I didn't hire more physical therapists and let them work with Myungki independently, or perhaps send her to a rehab institution, which would have freed me up to start another business or pursue other interests. In his view, I had sufficient financial resources available for extensive treatments. It was a valid question. My only rationale at the time was that I seriously doubted that Myungki would be able to last more than a couple of years after the mastectomy, a mere two years after the car accident. I poured my heart and soul into her recovery during that seven-year period so that I would not regret that I hadn't done enough for her and our daughters. I also felt it was extremely important for Myungki's emotional and mental recovery that I provide her with my utmost care and love.

There is no better medicine or therapy than the unconditional love and care a spouse can provide for their loving partner, especially for a patient with traumatic brain injury. I can now say with confidence that I did the right thing for Myungki and my family, and I have no regrets about the decisions I made along the way. Presented with the same circumstances, I would not hesitate to do the same thing all over again.

There is a wisdom taught by our founding fathers in Korea. When you approach life with all your might and sincerity, faith arises from it, and then love will follow, enabling you to care, share, and freely give your love to your loved ones and the people around you. I believe I have practiced this wisdom in my own life. Along the way, God helped me to realize who He is and who I am. Ultimate truth may be unattainable during our lifetime, but to have peace of mind concerning God and your spirit now in the present is better than spending your life in caves, temples, and churches repenting and seeking enlightenment and salvation. Making my way through the pitch-dark tunnels of life often seemed like a never-ending ordeal. The only thing I could do was to accept the challenges without complaint, give everything I had, and never give up hope.

—⁓—

CHAPTER 59

RECONCILIATION

On January 9, 2018, we held a family gathering for my mother's ninth memorial service at the Skyline Memorial in Portland. It was a beautiful sunny day, but extremely cold, and there was snow on the ground. My brother Sonsik, who was eighty-two years old and a retired elder of the Portland Youngnak Presbyterian Church, led the prayer and the rest of the service. All of my family members looked healthy and happy that day. Even my sister Woonsik and my brother Sonsik and his wife seemed to have reconciled their differences.

Woonsik smiled and walked over to me. "Abeom, can I talk with you privately?" My sister Woonsik calls me "Abeom" like my mom used to. It's very endearing and always reminds me of my mother.

"By the way, do you still have a couple of burial spots available adjacent to our mom's plots? Your brother-in-law, who is now approaching ninety, and I would like to be buried next to our mom when we die."

I had purchased a block of eight plots for our family burial site many years ago. I announced at that time that whoever wanted to be buried next to our mother was welcome to join her free of charge. I still had six plots left after Mom and my sister Yuni's long-time boyfriend were buried there.

For a second, I couldn't believe what I had just heard. I knew my mom was listening to this conversation between my sister and me. My joy was beyond expression. I was sure our mom had been waiting for this moment for a very long time, knowing that her kids would want to return to their own mother's warm and loving bosom.

"Absolutely, Sis. You are welcome to join us in the same site, free of charge!"

"No, no, no. I will pay for them," she insisted.

She said her own daughter Youngshin, who was an executive at a world-renowned athletic shoe manufacturer, had agreed to pay for the cost of the plots for her parents.

"Okay, in that case, I have a suggestion. Why don't you donate the cost of the plots to the Oregon Korea Foundation in honor of our mom, Yoo Taejung."

Happily, we all agreed!

"By the way Sis, how are you and brother Sonsik and his family getting along these days?"

"We are just fine and doing great! Don't you worry about us anymore!"

—⟋ⱴⱴ⟍—

CHAPTER 60

RETURN TO THE MOTHERLAND

You cannot cover the sky with your palms.

—Korean proverb

Not long after the anniversary memorial for my mother, I felt inspired to read her unfinished memoir, which I had put away years ago. My daughters had been encouraging me to write my memoir for them and their future children. They often asked me questions about what it was like growing up in Korea and how their father had started out life in the United States. I also wanted to reflect on my life in Korea in the hope of solving the mysteries surrounding my father's tragic death and his relationship with Kim Il Sung. I felt strongly that I owed it to my mother and father to find out the truth and pay proper tribute to their memory.

One year later, I had finished the first draft of my memoir. I sent my manuscript to an editor and publisher in the United States for her assessment. With her blessing and encouragement, I also sent a copy to a publisher in Seoul, South Korea, recommended by my friend Park Youngju. With a positive response from them as well, I decided to visit Seoul and search the libraries for an original copy of my father's two-volume book, *A Short History of the Overseas Korean Revolutionary Movement*, to confirm what I suspected about the partial copy given to me in North Korea in 1993. I also made appointments to meet with the Korean publisher, and the editor of a Korean newspaper who had written articles about my father and Kim Il Sung.

On October 11, 2018, my daughter Christine and I boarded a Korean Airlines flight in San Francisco and were on our way to Incheon, South Korea. The trip to Seoul was especially meaningful for me this time because I was on a mission, and also because I had my daughter Christine as my traveling companion. She had often expressed her wish to visit South Korea with me and she had finally found an opportunity to make the trip. I knew how much she would love to experience the vibrant city of Seoul and see the sights and taste the delicious Korean dishes of her parents' homeland.

The thirteen-hour plane ride on the Boeing 777 jet was smooth and comfortable. We landed at Incheon International Airport at around five-thirty AM the following day. After checking into the Shilla Stay Gwanghwamun Hotel, located in the heart of downtown Seoul, we rested a little while. Then we decided to have a traditional Korean breakfast of seolleongtang (ox bone soup with rice), before visiting the National Central Library, the largest library in Korea.

We were thrilled when the library clerk at the front desk returned from the rare books collection with a copy of the first volume of my father's book. Sadly, it was in terrible condition. The edges of the book were brittle and crumbling, and the words on the yellowed pages were barely readable. Even so, I felt like I was meeting with my father for the first time in sixty-eight years. I noticed my hands trembling as I held the worn-out book authored by my father. The library clerk had provided a special pair of gloves to protect the book while handling it, and with Christine's help, I was able to take photos of the entire book with my iPhone and save them in my file. Unfortunately, the second volume was not available at this library. I was disheartened, but grateful to have held my father's book in my hands.

A Short History of the Overseas Korean Revolutionary Movement (in two volumes, 1945, 1946), by Choi Hyungwoo (Il-chon), the author's father.

The following week, Christine and I went to the library at Korea University, my alma mater, in the hope of finding a better copy of my father's book. Back in 1985, while in Seoul on a business trip, I had visited this library with the hope of finding my father's book. The librarian did find a copy in the collection, but to my astonishment, it had been banned from the general public. Korea was under military dictatorship. No books or newspaper articles with pro-North Korean content were allowed to be read. Since we had no trouble checking out my father's book at the National Central Library the previous day, I did not expect a problem, but I was still a little apprehensive.

We were ecstatic when we found both volumes available in the library collection, and in far better condition than the copy at the National Central Library. I spent a great deal of time studying the content of the books from cover to cover and made photocopies with the idea of reprinting them in the future. Obviously, the censors of my father's book had not read it carefully, but hastily classified it with a red tag, and let this important contribution to Korea's history remain buried for thirty years.

In the preface of his book, my father, Choi Hyungwoo, wrote:

On this day of August 15, 1945, the iron chains of Japanese Imperialism were broken and the sound of the raging bells of independent Korea rang throughout the entire Korean peninsula. For thirty-six years since 1910 we have continued our resistance with blood and tears despite unimaginable suffering and oppression. It is still fresh in our memory that the Japanese massacred hundreds of thousands of innocent compatriots during the March 1st Independence Movement and the Gyeongshin Massacre. And yet, still not satisfied with these massacres, Japan the nation of robbers continued their oppressive measures on all Korean ideological movements, killed many revolutionary activists and implemented the policy of castration of the Korean nation.

At last, like the falling Japanese flags, Japanese imperialism is about to disappear from the face of the earth. The real construction of the resilient Korea that has more than four thousand years of splendid civilization will be restarted, and the complete independence of ten-thousand-year-old Korea will finally be realized.

As we turn the pages of this splendid history of the new century, we ought to acknowledge all the accomplishments made by the myriads of passionate revolutionary comrades with their heroic struggles. At the same time we must realize and understand [what is] the meaning of this huge contribution made for us by the peace representatives of the world, the allied forces, thus let us determine the future course of our country with utmost clarity.

In chapter nine of my father's book, "Yoha Farm and Nong Woo Hoe," he boldly stated on page 27 that the spirit and the goal of the independence movement would go beyond Nationalism, Communism, and Anarchism to "benefit broadly in the human world and devote itself to the welfare of humanity," as proclaimed by Korea's legendary founding father Dangun over four thousand years ago. He also reminded the Korean people never to forget how Korean independence was achieved through the help of the United States and its allies. He warned Koreans to wake up and give their all-out efforts to become one of the most civilized nations on earth. Reading this history so eloquently written by my father, I was deeply moved.

It was a revelation when I was finally able to compare the original text of my father's book with the pages of the ten-page excerpt presented to me and my mother at the luncheon with Kim Il Sung at his palace in 1993. I was startled to see that the names of the Korean Revolutionary Army (KRO) leaders Lee Jongnak and Chang Sobong and the year 1928 had been suspiciously erased from the page; a series of blank circles replaced the original words.

I already suspected the reason for these alterations. Before making this trip to Seoul, I had studied Kim Il Sung's *With the Century* to understand the significance of these historic names and dates. In his history of the movement, my father indicated that Kim Il Sung had served in the KRO under Lee Jongnak, the leader and founder of the Alliance of Gilheuk Farmers. Whereas, in Kim Il Sung's *With the Century*, he stated that Lee Jongnak had served under him, not the other way around. Kim Il Sung also stated that he was the one who had created the AOI (Alliance for Overthrowing Imperialism), as he later named it, not Lee Jongnak.

Interestingly, in my father's *Short History vol. 1*, there is a discrepancy as to the date when AOI was founded. In chapter nine, he indicated that it was founded in 1926, when Kim Il Sung was fourteen. However, on page 30, he stated that AOI was founded in 1930, when Kim was nineteen. Clearly, that was an oversight on my father's part. It is far more plausible that AOI would have been founded in 1930, after Lee Jongnak and Chang Sobong were arrested by the Japanese in 1928, not in 1926 as Kim Il Sung claims. Now it was obvious to me why North Korean scholars had to blot out the year 1928 and the names of the KRA leaders Lee Jongnak and Chang Sobong in my father's book. Especially since, years

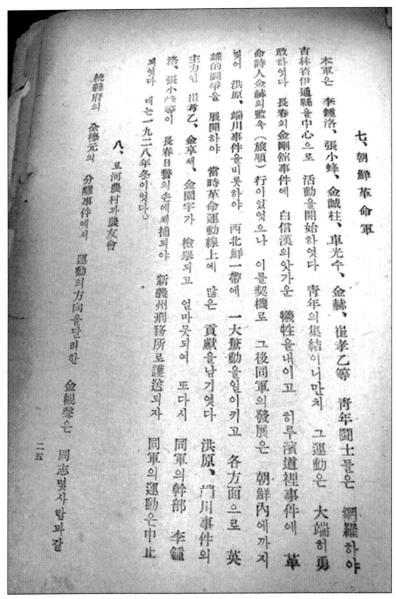

Photocopied pages from *A Short History of the Overseas Korean Revolutionary Movement,* in two volumes (1945, 1946) by Choi Hyungwoo (Il-chon). The page on the right is from the excerpt presented to me and my mother by Kim Il Sung in North Korea. The page on the left is from the original book I photocopied at the Korea University Library.

七、朝鮮革命軍

本軍은 金誠柱、車光洙、金赫、崔孝乙、○○○○ 等 靑年鬪士들은 網羅하야

吉林省伊通縣을中心으로 活動을開始하엿다 靑年의集結이나만치 工運動은 大膽히勇

敢하엿다 長春의金剛舘事件에 白信漢의앗가운 犧牲을내이고 하루濁里裡事件에 革

命詩人金赫의監獄(旅順) 行이있엇으나 이를契機로 그後同軍의發展은 朝鮮內에까지

뻗어 洪原、端川事件을비롯하야 西北鮮一帶에 一大驚動을일이키고 各方面으로 英

雄的鬪爭을 展開하야 當時革命運動線上에 많은 貢獻을남기엇다 洪原、端川事件의

主力인 崔孝乙、金享제、金國宇가 檢擧되고 일마못되여 또다시 同軍의幹部○○

○○○ 等이 長春日警의손에逮捕되야 新義州刑務所로護送되자 同軍의運動■■■

되엿다 때는一九××年冬이엇다。

凡、묘可襲け마늘反솜

later, Kim Il Sung ordered the execution of his former superior and comrade Lee Jongnak, who became a pro-Japanese traitor.

There is a reason why the founding date of AOI would be so important to Kim Il Sung and the scholars and editors who assisted with his memoirs. As Kim Il Sung stated in *With the Century*, "The AOI is the root of the party history and the date of its formation is the beginning of the Revolutionary Communist Movement." Naturally, to seal his reputation as the supreme leader, he would want to credit himself as the founder of the revolutionary organization that had fought to overthrow Japanese imperialism and reunite Korea. 1926 was the date he chose.

I found further evidence to support the year 1930 as AOI's birth year in a book titled *The North East Korean Revolution,* published in China in 1992; and in the article "Fabrication of AOI," by Cho Youngwhan, published in the online newspaper *All in Korea.* The author indicated that Kim Il Sung had changed the original name "Gilheuk Farmers Alliance" to AOI in 1930.

Another contradiction revealed by comparing my father's book with Kim Il Sung's is the location where AOI was founded. My father states that it was in Hwedeok, Manchuria. *With the Century* indicates it was in Hwajeon. Which account is correct? Are we looking at intentional revisions by those who assisted Kim Il Sung with his reminiscences? Or oversights, innocent mistakes? Was AOI founded in 1926 or 1930? Was it in Hweweok or Hwajeon?

Without further research into this conundrum, we can't say for sure. In my father's book preface, he makes a disclaimer about the accuracy of the information in his book and invites historians to assist him in confirming it:

I do admit that I am not the most qualified person to write this very important history, especially when there is not much data and information available. I will be ready to make any corrections and additions in future. Any and all constructive advice and teachings by scholars and historians will be welcomed.

Regardless of the accuracy of the facts, what I discovered by comparing these conflicting accounts casts doubt on the claims in Kim Il Sung's memoirs. Were it not for the blotting out of key information in my father's book, I would be willing to view this as an innocent mistake. However, the falsification of Korean history by the North Korean government is well known. The government would go to any lengths to assure the legitimacy of Kim Il Sung and his legacy as the sovereign leader. Now I understood why pages of my father's book were falsified and enlarged and put on display in the museum in North Korea. It was all a show and a travesty.

When I met with Choe Youngjae, a prominent journalist in Seoul and an expert on North Korean history, he confirmed that Kim Il Sung's memoir contained many fabrications, including reference to my father's books. In an article in *Asia Today*, Mr. Choe reported that 1926 was not cited as AOI's founding year in any of the books on General Kim Il Sung published in North Korea from 1946 to1968. Not until 1973, in *The Dictionary of Politics*, published in Pyongyang, is there a statement claiming that AOI was established on October 17, 1926. This leads me to believe that my father's account of this history may have influenced the authors of *The Dictionary of Politics*.

To this day, it is my belief that my father was taken to North Korea and executed as a traitor on November 5, 1950, after being captured in Seoul by North Korean soldiers on September 21st. Not until the 1970s, when researchers at the Party Research Institute in Pyongyang discovered evidence in my father's book to support Kim Il Sung as the sovereign leader (through Kim's claim to have founded AOI), would my father be seen in a new light—not as a traitor but as a patriot and friend of the Great Leader.

The author and daughter Christine visiting the DMZ in South Korea, 2018.

The history of the independence movement told in my father's book is important, because it was written by an honest journalist and activist who fought for Korea's independence and freedom. I felt that it was my duty to restore the missing pages of this history by exposing the lies, and render due credit to my father, Choi Hyungwoo, who never became a pro-Japanese collaborator but was true to Korea's independence to the very end.

❧

With Christine's support, I had accomplished my main purpose for our trip. I felt relieved and proud to have brought this information to light on behalf of my parents and our family legacy. We were now free to enjoy some of the attractions around Seoul. Christine had already learned how to navigate Seoul's superb and convenient underground subway system. But before we ventured out to do sightseeing, I wanted to show Christine the houses where I had once lived with my family.

When we reached the vicinity of my old neighborhood, not surprisingly, the houses from my childhood were long gone. Modern concrete commercial buildings had replaced them. However, the main roads and familiar alleys were still there. As Christine and I walked along, I shared memories from my earlier days, the good, bad, sad, and sometimes downright depressing. Walking up the hill toward Chunghyeon-dong, where my old house was located, I had a flashback of a fierce battle between the People's Army and the South Korean soldiers on this very hill. There were hundreds of casualties. I didn't witness the battle, but the ear-piercing sound of submachine gun shots is still painfully fresh in my memory.

We hired a private guide who drove us out to visit the Demilitarized Zone, or DMZ, the strip of land that divides the Korean Peninsula in half at the 38th parallel, established after the armistice agreement in 1953. Across the barbed wire fence, we could see the land and small mountains of North Korea. The scene looked beautiful and serene, but the South Korean soldier guarding the DMZ quickly reminded us of the hundreds of thousands of land mines still buried there; it would take years to remove them once peace was restored on the peninsula.

Next, we visited one of the four infiltration tunnels under the border between North and South Korea extending to south of Panmunjom. These tunnels were dug by North Korea to quickly move thousands of troops underneath the DMZ and invade South Korea. Although it was now being used as tourist destination by South Korea, we felt tension in our bellies. Since the truce in 1953, the Korean War has never officially ended. The world is watching to see what will happen in the next round of meetings between the United States and North Korea.

During our remaining days in Seoul, we visited Gyeongbok-gung Palace and the Museum of the Contemporary Arts. We also visited interesting night spots, such as the famous Gwangjang

Market in Dongdaemun, and tasted some delicious street food. I also took Christine to Gonghwachun in China Town, one of the oldest Chinese restaurants in Incheon. The number one popular Chinese dish for all Koreans, jajangmyeon, noodles mixed with black bean sauce, originated at this very restaurant, which opened its doors in 1908. We even went to the Korean cinema and watched the blockbuster movie, *An Si Sung (An Si Castle)*.

The highlight of our trip to Seoul, next to finding my father's books, was the invitation to visit my friend Park Youngju's beautiful palatial residence in Buam Dong, where he held a reception for the world-renowned guitarist Milos Karadaglic and his ensemble. Milos Karadaglic was giving a series of concerts for the general public, free of charge, sponsored by Park Youngju's company, the Eagon Group. Park Youngju is a remarkable businessman with true vision and great compassion for the Korean people.

On the day Christine and I were scheduled to leave Seoul, Youngju and his wife Inja invited us to join them for lunch at a charming Korean restaurant called "Poom," with a Michelin one-star rating. Christine was mesmerized by the food and the gracious hospitality. I was proud to have introduced my daughter to my dear friend, one of the most admired, respected, and successful businessmen in Korea.

On our return flight with Korean Airlines, Christine turned to me and said, "Dad, I truly had the greatest time of my life in Korea, your motherland. Thank you."

"My pleasure, dear. I am so glad you came along with me on this trip."

Upon arriving back home, I was happy to see Myungki in good health under the excellent care of Rita, her caregiver. Our eldest daughter Jennifer was stopping by for a visit that evening. She was on her way to Texas A&M University, where she was scheduled to give a violin performance and teach master classes. Our youngest daughter Didi called from New York to say that rehearsals for the second national tour of the hit Broadway musical *The King and I*, were going very well. She was playing the principal role of Lady Thiang in the show, a dream role for many Asian actresses. The opening night performance was to be held at the Wilson Center in Wilmington, North Carolina, on November 9th, with the last show of the season in New Haven, Connecticut, in May 2019. Myungki and I were looking forward to seeing Didi in the performance at the Keller Auditorium in our hometown Portland, Oregon, in January, where she would also receive the exciting news that she would make her Carnegie Hall debut on June 9, 2019, as soprano in Christopher Tin's, *Calling All Dawns*, presented by Distinguished Concerts International New York. The tour across North America to 48 cities was going to be a long and grueling journey for her and the rest of the cast. But we knew that Didi was excited to be fulfilling her lifelong dream. There was no question that she felt like the luckiest person on earth.

🦢

Compared to my parent's life, filled with so many trials and tribulations, my life has been richly blessed. Of course, I've had my own share of nightmares and suffering. But perhaps because of the many good deeds my parents and ancestors accumulated in heaven, God graciously gave me the courage to withstand all the challenges thrown in my path. The greatest gift I have received in life is that God allowed me to have a peek at who He is, while at the same time, planting a firm conviction in me that my spirit will forever reside in Him. This awakening truth has sustained me throughout my life.

—⟋⟋⟍—

IN PURSUIT OF COMMON SENSE

When I came to the United States in 1969, I did not hesitate to become a naturalized citizen when I had the opportunity six years later. I proudly accepted the United States of America as my home country. Like most naturalized U.S. citizens, however, I took a moment to reflect on this decision. To become a U.S. citizen meant giving up my Korean citizenship. And yet I didn't feel as if I was abandoning the motherland. The country that had nourished me in childhood and gave me my education would always be with me. If anything, the distance from Korea only made me feel more compassionate towards my family and everyone living in North and South Korea. I wanted everyone to be able to enjoy the freedoms I now had in America.

There is no such thing as a perfect country in our world. In spite of the ongoing domestic and international problems, the United States is still the best country on earth to live in. What makes this country great is the democratic system of government that allows people freedoms not enjoyed in many countries around the world. When individual human rights are protected by the law of the land, it propels the spirit of the people beyond any boundaries or limitations.

For me to become a U.S. citizen was an important step in my life from a political standpoint. It was also a practical decision, a matter of convenience, for a young man with aspirations in international business. I considered the whole world my home-land and believed that all of humanity has the God-given right to live wherever they choose. Because of the artificial boundary in my Korean homeland that divides the peninsula in two, tearing my own family apart, my freedom to exercise this right was espe-cially important. To restrict and bind people to a country for the sake of race, religion, politics, or for whatever reason, oppresses people and violates their human rights. It is absurd and crazy. Who has the absolute authority to say that North Korean peo-ple must live in the DPRK, or that Jews and Arabs must live in Palestine or the Gaza Strip?

At the beginning of his rule, Kim Il Sung started out as Chairman of the Communist Party, but gradually morphed into "The Great Leader." His party people made him a Godhead so that he could rule with absolute power without interference. Regardless of what Kim Il Sung and his heirs, Kim Jong Il and grandson Kim Jong Un, claim about their benevolence to the people, the end results of the Juche system in North Korea are rather stark and quite contrary to what we are led to believe about the success of their regime.

Korea is not only divided into two countries at the DMZ. North Korea itself is also divided in two. There is the elite so-ciety of the Pyongyang Republic and the Republic of everyone else, people like my brothers and their families. Clearly, it is a cult system fortified by brainwashing its people and protecting itself from the outside world with weapons of mass destruction. There is no freedom of any kind for its people, and the country is tight-ly closed lest any foreign influence be infiltrated. The country and its people are slowly atrophying. As a Korean descendant, I could not bear to witness the peculiar and horrifying phenomena of North Korea's system of government. Not only did it lack com-mon sense, it was beyond comprehension.

The South Korean government is not free from human rights abuses either. It has a long history of oppressing dissidents in the name of national security. Corruption at all levels of government and business was rampant until recent times. However, the country is making steady progress toward developing a government system that allows a considerable amount of freedom to its people. The miracle of the Han River brought forth economic prosperity to the nation of fifty million. Their economic system, like that of America, is flawed, but it is working, and its citizens know it. Above all, it is the protection of human rights that fosters the productivity and creativity of a nation. Where there is no freedom, people cannot exercise their right to pursue happiness. Without freedom, it's impossible to thrive. I believe it is important for a nation to have certain ideologies upon which to build its system that enable the people of the country to bond together. However, any system without basic human rights guaranteed to its people is like giving someone an automobile without air in the tires. They won't get far. Our world history has ample evidence of that.

A majority of the fundamentalist and monotheistic religions as practiced in South Korea and the rest of the world are not much different than Communism and its dictatorship. When people are confined to the beliefs of a certain religious denomination or institution that forbids them from acknowledging the views of other religions of the world, they are betraying their own core principal teaching of love and compassion. If you don't see and feel the divinity within others, how can you claim to know divine spirit within yourself?

Binding together a church congregation through blind allegiance, telling them their religion is the only way to salvation, is essentially the same as communist propaganda. It doesn't require a leap of faith for someone to become more tolerant of other religious beliefs. It is simply a matter of exercising common sense and keeping an open mind.

The truth we all are seeking, beyond any religious creed or political doctrine, is the truth that resides within ourselves. Practicing common sense is what will bring us enlightenment and salvation, not a sudden jolt of recognition about the holy spirit received in churches, temples, or holy shrines. The salvation and enlightenment received by the grace of God has to be a permanent one. If it comes and goes like the wind, and is not known within, it is not a true enlightenment. Even the great pillar of the Catholic Church, St. Peter himself, betrayed the Lord Jesus Christ three times the moment his life was in danger. He didn't realize who he was and who the Lord Jesus Christ was. Blind faith is fragile and dangerous. The knowingness based on common sense is the opposite, and I have no doubt it brings us closer to the truth.

Looking back on my life and the success I have achieved, I feel humbled. I was not blessed with great talent or intellectual genius. I was just one of those average kids on the block. But I was blessed with great parents who demonstrated the meaning of self-sacrifice, hard work, and faith in God. Because of them, I had the courage to pursue my dreams. Without my asking, many angels appeared on my path that helped me to know who I am and who God is.

The miracles in my life were possible because I trusted in my own common sense about God. I learned how to see His spirit working in my life. I did my share of prayers and service and I believe in their power. But rather than relying on thousands of hours of prayer or racking up good deeds required by the churches and religious institutions, with the promise of salvation in the next life, I found His spirit within me. God has endowed this precious gift of common sense in all human beings. If our common sense tells us that something is not right and doesn't make sense in our hearts, it cannot be the truth, whether we are talking about religion, business, or government affairs. We don't have to look to the higher authority of a church or government official to tell us what is right or wrong. Having trust in our common sense and being completely honest with ourselves in our personal lives and in our dealings with other people will bring us peace, happiness, and many miracles.

About the Author

KEN KOOKJOO CHOI was born in Beijing, China, in 1942 and grew up in Seoul, South Korea, before emigrating to the U.S.A. and becoming a citizen. He founded K-C International Ltd. in Portland, Oregon, and served as President and CEO until 2002. Mr. Choi served as President of the Korean Society of Oregon and as Chairman of the Oregon Korea Foundation in Portland, Oregon. Mr. Choi and his wife Hahn Myungki live in Northern California. They have three daughters.

46890478R00186

Made in the USA
Lexington, KY
01 August 2019